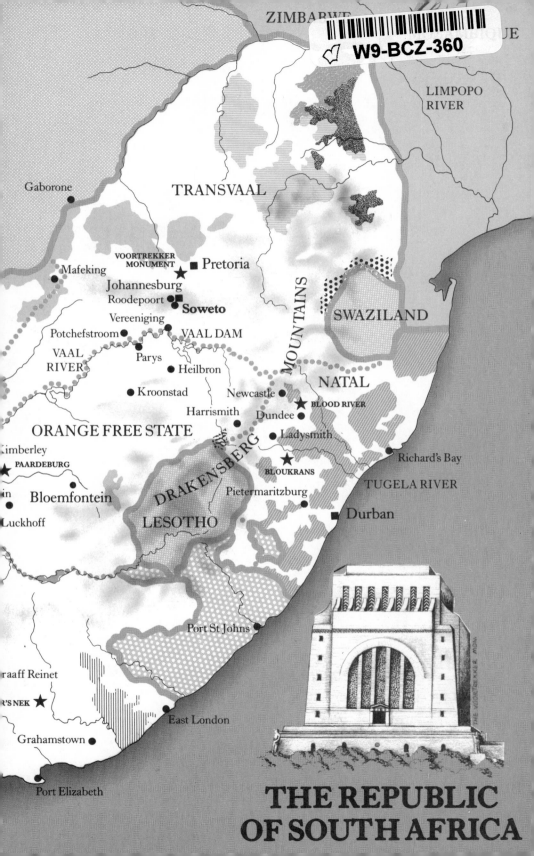

ZIMBABWE

MOZAMBIQUE

LIMPOPO
RIVER

Gaborone

TRANSVAAL

VOORTREKKER
MONUMENT

Pretoria

Mafeking

Johannesburg

SWAZILAND

Roodepoort

Soweto

Vereeniging

VAAL DAM

Potchefstroom

MOUNTAINS

Parys

VAAL
RIVER

Heilbron

NATAL

Kroonstad

Newcastle

BLOOD RIVER

Harrismith

Dundee

ORANGE FREE STATE

Ladysmith

Kimberley

PAARDEBURG

BLOUKRANS

Richard's Bay

Bloemfontein

DRAKENSBERG

Pietermaritzburg

TUGELA RIVER

Luckhoff

LESOTHO

Durban

raaff Reinet

Port St Johns

R'S NEK

East London

Grahamstown

Port Elizabeth

THE REPUBLIC
OF SOUTH AFRICA

THE WHITE TRIBE OF AFRICA

PERSPECTIVES ON SOUTHERN AFRICA

THE WHITE TRIBE OF AFRICA

South Africa in perspective

DAVID HARRISON

University of California Press
Berkeley and Los Angeles

For Vergie

University of California Press
Berkeley and Los Angeles
© David Harrison 1981

Library of Congress Cataloging in Publication Data
Harrison, David.
    The white tribe of Africa.
    (Perspectives on Southern Africa; 31)
    Bibliography: p.
    Includes index.
    1. Afrikaners — Ethnic identity. 2. Afrikaners —
Psychology. 3. South Africa — Race relations.
4. South Africa — Politics and government.
5. Afrikaners — Political activity. I. Title. II. Series.
DT888.H37   305.8′393606   81-24057
ISBN 0-520-04690-0   AACR2

CONTENTS

FOREWORD

David Harrison and I travelled together for many months in South Africa researching and filming for the BBC-1 series 'The White Tribe of Africa'. This book, which has its origin in those journeys, gives a far more detailed account of the dramatic story of the Afrikaners rise to power than was possible in the television programmes. It tells the saga from the earliest days, when the Afrikaner was the underdog to the Nationalist victory of 1948 and then explores the ways in which the Afrikaner has tried to consolidate his power and ensure the survival of his culture.

It is not easy to win the confidence of Afrikaner Nationalists as we quickly discovered. They tend to be suspicious of outsiders and defensive about their policies. They were at first reluctant to co-operate in our attempt to reveal their attitudes. It made the task seem daunting but David Harrison proved their match. He listened, without allowing his own views to intrude, and with patience and determination in equal measure, eventually coaxed some of the most reluctant Afrikaners in front of our cameras and onto the pages of this book.

The result is a fascinating and disturbing story which must interest anyone worried by the prospect of continuous turmoil, even race war in Southern Africa. But it has another dimension. For it is the old story of man's search for power and security, for a sense of identity and a measure of freedom even at the expense of his neighbour's. It is taking place in a harsh setting, under the glaring southern sun, where the contrasts of black and white and their conflicting interests make the story more lurid. But it is not so different at heart from how we have behaved and still behave under our gentler northern skies.

David Dimbleby   August 1981

vii

AFRIKANER PROLOGUE

Pretoria always seems to be ten degrees warmer than Johannesburg. The fifteen hundred foot drop in altitude is the reason, they say. Also, the city lies in a valley. That day in March 1970, after a sticky drive from Johannesburg, the difference seemed even greater.

Van Soelen Avenue was a cul-de-sac, a turning off Buffels Road in the suburb of Rietondale. The centre of Pretoria was not two miles away and that South African suburban-ness was already everywhere; a feeling of order and space. Black 'garden boys' going about the watering; black girls flopped out in the shade, gossiping. White ladies driving past from shopping or tennis in gleaming cars. There is never a dirty car to be seen in white man's land. The 'boys' see to that.

The steely-eyed woman at number one hundred and seventy was not welcoming. '*Ja*,' she said, 'what do you want?' I had an appointment with Jaap Marais, I explained. He was the deputy leader of the HNP, the *Herstigte* (Reconstituted) Nasionale Party, the right-wing group that had broken away from mainstream Nationalism the previous year. John Vorster had called an early election to stamp out the growth before it had time to take root. That was why I was there; to make a film about these Afrikaners who thought Vorster was a liberal.

'Mr Marais is not in', said the woman. I explained again that I was there by appointment. From the BBC, four p.m., Wednesday the twenty-fifth. I was sure there was no mistake. Mr Marais had confirmed it himself.

'He's not available. He's resting.'

At least that was better. Could I wait? Or come back later?

'No, I'm not going to disturb him. And even if I did, what makes you think he would speak to you?' The conversation was over.

That evening Marais was addressing a meeting at Primrose, thirty miles away near Germiston, a gold mining and railway town, the sort of place where the HNP were finding their best support. Blue collar

1

workers, particularly, feared that Vorster's promises to reduce discrimination against blacks on the shop floor could threaten their own jobs. We had hoped to film the meeting. My earlier chat with Marais was supposed to have cleared the way.

We decided to try again. Our cameraman was a South African named Ernie Christie. His Afrikaans was good. He was well-known locally. Perhaps we could talk our way in. As Marais arrived we seized our chance. He was apologetic about the afternoon but gave no explanation. He could not himself give permission to film, he said, but promised to ask the meeting. Would we wait outside?

In Afrikaans he explained to the audience about this *televisie span* (television team) who said they were from the BBC. They had told him they were interested in the meeting, as part of a film about the election, but he had only their word for it. What would happen to the film when it got back to London he could not say. With no more prompting, the assembly turned us down flat.

Three hours later, at the end of a long meeting we tried again. Marais was once more apologetic. I said we were still keen on an interview but would it not be better to be quite frank? If he wanted nothing more to do with us, he had only to say. No, no, it wasn't that. But these meetings can be difficult, he explained. He would be out of town for the next few days but we could come to his office in Pretoria at three o'clock the following Thursday and could film an interview then.

The next week, with camera and lights and questions we were back in Pretoria. The HNP office was on the first floor, number two hundred and twenty-five, Schubart Street.

We had come to see Mr Marais, I said. Sorry, replied the girl. He's not in. It was the day after April Fool's Day.

It was a hard lesson, repeated many times in the years to come. Many Afrikaners, and not only the more conservative, are deeply suspicious of outsiders, particularly foreign journalists. They feel the world makes no attempt to understand either their problems or their efforts to solve them; and for that they can find a ready reason. It lies, they say, in the reports and films of those who come to observe them.

The real Afrikaner, [said René de Villiers, an Afrikaner himself but far from a Nationalist,] is a man who longs to be accepted, a man who longs to be wanted, and to be loved. But he starts from the assumption that the rest of the world does not understand him. Therefore he simply writes off ninety per cent of what the world says about him. This is all part of the process of saying:

'If only the world knew the truth about us. Then they would understand. Then they would stop ascribing these motives to us.'

This book is an attempt to tackle the Afrikaner on his own ground, to probe some of his attitudes by going back to the events which helped form them and to the people who understand them. It is also an attempt to follow that particular strand of Afrikaner thinking which became the Nationalism of today. The account will trace the Afrikaners' fortunes from the dark days of the defeat by the British in 1902 to the election victory in 1948, the moment which finally gave the Nationalists control over South Africa and the opportunity to impose on all its citizens the political creed they called Apartheid. It also attempts to show the realities of a system which in the end, whether Nationalists claim to have been misunderstood or not, has brought subjugation where it promised freedom and which could yet threaten the very future of the Afrikaner people it sought to preserve.

In trying to tell the story of this White Tribe I have called on many Afrikaners; men like the redoubtable Henning Klopper, one of the founder members and first chairman of the Broederbond, the Afrikaner secret society that for sixty years has worked for the cause of exclusive Afrikanerdom. His bitter experiences in a British concentration camp during the War of Liberation and his disillusionment with his own Boer leaders afterwards explain a good deal about the birth of Broederbond Nationalism. When last I met this eighty-five-year-old Nationalist he was sitting up in a hospital bed, recovering from a heart attack. He was reading the same Bible his mother had given him when he set off for his first job in Johannesburg almost seventy years before. He said he had read it through well over seventy times.

For less peppery accounts of the making of the Afrikaner I am indebted to the patient Hennie Coetzee, Professor of Social Anthropology at the University of Potchefstroom, and to Piet Cillie, Professor of Journalism at Stellenbosch and longtime editor of *Die Burger*, the Nationalist newspaper at the Cape. Both gave extensively of their time and experience. So too did Riaan Kriel, a farmer in Natal, always ready to invite the 'Bloody British Communists', the BBC, to breakfast and lively debate. Koot Vorster, the brother of the former Prime Minister, a senior figure in the Dutch Reformed Church, never turned us away nor made any secret of his fears for the future of Afrikanerdom if Verwoerd's principles of racial separation were ever abandoned.

3

Eighteen months' work on the television series, *The White Tribe of Africa*, following other regular filming visits, provided the opportunity to meet some of the leading Nationalist politicians of the decade, John Vorster, Connie Mulder, Pik Botha, Jimmy Kruger, Piet Koornhof and, after Muldergate, P. W. Botha. Some of them took part in our BBC series and their filmed interviews, thanks to the sharp questioning of David Dimbleby, provided valuable material for this account.

On numerous film trips to South Africa my official point of contact with the government was the Secretary for Information, Dr Eschel Rhoodie. He once said during the filming of *The White Tribe* that he knew every contact we had made. He also threatened dire consequences if the series was not regarded by Pretoria as 'positive'. Three months after the programmes were all over we met again in very different circumstances. The so-called Muldergate Affair was at its height. Rhoodie's Information empire was in ruins; he was on the run from his former masters. After negotiations in Zurich and Cannes he agreed to a television interview with David Dimbleby to put his side of the story. Again these events and the insight they afforded have become part of this narrative.

For a completely different view of the Nationalist psyche I had the good fortune to be able to call on the lifetime experiences of several other Afrikaners. Beyers Naudé was a senior churchman and member of the Broederbond who had the courage to denounce publicly the secret society and all its works. But the state took its revenge; now he is banned and cannot be quoted. René de Villiers is a newspaper man, former editor of the Johannesburg *Star*, one-time Member of Parliament for the opposition Progressive Federal Party and now President of the South African Institute of Race Relations.

No one can question Ernie Malherbe's Afrikaner credentials and no one is better qualified than he to comment on the events of the century. His ancestors arrived with the Huguenots from France nearly three centuries ago; his grandfather helped found the first Afrikaans language movement. Ernie Malherbe himself was born in 1895. As a small boy he lived through the same War of Liberation as Henning Klopper. His father was imprisoned, his family lost everything. But at the end of it the Malherbes espoused not Nationalism but the broad South Africanism of Louis Botha and Jan Smuts.

Later as a member of the Carnegie Commission he spent three years studying the plight of his fellow Afrikaners, the 'Poor Whites'. It was the time when many attitudes towards race were being fashioned. Later still, as Smuts' Director of Military Intelligence during World

War Two he had a unique vantage point from which to study the machinations of the Broederbond and its uncontrollable offspring, the Ossewabrandwag. His wife served in Intelligence too. After the war Malherbe began another career and spent twenty years as Principal and Vice-Chancellor of the University of Natal with an insider's view on the changes the National government was imposing on the nation's educational system. To Dr Ernie Malherbe and his wife Janie, who made available their recollections and their writings, I owe a great debt.

Kowie Marais brought another insider's view. He was also once a member of the Broederbond, active in the Ossewabrandwag, working for the revolution which he hoped would sweep Nationalists to power in the early days of the 1939 War. But the call never came and he found himself interned at Koffiefontein with John Vorster. Marais once believed that Verwoerd's ideal of 'separate freedoms' for all the races in South Africa at least had a chance. But he changed his views, left the Nationalists and carried his opposition into parliament as the Progressive Federal Party member for Johannesburg North.

Kowie Marais provided some graphic detail about the Broederbond; more analysis of the role of this so-called 'cultural society' came from two books published in 1978. Both relied on extensive anonymous contacts within the organisation and on a close study of secret documents obtained from them. Without Hennie Serfontein's *Brotherhood of Power* and *The Super Afrikaners* by Hans Strydom and Ivor Wilkins it would have been difficult for an outsider to have grasped the full range of Broederbond activity.

I am indebted to Hennie Serfontein for more than just his writings; without his personal Afrikaner teach-ins and his generosity in allowing access to much of his source material our Afrikaner film series would have lacked much in authority and this narrative would have been the poorer. Hans Strydom, too, was generous with additional information. All of them, Kowie Marais, Serfontein and Strydom, underlined what Malherbe had already perceived during the war years, that the Broederbond's role has gradually changed, from safeguarding Afrikaner interests to conspiring to maintain Afrikaner Nationalist domination.

In attempting to chronicle some of the other changes taking place in South Africa I am further indebted to the South African Institute of Race Relations and to the Black Sash who make it their business to distinguish between what politicians say and what they actually do; to John Kane-Berman whose reporting must be as good as anything coming out of South Africa; also to Stanley Uys and Tertius Myburgh, two Afrikaner journalists who always had time for English questions.

At times when my quest kept running into the brick wall of Nationalism it was stimulating to spend a moment with Helen Suzman. She faced the full might of the National government alone from her opposition bench for thirteen years and still jokes about it. No observer knows better than she the workings of the Nationalist mind; except perhaps Alan Paton, equally ready to give his time to those of us from the BBC team who came to seek his advice. I am grateful to him also for permission to quote from his writing; grateful as well to Zach and Mona de Beer who always had space at table and who opened so many doors.

Not many new authors have literary agents as fathers and I have mine to thank for professional prodding and wise counsel. The book became, in fact, a family enterprise with a mother who kept me up to date with South African cuttings in one continent and a mother-in-law who did the same in another. Throughout, and for this especial thanks, I was sustained by my wife who had to endure all the pains of my authorship.

Much of the initial research was done for the BBC television series *The White Tribe of Africa* where I was surrounded by an exceptionally talented team, Mike Dutfield, Daphne Wood, Francis Gérard, Marshall Lee and the best reporter in the television business, David Dimbleby. Freelance cameraman, Alex Learmont with his knowledge of his adopted country and its language, was a constant source of ideas and with the BBC camera trio of Butch Calderwood, Tony Jacobs and Fred Downton, produced a filmed impression of South Africa, that will take a lot of beating. Without Marshall Lee's continuing encouragement and advice, plus discussions at every stage enriched by his expertise in both the history and politics of his own land, it is unlikely that this book would have ever appeared. That it has is thanks also to John Gau, former Head of Current Affairs at Lime Grove, for allowing me time to complete it, as well as to Ernie Malherbe, Sheena Duncan, Mona de Beer and especially René de Villiers for close reading of draft chapters. They were corrected and typed with feeling in Dorset by Kate Lee and in London by Julie Anderson and awaited at BBC Publications with kindly tolerance by Victoria Huxley, always ready with words of good cheer even when deadlines loomed.

A final word about terminology. In trying to understand Afrikaner Nationalism I have been somewhat confused by the widely used terms of *verligte* and *verkrampte*, meaning enlightened or moderate, and

6

reactionary or hardline. They have always seemed to suggest more difference than actually exists. Those dubbed with either adjective still appear to be equally wedded to the basic tenets of the Nationalist creed, separate black homelands, separate citizenship, separate parliaments, separate schools and separate living areas however much the so-called moderates may advocate the abolition of separate park benches or separate lifts. It seemed sensible, therefore, to avoid using the terms altogether.

What it has not been possible to avoid are the changing names of the government ministry which deals with black South Africans. It has evolved from the Ministry of Native Affairs to Bantu Affairs to Plural Relations. Now it has become the Ministry of Co-operation and Development. Perhaps the best comment on it all came from Percy Qoboza, editor of *The World*. In 1977 his newspaper was shut down and he was detained without trial for five months. When he was released he said: 'Let no one tell me there has been no change in South Africa. I went into gaol a Bantu and came out a Plural.'

1

'A Nation of Heroes'

The Afrikaners as described in the official guide to the
Voortrekker Monument

On the drive from Johannesburg to Pretoria on the Ben Schoeman
Highway, soon after Halfway House a pebble appears on the horizon.
It disappears occasionally behind the Transvaal hills but by the turn-
off to Pietersburg and Zimbabwe it has grown into half a brick. By
Sesmylspruit it looks like a stone blancmange. By Swartkop Air Force
base it is more like a radio-set in granite, 1940s style, complete with
latticed loudspeakers. Only as the highway sweeps round the last hill
before Pretoria, is South Africa's most important monument revealed in all its massiveness. It is the Voortrekker Monument, built
to commemorate the deeds of the Boers who rejected British rule and
trekked away from their beloved Cape to found their own two
republics.

One hundred and fifty years ago, the Boers had nothing but a
determination to escape from those who prevented them from living as
they wished. Today their descendants control the whole of South
Africa. They number only two and a half million but they dominate
the lives of ten times that number of other South Africans, white as
well as black.

The Monument is itself as much part of the story of the Afrikaners'
rise as the early events it records. When the foundation stone was laid
in 1938 to mark the centenary of the original trek, one hundred
thousand people were at the ceremony. As part of the celebrations, a
group of idealistic Afrikaners had set off by ox-wagon earlier in the
year to retrace the route their ancestors had followed, all the way from
the Cape to the site of the Memorial in Pretoria, nearly a thousand
miles to the north. The idea caught on. Thousands joined in, travelling from all over South Africa, by ox-wagon and horseback, by
bicycle and car. Afrikaners came together in an emotional pilgrimage
to pay tribute to their ancestors. It was the biggest gathering ever
known in South Africa. The tribe was united as never before.

9

The whole project was one of the first great successes of the Broederbond, the secret organisation that has done so much to bring the Afrikaners to their present position. The task which they had set themselves, and the reason why the Broederbond was formed in the first place, was to bring Afrikaners together. In 1938 there were deep divisions over how far Nationalists should collaborate with the old enemy, the English.

The symbolic trek and its Monument gave an emotional impetus to Afrikaner nationalism that had far-reaching consequences. 'Without the trek', claimed Henning Klopper, the first Chairman of the Broederbond in 1978, 'the Nationalist government would never have come to power as early as 1948.'

In the 1980s as Afrikaners face calls for change and criticism of the path they have chosen, their Voortrekker Monument still has its role to play. It has become the shrine where the faithful come for inspiration from the past, where those who have doubts about the present may be reassured.

'The Monument', says the official guide book, 'will arouse the pride of belonging to a nation of heroes . . . it will arouse and strengthen a love for the country for whose sake so much was sacrificed; and it will strengthen a faith in God in whom the people trust.'

To this Afrikaner temple are brought bus-loads of young South Africans to learn their lessons of the past. Up the wide steps past the official noticeboard:

Visiting Hours – Whites Daily 0900–1645
Non-Whites Tuesday 0830–1200

'We've been waiting for months for the Department of Works to take that notice down,' said the Monument Information Officer. 'But you know how it is with Government Departments.' Tuesday, says another notice, is the day when the restaurant is closed.

At the top of the steps the uniformed crocodiles are handed over by their teachers to the special guides from the Transvaal Education Department. They're friendly uncles, Afrikaners all, and they know the history that young visitors need to be taught. They start right there at the bronze statue of the Voortrekker Mother with her two children. It stands against the main wall, flanked by the steps to The Hall of Heroes.

The place of honour [says the guide] has been given to the woman because she made everything possible by trekking with her husband . . . by giving up her

10

The Voortrekker Monument, Pretoria, the shrine of Afrikanerdom

Bronze statue of the Voortrekker woman and children at the Voortrekker Monument. According to the official guidebook, 'The woman suffers but she does not look down. She looks straight ahead. The children do not look back. They look up'

home, by bringing her children, by being ready to face sickness and danger she helped bring civilisation to the heart of this black continent.

Carved on the wall behind are four black wildebeest. They are symbolic too.

The statue of the Voortrekker Mother and her children [says the guide book] symbolises white civilisation while the black wildebeest portray the ever threatening dangers of Africa. The determined attitude and triumphant expression on the woman's face suggest that the dangers are receding and that the victory of civilisation is an accomplished fact.

From the dominant position of the Monument there is little to contradict such Afrikaner optimism. On a clear day white South Africa seems to extend forever. Across the valley on the other side of Pretoria stand the Union Buildings, seat of the Afrikaner Nationalist Government since 1948, from where they have been impressing their grand design onto the map of Africa.

From the city itself rises the new *Volkskas* building, the People's Bank, started in 1934 from the sixpences and shillings of poor Afrikaners. Now '*u eie bank*' (your own bank) is the third largest in the Republic.

On the hill to the west are the head offices of ISCOR, the massive state-controlled Iron and Steel Corporation with a board dominated by Afrikaners, an example for all to see of how far the Boers, the farmers, have come in the world of industry so long dominated by English-speaking South Africans. Just over the hill to the south is the Atomic Research Centre of Pelindaba where Afrikaner physicists with Israeli know-how stir their nuclear brew.

From the Air Force Base at Zwartkop the jet fighters take off past the Monument – French Mirages, every last bolt made in South Africa, arms embargo or no. Within mortar range there is the military Ordnance Depot at Lyttelton, where row upon row of trucks, scout cars, armoured personnel carriers stand ready for any assault.

Over the hill lies the great military base of *Voortrekkerhoogte* (Voortrekker Heights). It used to be known as Roberts Heights after the British Commander-in-Chief during the Anglo-Boer War. Not surprisingly the Nationalists changed the name. It is now the camp where many young white National Servicemen are processed on their way to fight 'On the Border'.

On public days, like the anniversary of the Republic, men and machines come together to parade past the Monument, and the old Boer songs and the politicians' pep talks ring across the veld:

13

We seek peace and friendship with the great nations of the world [proclaimed Prime Minister Dr Verwoerd, in his Republic Day speech in 1966.] But we will not sacrifice this Republic and its independence. If we are forced to by aggression, we will defend it with all we have at our disposal. This republic is not to be taken away from this new nation which has come so far and is so proud of what it does possess.

At Voortrekkerhoogte too, although not quite so well-known, is an institution that in a different way also does its bit to preserve the republic. It is a work colony for blacks or 'Bantu' declared 'idle and undesirable' under Section 29 of the Urban Areas Consolidation Act No. 25 of 1945. Arrested without a warrant, sentenced without a trial, a black man can now be detained here for up to two years on the order of a civil servant, under a definition of idleness that has never yet applied to a white.

But these are no considerations for the uncles at the Monument. Their business, in the main hall, is heroes and tales of derring-do to inspire their respectful audience. The centre piece is the cenotaph, the symbolic resting place of trek leader Piet Retief and his comrades. 'It is set low,' say the uncles, 'so you have to bow your head in respect for those who have paid the ultimate sacrifice for South Africa – as the boys on the border are still doing.'

Retief is the best known of all the trekkers. His famous Grahamstown manifesto of February 1837 set out the reasons why he and his fellow farmers had decided to quit 'the fruitful land of our birth'. It tells why they could no longer stomach British rule, it tells of their sense of injustice that Britain could not, or would not, help them in their frontier troubles with the blacks, and indeed often punished them for taking reprisals against stock thieves.

The manifesto records the deep distrust of the missionaries, 'whose testimony is believed in England to the exclusion of all evidence in our favour.' It complains above all of the losses the farmers suffered through the abolition of slavery. Some compensation was paid, but by a deliberate act of British bloody-mindedness, could be collected only in London. It was, above all, the principle behind these British attitudes that most outraged Retief's sister, Anna Steenkamp:

And yet it is not their [the slaves'] freedom that drives us to such lengths, as their being placed on an equal footing with Christians, contrary to the laws of God and the natural distinction of race and religion, so that it was intolerable for any decent Christian to bow down beneath such a yoke; wherefore we rather withdrew in order to preserve our doctrines in purity.

14

Not all Boer settlers in the Cape shared these views. Many put up with British rule and came to accept a less feudal relationship with their brown and black workers. Indeed ties between master and servant were sometimes very close. It was not just passing sailors who produced so many pale skins among those now called Cape Coloureds.

The Dutch Church in the Cape offered no blessing to those who trekked. The Church was part of the establishment and gave its support to the government of the day even if it was British. Between the Boers who lived comfortably on their fertile farms in the Western Cape and the restless frontiersmen five hundred miles away to the east there were already differences. The trek would make them even greater.

At the Voortrekker tomb in the Monument the uncles do not spend long on the reasons behind the Boer exodus: 'There really isn't time.' And every white South African knows what happened to Piet Retief. How he led his party of trekkers across the Drakensberg mountains only to be murdered by Dingane, the Zulu king, when he had just signed a treaty giving the Boers great tracts of land; how the Zulus then slaughtered the men, women and children camped in the foothills of the Drakensberg around Bloukrans; and how the Boers, helped by God and guns, got their own back at the Battle of Blood River on 16 December 1838, the key date in the Afrikaner calendar, the focal point of the whole of the sacred history.

And at noon on 16 December each year [says the guide, pointing out a pin-prick of light in the roof] through that hole up there in the dome, a ray of sunlight, the light of civilisation, falls directly onto the cenotaph. It falls onto the words you see there, from the National anthem: '*Ons vir jou, Suid Afrika*' – 'We for thee, South Africa'.

Around the marble frieze in the Hall of Heroes the guided tours move, twenty-seven panels of the Afrikaner version of the trek; a welcome here, a treacherous attack there, a brave deed, an Act of God. The text for the uncles is taken from the Offical Guide, page thirty-one.

It is nonsense to suppose that the interior of Southern Africa belonged to the Bantu and that the white man took it away from him. The Bantus penetrated from the north almost at the same time as the white man entered the south. They had equal title to the country. The Voortrekkers wished to partition the country and live in peace because they had already experienced enough trouble in the Cape. But the Bantu were not amenable to reason. He respected only one thing and that was force.

It is a comfortable view but unfortunately not quite true. Non-

Nationalist historians now accept that the Transvaal, the destination of many of the Voortrekkers, was the home of black people as early as the fifth century. They moved in swirling currents, expanding steadily south. Portuguese sailors, shipwrecked on the Transkei coast in 1554, reported settlements of people 'very black in colour with woolly hair'. The tribes who were eventually absorbed into the Zulu had been fighting over Natal for a hundred years by the time Piet Retief's wagons rolled over the Drakensberg.

As for the Cape, to which white settlers – Dutch, German, Huguenot and later British – helped themselves after the first landing in 1652, it had been the hunting ground of the San people, brown-skinned Bushmen, for centuries. Occupying the land with them were the Khoikhoi. They were brown-skinned too. Nomads and stock owners, they had long been trading with black men further north in cattle and cannabis, iron and copper. But the San and the Khoikhoi do not appear on the Voortrekker frieze.

One central figure who does, of course, is Dingane, the Zulu king. 'To them he's a god,' says the guide, pointing to the black camp followers carved in the marble:

With a flick of his hand he can cause your death. When you come to him you kneel down. Even if you're an *induna* [head man]. This man, with his hands cupped, he's the receiver of the royal spit. It must never fall on the ground.

Retief had drawn up a written contract. Before witnesses Dingane is actually making his cross on it. Because of course he can't read . . . But the signing of a treaty meant nothing. At a word from Dingane, Retief and his whole party were cruelly done to death. You see the clubs and the native holding a rock. They were all killed. Every one of them.

Dingane was not yet satisfied. Within hours of the massacre he had dispatched three Zulu regiments, or *impis*, to attack the Boer families waiting in the foothills of the Drakensberg. Their wagons were scattered on the banks of a score of mountain streams. Many of the men had gone with Retief; others were away hunting or searching for possible farm sites.

What followed is seared upon the Afrikaner soul as no other event in their history. The impis fell upon the defenceless wagons in the blackness of night. Forty men, fifty women and one hundred and eighty children perished and so did over two hundred Hottentot servants. It was February 1838, the year of Queen Victoria's coronation, the year the Westminster parliament finally voted to free all slaves.

16

And what does this mean for us? [asks the guide at the end of the story] We shall live, we shall die for you, South Africa. They are the words on the cenotaph. Here are children, Retief's own son, Voortrekker children who laid down their lives . . . Voortrekker children who died for South Africa.

The Boers' first attempt at retribution failed. In April 1838 a force of over three hundred and fifty men rode out under Uys and Potgieter, but the two leaders were barely on speaking terms. They failed to co-ordinate their attack on a large Zulu force and Uys was killed. Back in the laager Potgieter was blamed for the defeat and in pique took himself and his men back over the Drakensberg to the Highveld.

It was seven months before the Boers tried again, under a new leader, Andries Pretorius. Towards the end of November 1838 he led a heavily-armed unit, known as a *commando*, deep into Dingane's territory. Each night they drew their wagons into a laager in case the Zulus attacked. Each night too, as battle approached, they repeated a vow that if God gave them victory they would keep the day forever as a day of thanksgiving.

On the night of 15 December the commando was in position on the banks of the Ncome River: sixty-four wagons, three cannon, *veghekke*, literally 'fighting gates', lashed between the wheels, lanterns tied to the whipstocks; the oxen and horses were all inside the laager. At dawn, one of the Boers recalled, 'the whole Zulu kingdom sat there'. There were ten thousand warriors at least, commanded by Dingane's best generals. But six hours later three thousand Zulus lay dead, their assegais no match for guns. The river ran with their blood. The trekkers suffered three wounded. It was a brilliant victory, at what was known from that day as the Battle of Blood River. Now every year on 16 December, at hundreds of services all over South Africa, to mark what is now called the Day of the Covenant, the faithful give thanks and renew the vow the trekkers took before the battle.

But who had really won the victory?

George Chadwick is a historian from Durban and a member of South Africa's National Monuments Council. He is also on the Board of Trustees of the Museum attached to the Voortrekker Monument. He says that serving under Pretorius were four hundred and sixty-four Voortrekkers and their six commandants; there were also three Englishmen from Port Natal: Parker, Joyce and Captain Alexander Biggar, and approximately a hundred and twenty black Port Natal scouts, almost certainly armed with muskets. At the Battle of Tugela earlier that year the scouts had used them to great effect, firing in volleys. Also in the laager were black 'leaders' for the oxen, and drivers for the wagons as well as coloured *agterryers* (after-riders) to take care of the spare horses. Chadwick puts their joint number at over two hundred; a total of around eight hundred, by no means the exclusive Afrikaner force of Nationalist legend.

But those who would put the record straight perhaps do so at their peril. In March 1979 a curious event occurred at a University symposium in Pretoria. Professor Floors van Jaarsveld, a respected historian from the University of Pretoria and very much a figure of the Afrikaner establishment, was in the middle of an address about the Day of the Covenant; he had just suggested that it was time to make the event less of an exclusive Afrikaner festival.

A line of protesters filed into the hall and up onto the stage, lifted him off his feet and daubed him with tar and feathers. Then they hoisted the flag of the old Transvaal Republic, the *Vierkleur*, and announced that they would not tolerate such 'blasphemous' attacks on Afrikaner history and religion.

Blood River still matters, of course, because it offers the perfect symbol for the Afrikaner Nationalist view of South Africa today – a gallant, God-fearing country surrounded by the forces of evil. It is the theme of countless politicians' speeches ever 16 December:

South Africa is on the brink of another Blood River, and this might be the beginning of the most vicious battle in South Africa's existence . . .

Dingane still threatens South Africa in many forms, International Communism and Pan African Nationalism . . .

The times call for a new covenant among all the peoples of South Africa so that the forces of order can be pitted against those of Marxism . . .

As the Afrikaner Volk had once resisted the impis of Dingane at Blood River, so too, the South African Volk should brace themselves against the assault of the new Russian Imperialism.

On the site of the Battle stand sixty-four life-size bronze wagons, in the form of the original laager. They cost the tax payer a small fortune. Every 16 December, as at the Voortrekker Monument, the faithful come to renew the Covenant. It is a remote spot and many camp overnight to enjoy a full twenty-four hours of Afrikaner *Volkfeeste*. On the first evening there is a concert of Voortrekker songs, *Boeresport* like tug of war and sack races, followed by a barbeque, known in Afrikaans as a *braaivleis*, organised by the local branch of the *Rapportryers*, the political Afrikaner version of Rotary.

The sixteenth begins with the raising of the flag, prayers and the National Anthem. Then there is a full church service with a sermon about the importance of the vow and the missionary role of Afrikanerdom, followed by a lengthy political version from an invited speaker. No Afrikaner public figure worth his *boerewors* (sausage) will fail to be on his feet somewhere in South Africa that day. The *Federasie van Afrikaanse Kultuurverenigings* – FAK – the Broederbond front organisation that co-ordinates such events, believes there are at least five hundred ceremonies each year.

The climax at Blood River itself comes in the centre of the laager with the laying of a wreath and the vow:

Here we stand before the Holy God of heaven and earth, to make him a vow that if he will protect us and deliver the enemy into our hands we will observe this day each year as a day of thanksgiving, like a sabbath. And we will also enjoin our children to take part with us for all the coming generations. For the honour of His name shall be glorified and the glory of the victory shall be given to Him.

At many ceremonies there is another striking ritual. Every person present takes up a stone and, just before the vow, lays it on an evergrowing pile, the symbol of united Afrikanerdom. These can be stirring moments, even for an outsider, but the implications are clear. The victory at Blood River which Afrikaner Nationalists claimed as the triumph of civilisation over barbarism was, however camouflaged, the victory of whites over blacks. Civilisation equals white, barbarism equals black. In Rhodesia Ian Smith insisted only that government should remain in 'civilised' hands. Every Rhodesian knew exactly what he meant.

For all that Afrikaners read into the victory, it did not really mark the start of a new era. The battle did not destroy the Zulus' military power. It took another forty years and the more sophisticated firepower of the British army to do that, and not before the 24th Regiment of Foot had suffered one of the worst defeats in British military history when the Zulus surprised them at Isandhlwana on 22 January 1879.

The victory at Blood River did, however, allow the Boers to set up their own republic in Natal, away from British rule – which was the reason for the trek in the first place – but it was a short-lived triumph. And for that the Boers had only themselves to blame. Two weeks after the battle, at the end of December 1838, Pretorius sent a heavily-armed commando further into Zululand to try to recover the cattle the Zulus had stolen after the massacre at Bloukrans. They rode straight into an ambush and six Boers and the Englishman, Alexander Biggar, were killed. In the confusion the Boers also managed to shoot a number of the Port Natal Scouts who were on their side, and they recovered only some of their cattle.

For a year afterwards Pretorius sent demands to Dingane for more cattle, claiming as many as nineteen thousand. Dingane replied by sending two hundred oxen and two indunas, Dambuza and Khambazana, to negotiate. Pretorius had both of them executed and stepped up his demand to forty thousand cattle. Then he sent out another commando and a force of Zulus who had deserted from Dingane. The Zulus met in bloody battle, after which the Boers ranged through the whole territory stripping kraal after kraal, returning in triumph to Pietermaritzburg, the new capital of 'The Free Province of New Holland in South East Africa', with a cool thirty-six thousand cattle. They also had with them over a thousand 'orphaned' Zulu apprentices who were put to work in Voortrekker homes.

For his services they proclaimed Mpande, the leader of the deserters and also Dingane's half-brother, as the new King of the Zulus, charging him eight thousand head of cattle for the honour.

The Boer farms along the foothills of the Drakensberg were still suffering from counter-raids, both from dispossessed Zulus and from parties of Bushmen who lived in the mountains. In December 1840 Pretorius took two hundred men and wiped out a clan who they believed were cattle thieves, clearing their kraals for good measure. The same year, Dingane was killed by a rival tribe and as news of his death spread, thousands of refugees who had fled before his regiments returned to their old grazing grounds. But now they were occupied by the Boers. In August 1841, the Boer Volksraad in Pietermaritzburg voted in favour of a simple solution. Only five families of Zulus would be allowed on each farm. That, of course, ensured a convenient labour force. The rest would be moved off to special reserves. So began the disputes over territory that are still not settled today.

In 1975, at a party in Durban, an Afrikaner businessman was talking about the problems he was having with the Zulus who were still living on a farm when his family bought it. They already had nine farms in Natal. 'We wanted to buy the Zulus out,' he said. 'We didn't need any more labour. But they just wouldn't go. Do you know what we had to do? We had to burn their kraals down. It was a terrible shame.'

In 1841 the Zulus did at least have someone to listen to their complaints, Sir George Napier, Governor-General of the Cape Province. Britain had already made one half-hearted attempt to annex Natal and the Boers' continuing ill-treatment of the natives hardened Colonial Office resolve. In May 1843 Napier announced in Cape Town that Her Majesty Queen Victoria intended to adopt Natal as one of her colonies. When the Union Jack was hoisted in Port Natal it was too much for many of the Boers. Susanna Smit, wife of the one pastor who had been with the trek right from the Cape, led a delegation of wives to Pietermaritzburg to see the Honourable Henry Cloete, the new British High Commissioner. At this famous encounter she listed the Boer grievances, and ended: 'We would rather go barefoot back over the Drakensberg to meet our independence or our death, than bow down before a government which has treated us as the British have done.'

The Afrikaners of northern Natal raised a statue to her only two years ago. It stands on the very edge of the Drakensberg escarpment at the spot where Piet Retief had led the Boer wagons down into the promised land. Her feet are bare. Her face is turned away from Natal; and that is where three-quarters of the Boer settlers went in 1843, back over the mountains – the way they had come. So the Trek went on. But the British were always one step behind.

The families who heaved their belongings back over the Drakensberg soon became part of two new Boer Republics. In 1852 the British agreed to recognise, 'the fullest rights of the emigrant farmers beyond the Vaal River to manage their own affairs and govern themselves according to their own laws.' As part of the deal the British gave up 'all alliances whatever and with whomsoever of the coloured nations'; the Transvaalers said they would give up slavery. Two years later the British granted similar independence to the Orange River Territory, mainly because it was costing Whitehall too much to supervise.

The new Republics certainly did not see eye to eye. They almost went to war when a Transvaal leader tried a coup in the Free State. Such unbrotherly arguments suited successive British High Commissioners in Cape Town who had no wish to see any amalgamation of the Boer forces.

Then diamonds were discovered in an area jointly claimed by the Transvaal, the Free State, two black tribes and the half-caste Griquas. Diggers flocked in, many of them English, and founded their own pocket republic. To settle everybody's arguments Gladstone's government took over the whole lot as a British Colony in October 1871.

Within six years Britain was to also annex the Transvaal. The Boer republic was in a parlous state. The Transvaal pound was worth one shilling; the Transvaal borders were being crossed with impunity by hostile black tribes. The Boers seemed to have lost the will to defend their new territory. In the Pretoria Assembly, the *Volksraad*, the bickering was endless. The Dutch church, already an offshoot from

21

the mother church in the Cape which had refused to give the Trek its blessing, was riven by dissent and had split into two sects. Three hundred families, disillusioned with their new republic, had trekked off once more into the interior. They went right across the Kalahari Desert, suffering terribly in what became known as the Thirstland Trek, and spent years in today's Angola before eventually finishing up in South West Africa.

When intelligence reports to London suggested a British presence in the Transvaal might not be entirely unwelcome, Lord Carnarvon, the Secretary for the Colonies, dispatched an envoy, Sir Theophilus Shepstone, to Pretoria. Scenting what was in the wind, the Vice President of the Transvaal, Paul Kruger, led a protest to London but to no avail. Carnarvon turned down flat Kruger's request to let the burghers say what they thought at the ballot box. On 12 April 1877, Shepstone, formally proclaimed the annexation of the Transvaal in the name of Her Britannic Majesty.

But on the ground in South Africa, Her Britannic Majesty's soldiery faced more than they could handle. In January 1879, the Zulus had given them a beating at Isandhlwana. In the Transvaal the senior British administrator, Colonel Sir Owen Lanyon, had neither the men nor the manner to control the recalcitrant Boers; he was known to be making a lot of enemies by treating the burghers like regimental recruits. It did not help that his swarthy complexion was so tanned that the Boers thought he was 'nothing but a nigger'.

In November 1880, Lanyon's heavy-handedness over a tax debt of twenty-seven pounds and five shillings led to a riot in Potchefstroom. Shots were fired though it has never been established who pulled the first trigger. Symbolically, on 16 December, the anniversary of Blood River, the Boers hoisted the Vierkleur, the four-coloured flag of their Republic. The first War of Liberation had begun. Within four days the Boers annihilated a British column, catching them unawares as they were marching to Pretoria. The band was in the middle of playing, 'Kiss me Mother, kiss your darling Daughter'. Three more British defeats followed, the last at Majuba Hill so conclusive that Afrikaners were still lighting bonfires to celebrate that and other British reverses right through the 1939 World War. 'Remember Majuba' was long a rallying cry.

Gladstone's new Liberal Government, beset with the Irish problem, was happy to give the Transvaal independence again without further ado. Westminster reserved for its own jurisdiction only foreign relations and some aspects of native affairs; the rest was handed back to Pretoria. The Boers went back to their farms, confident that the Lord was on their side and likely to remain so in any future conflict. Then, incredibly, the whole cycle began again.

In 1886 gold in undreamed of quantities was discovered on the Witwatersrand. *Uitlanders* (foreigners) poured into the Transvaal. Kruger's Republic was being overrun, every Afrikaner susceptibility ignored.

Cecil Rhodes, the Prime Minister of the Cape, with one eye on his vision of Union Jacks all the way up Africa, the other on the gold, hatched a flimsy excuse to invade the Transvaal. With a nod and a wink from Whitehall he launched the infamous Jameson Raid, which took its name from a doctor, Leander Starr Jameson who led an armed band into the Boer republic. His arrival was to have been the signal for a general uprising of the uitlanders. But the whole episode was a disaster, badly planned and executed. The uprising never took place; Jameson and his sorry troop were captured. To President Kruger and his Boers it only underlined what they had really known all the time, that the British could never be trusted; and what was more they were incompetent.

'Before the Jameson Raid,' recalls Kowie Marais, former judge and from 1977 member of Parliament for the Progressive opposition, 'my father used to write his love letters to my mother in English. It was the smart thing to do for middle-class Afrikaners. After the Jameson Raid he never allowed English to be spoken in the house again.'

Negotiations between Pretoria and London dragged on for three years. The nominal issue was a vote for the uitlanders who worked the gold mines. But the Boers were as reluctant to give the franchise to them as they are to today's black uitlanders who keep the Nationalist economy going. Kruger, of course, knew that was not all. 'Her Majesty's subjects', he complained, 'demanded my trousers. I gave them and my coat likewise. They now want my life; I cannot grant them that.'

The Boers' ultimatum to Her Majesty's Government, approved by the Volksraad, was delivered to Colonial Secretary Joseph Chamberlain at 6.15 on the morning of 10 October 1899. It demanded that all British troops in the Transvaal should be withdrawn and that those on the high seas on the way to South Africa should be sent back. All disputes between Britain and the Transvaal should go to arbitration. If Her Majesty's Government failed to comply within forty-eight hours the government of the South African Republic would, 'with great regret be compelled to regard the action as a formal declaration of war.'

Chamberlain could not have been more pleased. Her Majesty naturally rejected the ultimatum. The Boers had fallen into the trap of presenting themselves as the aggressors.

In the block of flats for retired people where she lives in Mears Street, Pretoria, Mrs Hettie Domisse does not see it quite like that. Her husband fought right through the war and survived to rebel again against the British in 1914 when they tried to send him to South West Africa to fight the Germans.

'This war,' she says, 'this Boer War, was the stupidest war the English ever carried on, because all that they achieved was to consolidate the Afrikaner Nation, from the bottom of the Cape, right up to Transvaal.'

2

'The stupidest war
the English ever carried on'

Mrs Hettie Domisse on the Anglo-Boer War

Henning Klopper was nearly five when what he calls the 'English War' began in October 1899. His first memory is of a long trip, a trek from the family farm in the Free State across the Drakensberg to take his brother back to the front. Christoffel, the eldest of six Klopper boys, had joined up immediately but in one of the first engagements had been wounded in the back by shrapnel; after some hospital treatment and a brief rest at home he was returning to his commando at Ladysmith. Klopper's father was there too with the Boers besieging the town.

In the first weeks of the war, three Afrikaner columns had invaded Natal. The British forces, with reinforcements still on the high seas, had withdrawn to Ladysmith, an important railway junction on the line between Natal, the Free State and the Transvaal. There, for four months, the Boers encircled them.

Mrs Klopper had loaded the family wagon with provisions for her menfolk because, as Henning Klopper put it: 'the Boers had no commissariat to provide food, every burgher had to find his own.' She put the two brothers up on top and off they went. Christoffel's horse and a couple of spares walked behind.

'My brother could walk [said Klopper] but he couldn't ride a horse, so we had to take him by ox-wagon. He didn't want to stay at home any longer. He wanted to get at the enemy.'

Such patriotic impetuosity on the part of the young Boers was not shared by the Boer leaders. Old General Joubert for one had rationalised his decision not to launch his champing horsemen on the fleeing British force as they fell back on Ladysmith, by saying: 'When God holds out a finger, don't take the whole hand.'

This curious piece of tactical reasoning might have consoled the General's conscience but it hardly accelerated the Boers' war effort. The fact is that the Boers failed to capitalise on their initial numerical

25

A Boer picket at Ladysmith where the British garrison of twelve thousand was besieged for four months

and military advantage and drive deep into Natal and the Cape. Instead they occupied themselves with sieges of Mafeking and Kimberley in the Cape, as well as Ladysmith, all three towns only just beyond the borders of their own Republics. It was as though the Boers felt they had gone far enough and now they should wait for Britain to treat with them as they had done after Majuba in 1881. But this time the British terms were all-out war and they were mobilising the might of the British Empire to fight it. Whatever opportunity the Boers might have had of neutralising the British threat was lost. They went on the defensive as though this was the best way of beating the British. By the end of the year when Lord Roberts took over the command of the British forces it was already too late.

Writing in a prisoner-of-war camp in India, a young Transvaler, Dietlof van Warmelo, had his own view on the Boers' caution:

It can be explained in this way [he wrote]. We were accustomed to fighting against Kaffirs, who hid in woods and mountains, and against whom we had to advance with the utmost precaution, so as to lose as few lives as possible. So we were too cautious in the beginning of the war. We would not make a great sacrifice to win a battle.

As it was, the Boers now faced a war that would result in the deaths of one-sixth of their entire population.

In February 1900, Roberts' forces, advancing from the Cape, inflicted the first heavy defeat on the Boers at Paardeberg, just inside the Free State near Kimberley. General Cronje and four thousand burghers were taken prisoner and the British swept north into Boer territory. When they reached Bloemfontein, Klopper's mother, back on the farm near Heilbron, waited no longer. 'We inspanned the wagon and fled,' said Klopper. There were ten of them: Klopper's mother, three teenage daughters and a baby sister born the year the war broke out, plus Henning and four of the brothers, all older than him. Then there was, 'the boy who drove the oxen', a black man named Speelman.

Eighty years later Klopper still remembers the oxen. 'The right leader was Platberg. Next to him was Wildeman. The next two were Donkerland and Witbooi. The two rear oxen were Appel and Stella-land.' Speelman had been in charge of that particular span for years. Klopper's father never allowed him to strike any of the oxen. 'He should speak to them and if he should have to use the whip he should just catch them under the belly, just with the point of the whip.'

With them they took a wagonload of *padkos* (provisions), a kettle, blankets and some of their Afrikander cattle. They left behind all their sheep, 'my parents told me we had four thousand very fine Merino stock', and they left behind their beloved geese. For months the little group moved north, avoiding other families, afraid that the British would pick on several wagons while they might leave a single family alone. Sometimes they saw the British soldiers in the distance.

'The others were looking with field glasses to see what was happening, and I would also look. You could see them in their regiments, marching. It looked as if the whole world was moving up and down.' For a little boy it was something of an adventure but they all had a good idea of what would happen if the British caught them. 'I knew that we were fleeing from them. From what we had heard we thought they were savages.'

They crossed the Vaal River into the Transvaal. To them it was a different country. 'We were two separate peoples. Although we were all Afrikaners, we had a different system to them, a different way of life almost.' But at Heidelberg they were warned of a great concentration of British troops and they turned back. They had gone about eight miles back over the Vaal River, a day's march, when they came across a large group of families, outspanned, waiting. They travelled right through them, moving fast. The oxen knew they were heading for home. Just as they were clear of the stationary wagons they saw British soldiers coming up behind on horseback. From in front there was firing; a dozen or so burghers retreating, moving from cover to cover, dismounting and firing.

Jan Klopper, aged fifteen, jumped on his horse.

'Look,' he said to my mother, 'I'm not going to allow myself to be captured by the British.' And he stuck out his hand to my mother and he waved her goodbye. He didn't have a hat. He didn't have a gun, didn't have a blanket, a change of clothing. It was midwinter. He didn't know where he was going, where he was going to get his next meal from. But nothing in this world would stop him. He wouldn't allow himself to be captured by the British, not at any price. He'd sooner be dead. He just rode away. Why they didn't shoot I don't know. Perhaps they couldn't fire when they were moving.

As the leading soldier passed the wagon the oldest daughter shouted:

'For God's sake, don't harm the boy.' Her name was Christina. She could speak English. And he took his sword and made a strike at her but she fell back in the wagon and he didn't touch her. Of course I don't want to hold it against the man. It was in the heat of battle, and it was a life for a life. And he did it perhaps unthinking.

The soldiers chased the Boers out of sight, but before long they were back. They made the Kloppers turn their wagon around and head back towards the other families. Then the whole convoy, under guard, set off for Heidelberg. 'And there,' said Klopper, 'they loaded us on an open coal truck.'

Three hundred miles to the south-west, in a Free State town called Luckhoff, another Boer boy had also been having his first taste of the war. Ernst Gideon Malherbe was born in November 1895. Ten months younger than Klopper, he was not quite four when the fighting began. His father was the *Dominee*, the vicar, of the local Dutch church. Most of the congregation had joined the district commando, and the Dominee became their chaplain. Before the British invaded, they came to church on Sunday with their bandoliers and rifles. Ernie Malherbe never forgot them. 'I remember how these men sat there with their guns. And when they stood up for a hymn or a prayer the butts knocked on the floor. It made an extraordinary sound in the church.'

At other times Malherbe's father drove out to the commando to hold Sunday service in the veld. Young Ernie went with him in the pony and cart. The Dominee always took his Mauser, and he always took his fiddle on which he played the hymns. Once, they went to Magersfontein where in December 1899 the Boers had won one of their early victories, inflicting heavy losses on the Highland Brigade. 'When we arrived the men made quite a fuss of me. They hadn't seen a small child for so long.' Malherbe remembered going to see Long Tom, the famous field gun. One of the men, thinking to give the boy a treat, put him up on the barrel, hot from the blazing sun. 'And of course my legs were bare and I let out a yell because it burned my bottom. That's one of my most vivid memories of the war.'

As the British troops swept north from the Cape Colony, early in 1900, Luckhoff fell into their hands. The Dominee was ordered to appear before the British commandant, a Colonel McCracken; he had already arrested one of the church elders. Malherbe recalled how his father told him that McCracken threatened to arrest him too, but said he would give the Dominee a chance on one condition: 'That you stop preaching war and introducing politics into religion. I heard about you in the Cape a month ago already.'

'Excuse me, Colonel,' my father replied. 'I have never introduced politics into religion but what I have decidedly tried to do is to introduce religion into politics.'

Would he be allowed to pray for his own leader, President Steyn of the Free State Republic? 'I would hardly advise you to do so,' said the Colonel.

Not long after a new Commandant arrived. Dominee Malherbe was arrested and sent to the Castle in Cape Town as a prisoner of war. Malherbe's mother took her two children, Ernie now six and Rachel aged four, and set off for her parents' home at Malmesbury, thirty miles outside Cape Town. Somehow her father, also a church Minister, had arranged a pass to allow them through the British lines.

The station at Belmont was patrolled by British soldiers. Just before the train pulled out Rachel spat at them and shouted: 'Sies, julle kakies!' – 'you dirty khakis!' Mrs Malherbe was so frightened that she hid her daughter under the seat.

'I don't know until this day how my grandfather managed to obtain permission for us to get on the train. It is quite a miracle that we escaped because the other people of Luckhoff, all the women and the children, were put into concentration camps.'

In the open coal trucks they had been forced to board at Heidelberg, that is exactly where the Klopper family were now going.

There were four families in each truck. One in each corner. In their corner were Henning Klopper's mother and, after his brother Jan had ridden off into the veld, eight children. Their oxen, their Afrikander cattle and Speelman who had been with them as they fled before the British, they left behind. They never saw any of them again.

They were ten days on the trucks, with little water, no proper sanitation, and no chance to wash. Sometimes the train was shunted into a siding to let other trains past carrying soldiers or prisoners of war. Back into the Free State they went, finishing up at Kroonstad, barely a hundred miles from Heidelberg.

When we got there we were taken to a sandy hill, a God-forsaken place alongside the Vals River [said Klopper]. It was winter then, and the river was very low. And they gave us a bell tent and said: 'There you are.' Eventually we got a second bell tent and that is where we had to live. There was no protection. In the summer you could almost not live for the flies. And the sanitation was an open hole with small lavatories erected for all the people. You could imagine how disease could spread.

Fresh water was rationed. It was delivered each day by mule cart. The Kloppers had only a small bucket, so they could take about a gallon and a half, morning and evening. Young Henning's job was to go and fetch it; and it was a long way to the cart and back. The food, he says, was terrible. 'We couldn't get milk, we couldn't get butter, sugar was very scarce and the meat – the mutton that we got was in such a condition that it was uneatable.'

Under Kitchener's policy the Kloppers were lucky to have meat at all. Thomas Pakenham, in his comprehensive history *The Boer War*, records that there were two scales of rations for what Whitehall called 'refugees'. No meat for families whose menfolk were still out on commando. It provided 'both a useful economy and an encouragement for the men to come in and surrender.'

It means, [said Liberal member Lloyd George in a parliamentary debate] that unless the fathers come in, their children will be half-starved. It means that the remnants of the Boer army who are sacrificing everything for their idea of independence, are to be tortured by the spectacle of their starving children into betraying their cause.

Rations in the camps did improve later but they were never as much as the troops received.

The blacks who had been workers on Boer farms were put into British labour gangs. Their families went to separate concentration camps but nobody bothered much about them. The daily mainten-

One of the British camps where 'concentrations' of families of fighting Boers were held during the Anglo-Boer War

ance allowance for Boers was 8½d a head, for blacks it was 4½d. Over thirteen thousand blacks died.

The families of Boers who had stopped fighting and gone home were treated better; but these *hensoppers* or 'hands-uppers', as the Boers called them, were much despised by those who fought on and the commandos under Botha, Smuts and De la Rey made it official policy to drive them from their farms.

As the war progressed British strategy was quite simple. Although they vastly outnumbered their opponents they could not catch the lightly-armed Boer guerrillas; so the British High Command resolved to deny them the support of the farms that fed and sheltered them. They blew up the buildings, killed the cattle, burned the crops and put the women and children into the world's first concentration camps. The British High Commissioner for South Africa, Lord Milner, was quite clear about the intention. It was, he revealed, 'to knock the bottom out of the great Afrikaner nation for ever and ever Amen.'

The Kloppers were part of the reason why Milner failed. As well as his brother and father, both of Henning's grandfathers had volunteered. One, on his mother's side, was sixty-six when the war started. He was captured and sent to India.

Some of the millions of cattle and sheep slaughtered by British troops as part of the scorched-earth policy to deny supplies to the Boer guerrillas

'My other grandfather,' said Klopper, 'was eighty-six. He was taken on the battle field because his horse was too lively and he couldn't mount when the British charged. So he was captured and he died in captivity.' He was not the first Klopper to shed blood for the cause. In Dingane's kraal in Natal there is a monument to the seventy burghers who were murdered with Piet Retief. Among the names are four Kloppers and four Dreyers who were 'relations by marriage'. Another man of the family had stayed behind with the wives and children at Bloukrans. He and his wife were killed when the Zulus attacked. Only the children escaped.

Henning's brother Jan, who had jumped on his horse and fled just before the family was captured, survived and fought throughout the war. Christoffel, the other brother, stayed at Ladysmith until the British raised the siege. He also fought at Spion Kop, where the Boers drove a numerically superior British force from the top of that blood-stained hill. Later he became part of General Louis Botha's staff. Eventually he too was captured by National Scouts, Boers who fought on the British side. He was shot in the legs by a man he thought was 'one of our people'. He too was sent to India as a prisoner of war.

Klopper is still enraged at the lot of many of those who were captured:

Why didn't the British take the prisoners of war to civilised countries, to Australia or New Zealand? Why did they take them to non-white countries? Is it because they wanted to hide their sins? They didn't take any to Britain. They dared not. But why Burma? Why Ceylon? Why India? Why?

Klopper believes that many Boers joined the British because they had to choose between that and being shipped abroad:

We are not seafaring people at all. It was a terrible punishment to send people by ship. We are a people accustomed to the land, and people were so afraid of the ships that they would do anything – join the British, become a National Scout, anything.

Whatever the reason the Boers had for changing sides it is estimated that a fifth of all fighting Afrikaners were on the British side by the end of the war. Klopper cannot forgive them. The Hensoppers perhaps, if they just gave up. The National Scouts are another matter:

To this very day there are people, descendants of National Scouts, that the greater body of Afrikaners won't associate with. I can go and point you out the families. We still distrust them to this very day. And we'll distrust them to our death.

Not all Boer prisoners of war were sent abroad. Chaplain Malherbe was first imprisoned in the Castle at Cape Town and then a short distance away at Green Point. As a Minister of the Church he received certain concessions. While he was in the camp he studied for a law degree and even persuaded the British to allow him out occasionally to play first violin in the Cape Town City orchestra, 'for which he earned £1'.

At the parsonage in Malmesbury, thirty miles away, the Malherbe children lived quite comfortably: 'There were horses and there were beautiful trees around the house, and several acres of open ground'. Then one day the British came and requisitioned the whole lot: 'They turned it into a khaki camp while we were living inside the house. We were completely surrounded by the khakis. There must have been a thousand or more judging by the tents.'

By now the Malherbes' home town at Luckhoff had taken the full force of Kitchener's scorched earth policy. Most of the houses had been destroyed, and the troops had smashed up the pews in the church for firewood. In a contemporary account called *On the Heels of de Wet*,

A contemporary drawing from the *Illustrated London News*. The caption read: 'Burning the farm of a treacherous burgher'

published in 1902, a British Intelligence officer described what happened when the soldiers reached the Malherbes' home:

The brigadier had planted his little red pennant in front of the villa of the absconded predikant. It was the only house in the area which had any pretension to decorative finish, but when the staff took over it was a sorry pigstye . . . The ruthless hand of man had ransacked each drawer and crevice and all that calls for the sacred care of woman lay tossed and tumbled on the dirt floor and passage.

When the soldiers had taken what they wanted, they burned the Dominee's home to the ground. What upset Malherbe's father most was that his library was destroyed.

'As children,' said Malherbe, 'we had a hatred of them, knowing what they had done . . .'

3

'It wasn't war, it was deliberate murder'

Henning Klopper on British tactics in the Anglo-Boer War

At Kroonstad concentration camp Klopper's ten-year-old brother was the first of the family to die. He developed typhoid, was taken to the military hospital but survived only a few days. It was the practice to give typhoid patients virtually nothing to eat, and Klopper is quite convinced that is what killed his brother. 'Just before he died he said to mother, "Mother just feel – you can feel my backbone through my stomach. I am dying of starvation."'

One night soon after, one of his sisters awoke, singing a hymn, 'and my mother said "You can't make a noise, you can't sing anything. It's not done. They'll come and arrest us." And about a week after that she became ill, she went to hospital and she died too.'

For her last few days, because there were so few hospital staff, she was nursed by another sister. Then she too fell sick, and it was Klopper's turn to help.

I found her with her arms and legs strapped to the bed. All the others were ill and couldn't visit this sister, they were all in bed. I was the only one that could move.

I came to her bed and saw countless numbers of flies round her face. She couldn't move away the flies because she was strapped down to the bed. Her mouth was wide open trying to get breath. And the flies were moving in and out of her mouth, her nose and everywhere and there she was, almost in the throes of death with nobody to attend her, nobody to do anything for her.

I moved away the flies as much as I could but what could I do? I stayed there for possibly an hour but I was only a little boy. When I told my mother, she broke down and was very ill. She couldn't even attend the funeral. I was the only one of the family well enough to go.

And when she finally was dead and they took her off the bed, they found that the bedpan had been under her, possibly for days, because she was all raw underneath.

Twenty-six thousand women and children died in the British concen-

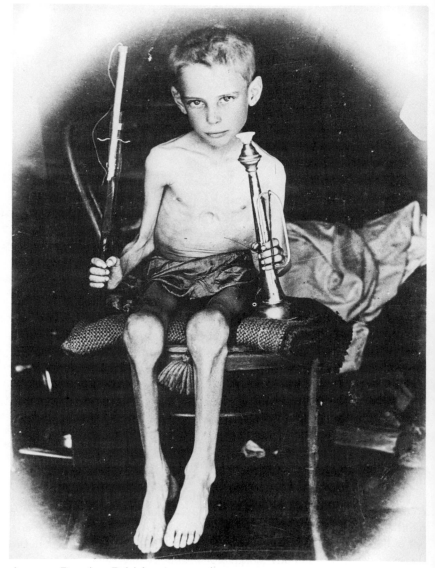

A young Boer in a British concentration camp

tration camps. Klopper remains convinced that if the British public had only known, 'there would have been civil war. And if there hadn't been civil war I would have said they were a lot of savages.' He is equally convinced, against all persuading, that people in Britain still refuse to acknowledge what was really happening.

It matters little today that the British Commander-in-Chief, Lord

Kitchener, had actually tried to make a deal with the Boer leader, Louis Botha, that he would spare the farms and the families of burghers on commando if Botha would agree to leave in peace those who had surrendered or who wanted to remain neutral. Botha would not agree. The fate of the women and children was thus sealed.

At the time, the War Minister, St John Broderick, certainly claimed that the refugee camps were well-run and were designed to encourage the Boers to come in and surrender; later that the camps were a military and a moral necessity. The commandos had to be deprived of food, and how could the women and children be left to starve? *The Times* correspondent, cabling from Bloemfontein, stressed that the death rate in the camp there was 'rapidly decreasing' when the reverse was true. Milner was prepared to argue that in any case the responsibility for the deaths should lie with the enemy. 'The problem was not of our making,' he said in a despatch, 'and it is beyond our power to grapple with it.'

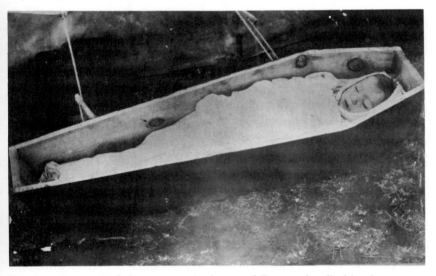

Twenty thousand of the twenty-six thousand Boers who died in the concentration camps were less than sixteen years old

There were reports and editorials in *The Times* saying that the Boers were quite used to living in confined surroundings, did not like fresh air and never gave milk to their children anyway; and it was all for their own protection that they were being put into the camps. Seventy-five years later similar arguments were put forward by apologists for the policy of herding black farmers into protected villages during the

Rhodesian War. It took a middle-aged English spinster named Emily Hobhouse to bring home to the British the full horror of what was really happening in South Africa. Her reports, speeches and paintings after visiting camps in the Free State and Transvaal finally aroused the national conscience.

On a visit to the camp at Aliwal North she wrote:

I began to compare a parish I had known at home of two thousand people where a funeral was an event – and usually of an old person. Here some twenty to twenty-five were carried away daily . . . The full realisation of the position dawned on me – it was a death rate such as had never been known except in the times of the Great Plagues. The whole talk was of death – who died yesterday, who lay dying today, and who would be dead tomorrow . . . It was all kept very quiet, after a while the corpses were carried away at dawn, and instead of passing through the town, approached the cemetery another way; many were buried in one grave.

In Parliament, Lloyd George, a member of the Liberal Opposition, pinned down the government to a debate in June 1901.

We want to make loyal British subjects of these people. Is this the way to do that? Brave men will forget injustices to themselves much more readily than they will insults, indignities and wrongs to their women and children . . . When children are being treated in this way and dying, we are simply ranging the deepest passions of the human heart against British rule in Africa . . . It will always be remembered that this is the way British rule started here, and this is the method by which it was brought about.

These are exactly the feelings that Henning Klopper remembers today.

The only conclusion I could draw from that war is that Milner and Kitchener were out to break the backbone of the Afrikaner, and their backbone consisted of their womenfolk. And to destroy as many women and children as they could. Otherwise you can't excuse a war campaign of this description.

And can you recollect any war in this history of mankind where such a ferocious war had been fought against a small community? It's not war, it's deliberate murder.

Emily Hobhouse never went to the Kroonstad camp where the Kloppers were held, but other investigators did. One report in November 1901 drew attention to the crematorium the military had established close to the camp, and to their refusal to move it. The Committee of Women, led by Mrs Millicent Fawcett, who came out from Britain the same year, noted that Kroonstad had an 'extremely bad' water supply.

At Heilbron, fifty-five miles away, they found that most of the camp

Cartoon from an Amsterdam weekly (October 1899) with Queen Victoria saying to Joseph Chamberlain, Secretary for the Colonies, 'I wash my hands in innocence'

inmates were healthy until hundreds of patients with measles were sent there from Kroonstad and infected them too, causing many deaths. A three-man committee of consuls of foreign powers represented in Pretoria found that the death rate in the camps at Kroonstad and Bloemfontein was fourteen times the normal rate for Pretoria, with deaths among children increasing at an alarming rate. After the war Emily Hobhouse met a small girl who had lost six brothers and sisters in the Kroonstad camp. Just outside Bloemfontein there is a memorial to those days of suffering; it is called the *Vrouemonument*, the National Womens' memorial, and bears the simple inscription: '*Aan onze heldinnen en liewe kinderen*' – 'To our heroines and beloved children.' '*Uw wil Geschiede*' . . . 'Thy will be done.' Emily Hobhouse is buried here too.

A visiting English newspaper editor, Geoffery Crowther, once said: 'No Englishman can understand South African history until he has seen this shrine.'

Today, many ordinary Afrikaners seem ready to forgive the events of three-quarters of a century ago but their Nationalist masters remain unwilling to let the wounds heal. Nor is it just a question of remembering old martyrs; new ones are still being created. On 27 May 1978 a memorial was unveiled to one such discovered hero at Graaff Reinet in the Eastern Cape. He was Kommandant Gideon Scheepers who had been executed by the British on 18 January 1902. The ceremony was part of the events to celebrate thirty years of Nationalist government. Prime Minister John Vorster was the guest of honour. Six months before, he had won the biggest election victory in South African history. English voters by the thousand had gone over to the Nationalists. Pamphlets from Eschel Rhoodie's Department of Information already spoke of the new 'Anglo-Afrikaner Nation'.

That togetherness was not much in evidence in the bright sunshine on the hillside at Graaff Reinet. This was a tribal affair. English South Africans, if they were there, had little to say. 'This is something that God has given us in a wonderful way,' said one of the organisers, Mrs Jane Retief, to me. 'If you are going to give a turn to this, to use this against our country, then you are going against the will of God.' There was a girls' choir from the local *Volkskool* (the people's school) dressed in long black robes, their hair tied back in traditional buns. They recited a dirge called '*Gebed om die Gebeente*' – 'Prayer for the bones' – that told of the legend of Gideon Scheepers, the story of a mother searching for the body of her son.

Scheepers was the leader of one of the commandos that penetrated deep into the Cape Province, towards the end of the war, to harass British lines. A young lawyer named Jan Smuts led a similar band. The Cape was British territory, so any local Boers who joined the invaders were technically in rebellion against the Crown. If caught they were tried for treason. Over fifty were executed. Those deaths still rankle with the Afrikaners as further British crimes. At twenty-two, Scheepers was one of the youngest Boer leaders. He was a romantic figure, who became a folk hero – wrecking trains, burning

Kommandant Gideon Scheepers, twenty-two-year-old guerrilla leader

the farms of Boers who collaborated with the British. There were about two hundred and fifty in his commando. They wore distinctive white bands around their hats. Many were teenagers who should have been in school. Once they rode into the small town of Uniondale, released all the Boer prisoners in the gaol, locked up the magistrate, burned all the records and hauled down the Union Jack. Scheepers then rode through the main street with the Union Jack tied to the tail of his horse.

But Scheepers' men also flogged and shot natives who helped the British, looted as well as burned farms, and executed Boer 'traitors'. Once when they caught two Boers they believed were spies, Scheepers made them draw lots; one carried a message back whence he came, the other was shot. For months the British hunted the Boer commando but Scheepers remained uncatchable. Then in September 1901 he fell sick. Soon he was too ill to ride, and was left behind at a farmhouse where the Khakis quickly found him. He was sent to hospital and then put on trial at Graaff Reinet, ironically on 16 December.

'Thirty accusations were brought against me of "murder"', Scheepers wrote in his diary. 'Seven of "arson", "rough" handling of prisoners, "barbaric" treatment of kaffirs etc.' Technically he was not a rebel at all. He was born on a farm near Middleburg in the Eastern Transvaal, the second of ten children. At the age of sixteen he had enrolled in the *Transvaal Staatsartillerie*, transferred later to another artillery unit in the Orange Free State. After gaining a reputation as a scout he had been given his own marauding commando and sent into the Cape Province. None of these considerations deterred his British military prosecutors.

Scheepers was particularly incensed at the accusations that he had ill-treated blacks, and that blacks were allowed to testify in court and even act as gaolers. 'We Afrikaners,' he wrote, 'will never find justice under the English. Everything is for the kaffirs.' It was hardly true,

Execution of Scheepers by a British firing squad, 18 January 1902

but Scheepers did not live to find out. He was judged guilty and sentence of death was read out to him in front of the townspeople, assembled under British orders, in the main square of Graaff Reinet. Scheepers was taken by ambulance to a hillside outside the town, tied to a chair, blindfolded and shot by a squad from the Coldstream Guards. In *The Great Boer War*, Byron Farwell tells the end of the story: 'Scheepers' body was cut loose, put on a blanket and carried to the grave. As they were about to lower it an officer called "Let him drop". He was dropped.'

'When the adjutant ordered us to drop him,' said one of the soldiers later, 'it made me feel sick.'

At the end of the war Scheepers' parents came to Graaff Reinet to look for their son's grave, but could not find it. When later it was discovered, the body was missing and Scheepers' last resting place is still unknown. Two of his sisters were at the ceremony on that hillside seventy-six years later. Mrs Aletta Beukes, eighty-five, unveiled the memorial; Mrs Mimi Erasmus, eighty-one, laid a wreath. She was helped forward by a young man named Gideon Scheepers, grandson of the hero's brother.

The inscription in Afrikaans reads: 'Kommandant Gideon J. Scheepers 4/4/1878 to 18/1/1902. Shot one hundred metres north of this memorial. He lives on in this land, now and for ever.'

In his address, Prime Minister John Vorster said: 'If we are asked why in 1978 a memorial should be erected for a man who died in 1902, then the answer is simple. The life and work of this man was such that history placed him in the heroes' gallery and nothing and no one can deprive him of that place.'

With the steady elimination of the commandos in the Cape, with the lines of British blockhouses which stretched far across the Free State and the Transvaal, with the decimation of the civilian population in the camps, the end of the war was not long in coming. At the negotiating table the Boers tried desperately to keep their independence, but Milner and Whitehall would have none of it. As far as they were concerned the Free State and the Transvaal were British. The Boers asked for an armistice so that their guerrilla leaders could be consulted. They all met in a marquee provided by the British at Vereeniging on 15 May 1902: thirty commando leaders from the Transvaal, thirty from the Free State, and the Afrikaner politicians. The Boers who had helped the British cause, the Hensoppers and the

National Scouts, had no part in the discussions; nor, of course, did any black man. Some of the commando leaders were for continuing the war. Others, like one of the senior Generals, De la Rey, spoke of the hopelessness of their position:

There has been talk of fighting to the bitter end. But has not the bitter end already come? Each man must answer that question for himself. You must remember that everything has been sacrificed – cattle, goods, money, wife and child. Our men are going about naked and our women have nothing but clothes made of skins to wear. Is not this the bitter end?

General Botha spoke of the critical shortage of supplies to the commandos and another growing problem – the kaffirs, he said, were increasingly attacking families on those of the isolated farms that were still intact. And many of their own kith and kin were now on the British side. General de Wet was for fighting on. He would not agree to giving up any part of Boer territory, not even the gold fields.

General Smuts believed that they no longer had any choice:

We have not continued the struggle aimlessly. We did not fight merely to be shot at. We commenced the struggle and continued it to this moment because we wished to maintain our independence and were prepared to sacrifice everything for it. But we may not sacrifice the Afrikaner people for that independence . . . Brothers, we resolved to fight to the bitter end; let us admit like men that the end has come for us – has come in a more bitter form than we ever thought possible.

After much argument the Boers agreed to a ceasefire if the British would allow them to keep protectorate status, surrendering control of foreign policy. A committee of five was delegated to treat with Milner and Kitchener in Pretoria; Botha, De la Rey and Smuts from the Transvaal, Hertzog and de Wet from the Free State. Smuts and Hertzog were the two legal experts – Smuts was Attorney General in Pretoria before he went to fight. Barry Hertzog was a judge.

Milner rejected their proposals outright. Ten days of bitter negotiations followed. At the end of it, Hertzog and Smuts and the English legal men drafted the Treaty of Vereeniging: the burghers would lay down their arms and acknowledge King Edward VII as their lawful sovereign. In return, 'as soon as circumstances permit, a representative system tending towards autonomy would be introduced.' The British would pay £3 million in reparation, prisoners of war who took the oath of allegiance would be repatriated, Cape rebels would go free on the same terms but would lose the right to vote. Some Dutch as well as English would be taught in the schools.

Milner gave the Boers forty-eight hours in which to sign. The five delegates took the train back to Vereeniging for the decision. It was made in the British marquee soon after two p.m. on 31 May. Only the commando leaders had a vote. The count was fifty-four to six in favour of peace.

'How great was the emotion,' wrote the official reporter. 'I saw the lips quiver of men who had never trembled before a foe. I saw tears brimming in eyes that had been dry when they had seen their dearest laid in the grave.'

An hour before the deadline the delegates were back in Pretoria. 'I have just come from signing the terms of surrender,' Milner wrote to a friend. 'And if anything could make me relent towards the Boers, it was the faces of the men who sat around the table tonight.' As A. N. Pelzer wrote in 1979 in the long-awaited approved version of the history of the Broederbond: 'On 31 May 1902 the citizens of the two republics stood next to the open grave of their freedom'.

The Boers were not the only ones to be disillusioned by the British terms. Article 8 (Clause 9) of the Treaty stated there was to be 'no franchise for the natives until after the introduction of self-government'. That one sentence killed all hope of a vote for black South Africans and opened for them a future without the franchise that still has no horizon today. Few in Whitehall could have been unaware that the constitution of the old Republic of the Transvaal allowed, 'no equality between the coloured people and the white inhabitants either in church or state'. The prospect of ending such discrimination had stilled many British consciences uneasy over the war. There was no reason to suppose that such a fundamental Afrikaner attitude was about to change. Milner and Chamberlain chose to shelve the whole issue of the black vote and evade the responsibility for millions of black British subjects whom they had not hesitated to use to help win the war. But then, as Milner had written to future Liberal Prime Minister Henry Asquith in 1897, 'You have only to sacrifice "the nigger" absolutely and the game is easy.'

So the *Tweede Vryheidsoorlog*, the Second War of Independence, drew to an end. The fighting burghers rode in from the veld and surrendered. There were over twenty-one thousand of them. They had been pinning down an army twenty times that size. They had lost seven thousand in battle: the British dead numbered twenty-two thousand, although many of them, like the families in the concentration camps, perished from disease.

When Smuts explained the ceasefire terms to his commando, a

voice cried 'Jan Smuts you have betrayed us'. Some fired off their last rounds and then smashed their rifles rather than give them up. De Wet wrote of his grief 'at the burial of my nation'. Nonetheless in his memoirs, *The Three Years War*, he directed some unexpected advice to the Volk: 'Be faithful to the new power. Loyalty repays in the end. Loyalty is worthy of a nation that shed its blood for freedom.'

It took nine months to clear the many thousands of families in the concentration camps. The Kloppers were still at Kroonstad and Henning's father came to collect them. He took them to his own father's farm at Parys. On the way from Kroonstad Klopper remembers a whole kraal full of the skeletons of cattle. At Parys the house had been burned down and everything in it.

We had nothing – no furniture, no cooking facilities. We didn't have a stove, and if we had had a stove we had nothing to put on the stove not in the way of either utensils or food . . . And they had killed everything, every chicken and every pig and every sheep – every animal on the farm. There was nothing on the farm. Nothing on any farm.

Malherbe's family had lost everything except his father's violin which he kept with him throughout the war, and his mother's tennis racquet. One of the members of the Dominee's congregation had picked it up some miles from their home, saw her name on it and sent it back to Malmesbury. Long afterwards the Dominee received a letter and a parcel from a William Dean in Manchester. He had been one of the soldiers who had ransacked the house at Luckhoff. He had taken two books, put them in his saddle bag and then posted them from Bloemfontein to his father, a Sunday school superintendent who also ran a bookshop in Manchester. In the parcel were the two books: *The Science of Religion* and *A Threefold Gift of God*. Malherbe's father's name and address were still inside the front cover.

When the war ended the British held thirty thousand Boer prisoners, most of them in camps outside South Africa. All had to take the oath of allegiance to King Edward VII before they were repatriated. In camps in India and Ceylon so many refused that, eighteen months after the armistice, the British had to ask one of the Boer heroes, General De la Rey, to go there and persuade some five hundred *bittereinders* that it was in their own, and the country's, interest that they take the oath and come home.

In Bermuda some sixty Boers still held out. They would not take the oath. They would not work. They refused the offer of free passage to any country of their choice. When the military authorities turned them out on the streets of Hamilton the police arrested them, but in gaol they still refused to work and were put on bread and water. When they were released they sat outside the gaol until they were rearrested. Eventually some took the oath and some drifted away from Bermuda. Some married local girls and there is a story that twenty-five years after the end of the war one Boer was still proclaiming himself a citizen of a republic which no longer existed.

In South Africa, British efforts to help the Boers start life again were vigorous and well-organised. Westminster had agreed £3 million for reparations under the terms at Vereeniging; Milner spent over £16 million. But after all, the British could afford it; they now owned the richest gold mines in the world. The money went on grants and loans, on providing ploughs, seeds and some rations until the Boers could feed themselves, and on veterinary services to combat stock disease. There were, not surprisingly, complaints that the hensoppers did better than the bittereinders. But five years of drought from 1903 made recovery painfully slow, and other measures that Milner was now taking only increased the bitterness that so many of the Boers felt.

As the Boers tried to pick up a living on their devastated land, Henning Klopper believes there was one feeling above all which sustained them:

We had not surrendered unconditionally. Our Nation has never surrendered unconditionally – not to the British nor anyone else – and never will.

When we made peace in 1902 it was an understanding between the leaders of the Afrikaner people that they would fight for their freedom at the very first opportunity.

That opportunity was not long in coming, but when it did not all the Boers were on the same side.

4

'*I am a donkey*'

Notice hung round the necks of Afrikaners caught not speaking
English at school

With the defeat of the Boers in 1902, the Republics of the Transvaal
and the Free State were no more. They had become part of the great
British Empire and their new overlord was the British High Commissioner in South Africa, Baron Milner of St James and Cape Town.
In war Milner's aim had been to, 'knock the bottom out of the great
Afrikaner nation'. In peace he intended to complete the task. Language was to be the weapon. The Boers were to be made into British
subjects, speaking the King's English.

The Boer's own language, Afrikaans, was at a critical stage of its
young life. In written form it hardly existed. School text books and the
Bible were still in High Dutch, the official language of the two Boer
Republics, although that was a long way from what was spoken on the
farms and in the veld. Afrikaans had been evolving steadily from the
days of the earliest settlers in the Cape. The Dutch they spoke soon
lost its links with the Low Countries. Seasoned with French and
German, spiced with words from Malaya and Madagascar brought by
the slaves, the language of the Cape soon took on a sound of its own.
The Hottentots found it no easier than the sons of the first settlers to
manage the declensions, the case endings and the other refinements of
High Dutch. They made do with the simplified dialect their masters
and mistresses used and simplified it still further.

When the British arrived at the start of the nineteenth century they
did their best to suppress both this Cape language and its mother Dutch. I
1822 the Governor of the Cape Colony, Lord Charles Somerset, issued a
proclamation that English was to be the only language of the courts and
schools, even though Dutch settlers outnumbered the British by eight
to one. He imported English, and especially Scottish, teachers and
ministers to put their stamp on education and religion. But many Presby-
terian Ministers found themselves so much in sympathy with the Calvin-
ism of the Dutch that they were themselves absorbed.

48

As for the early schools, many parents simply kept their children away to avoid having them educated in English. In 1828 in the Government schools in Cape Town there were 675 pupils; eleven years later the combined attendance was eighty-four.

Those Cape-Dutch-speaking children who did go to school found themselves learning all the facts of arithmetic, geography and history in a language they did not understand. The history was the history of England starting at 1066. It was much later before something called 'Cape History' was included. The syllabus in the primary school was exactly the same as the one used in schools in England. School Readers were all imported so the little Boer boy would pick his way through stories about primroses, lifeboats and nightingales and learn how to take them down in dictation.

Contemporary records show just how unsatisfactory the imposed British system really was. In *An Epitome of the State of Education at the Cape of Good Hope for the last Twenty Years*, published in Cape Town in 1841, J. C. Golding painted an unflattering picture of the quality of the imported teachers:

The teachers to whose guidance the government schools have been entrusted ... seldom possess the qualities absolutely requisite; many of them can neither understand nor speak Dutch though they have to teach a *Dutch* population. Most of them are crude, illiterate and prejudiced. Are these the persons to teach a people differing from themselves in habits, manners, religion and language? Few tasks can be found more difficult than that of instructing a rude people, distrustful of their teacher.

When F. L. Rothmann went to school in Swellendam in 1865 all the lessons he received were in English, and the children were forbidden to speak anything else. Anyone who did was given a large key as a mark of disgrace which was handed on as quickly as possible to the next offender. Years later, Rothmann's sister Miemie Rothmann, who wrote and became famous under the pen name MER, described his schooling: 'Reading, writing and reckoning, and above all not speaking Dutch, this constituted the whole of his education'.

Such formal insistence on English succeeded in Anglicising many of the Cape colonials. Some even aspired to Oxbridge accents and English manners. But others, the Malherbe family among them, had no intention of allowing their language to be uprooted. Ernie Malherbe can trace his Afrikaner lineage back through eight generations to the day when his Huguenot ancestor, Gideon Malherbe, stepped off the sailing vessel, *Die Voorschoten*, in Cape Town harbour in 1688. But there is no date in almost three hundred years in Africa that means more to the family than 14 August 1875. On that day a group of young Afrikaners held a meeting in the home of Ernie's great uncle, Gideon, in the town of Paarl, not far from Cape Town. On that day they founded what was called *Die Genootskap van Regte Afrikaners*, the Society of True Afrikaners. Its aim was to help Afrikaners establish a real identity, 'to stand for our Language, our Nation and our Land.'

The young men of the Genootskap faced a considerable task. They had to be discreet because they did not want trouble with the English authorities. Many of their own volk mocked their efforts. As Ernie Malherbe's wife Janie wrote later, they ridiculed these, 'young school masters and little wine farmers' who had, 'got it into their heads to elevate a Hotnot language into literary form'.[1]

Undeterred, they set about writing a history of South Africa, 'in the language of our people'. They composed an Afrikaans anthem which rang with their belief in God, their land and their language. In 1876 they produced their own newspaper, *Die Afrikaanse Patriot*, the first publication to be made in Afrikaans. The editor was the local Dominee, Stephanus du Toit, whose son later became famous as 'Totius', one of Afrikanerdom's most revered poets. The newspaper itself was printed in the house of Ernie Malherbe's grandfather, Ernst Gideon, who also helped foot the bill.

'An Afrikaans newspaper! Who would have believed it! A newspaper in our own language!' So chirped the first editorial. It was an emotional moment. 'There are Afrikaanders with English hearts,' the editorial went on, 'And there are Afrikaanders with Dutch hearts. Then there are Afrikaanders with Afrikaans hearts. These we call the TRUE AFRIKANERS and these, particularly, we call on to stand by us.'

The paper soon took a political stance. When the British annexed the Transvaal in 1877, du Toit's weekly editorials were quick to condemn this extension of imperialism.

Such was the atmosphere in which Ernie Malherbe's own father grew up. Virtually from birth he breathed in the Afrikaners' struggle for their own language and their own identity. He was seven when the Genootskap was founded. Afrikaans writers and poets experimenting in their new language, spent hours in his uncle's home. The fact that Gideon had four eligible daughters did nothing to reduce the visitors. One of the regulars was Dominee J. D. Kestell, who later rode with De Wet in the Anglo-Boer War; he was the official secretary at the Peace of

---

[1] *Predikante-Prestasies en -Petaljes (Clerical Feats and Fun)* by Janie Malherbe, Maskew Miller, Cape Town, 1950.

Vereeniging and later still a hero of Broederbond-inspired nationalism. Together these young idealists were every bit as much Afrikaner
pioneers as those who had trekked away in their ox-wagons to found
the new republics forty years before.

And in the Republics of the Free State and the Transvaal what
quickened the Afrikaner's spirit quite as much as the right to govern
himself, was the freedom to use the language of his choice. Shortly
before the outbreak of the 'English War', F. L. Rothmann left his
birthplace in the Cape and travelled north to throw in his lot with the
Transvaal. What he found there thrilled his Afrikaner soul.

Instead of the home language being eschewed and despised, [wrote his sister
Miemie Rothmann] it was the official language in its Netherlands form but
most familiar. It was the language of the Volksraad, of justice, of public
services, of the schools.

Instead of Cape History being a despised fragment in an English school
book, it was here studied as an honourable episode . . . Newspapers could be
read in Dutch and all the people revelled in their independence and all its
manifestations.

Now the Boer defeat in 1902 looked to put an end to all that. Milner,
unmindful of history, proposed to attempt what Somerset had failed

Left: Lord Charles Somerset, Governor of the Cape Colony, 1814–1827,
and *right* Lord Alfred Milner, High Commissioner for South Africa,
1897–1905, who both tried to suppress the development of Afrikaans

51

to achieve eighty years before. He would get rid of the Boers' written and spoken language once and for all; and there was no better place to start than in the schools. The whole educational system of the Transvaal and the Free State was swept away. Gone were the Dutch superintendents, inspectors and officials and the local elected school committees that had some say over the appointment of teachers. There was not a single Dutch name on the new list of school inspectors. They were all English. Teachers were appointed by the central English authority. Local parent committees were ignored.

All teaching in the government schools had to be in English with the exception of three hours a week for Dutch, plus a further two hours that could be used for religious instruction in the mother tongue. It made no difference to Milner that for ninety per cent of the rural population virtually all their education would now be in a foreign language. That was how the Boers were to be anglicised.

The two hours of Dutch for religious instruction posed a particular dilemma for the Dutch church. A headmaster could, at his discretion, devote them simply to giving his pupils more teaching in the Dutch language, but if he did they would have no Bible study. It was an impossible choice for the Boers, but one that the British had posed them quite deliberately.

In a letter written in July 1903, the Colonial Secretary, Joseph Chamberlain, explained his 'highly ingenious' law. 'The fact is, we are in this matter engaged in a fight with a very astute adversary [i.e. the Dutch Reformed Church] and there is no harm, in my opinion, in using the wisdom of the serpent against it.'

Milner attached particular importance to school text books, in particular history books: 'A good world history would be worth anything . . . Everything that makes South African children look outside South Africa and realise the world makes for peace. Everything that cramps and confines their views to South Africa only . . . makes for Afrikanerdom and further discord'.

Even the Corinthians, the famous English amateur football team, the epitome of the English sporting spirit, unwittingly played Milner's game. They came out on a two month tour in 1903 and trounced South Africa 5–0 in a Test match, emphasising to all present, including Milner himself, that British was best.

Milner also imported English teachers, as Somerset had done. The majority of them knew no Dutch, but it was their responsibility to see that the Dutch children received their minimum three hours of instruction in their mother tongue.

Henning Klopper knew what it was like to be one of the pupils:

We were taught by foreign teachers, by English teachers, all from England. We were an Afrikaans-speaking community, we'd hardly heard English spoken before in our lives. The only English we had come in contact with was during the war and after the war.

We had a lady from Lancashire, she had to teach the little ones, and when she spoke to you, you couldn't understand her. I couldn't understand her. I don't suppose I would understand her today. She had such a dialect, such a broad dialect.

Klopper's father did not tolerate that for long. He took his children away from the government school and found a private teacher from Holland. The Dutch church soon organised their own schools; by 1906 there were at least two hundred in the Transvaal and the Free State where young Afrikaners could be taught by teachers chosen by the local community, in the language spoken and read at home.

Milner also planned to introduce large numbers of English settlers to outnumber the Afrikaners. He hoped for ten thousand within a year, but nothing like that number arrived. Professor T. R. H. Davenport, in his modern *History of South Africa*, maintains that if possible Milner would have withheld political power from the whites in the two colonies he governed until the immigration figures improved, with the argument that 'if, ten years hence, there are three men of British race to two of Dutch, the country will be safe and prosperous. If there are three of Dutch and two of British we shall have perpetual difficulty'.

Milner was clearly an able administrator and had capable men around him. To him must go much of the credit for resettling the families from the camps and the prisoners of war, as well as restarting the country's agriculture. He soon had the gold mines working too, albeit with imported Chinese labour. But nothing he did in South Africa will make Afrikaners forget his attempts to suppress their language.

'Had it not been for Milner and his extreme measures,' says Kowie Marais, former judge and later Progressive Federal Party spokesman on Education, 'we Afrikaners would probably all quite happily have been speaking English by now. By his opposition to our language, he helped create it.'

Milner himself was not long in a position to influence directly events in South Africa. His downfall came over the issue of Chinese labour in the gold mines. Since insufficient Africans were prepared to work below ground for the wages offered, the British cabinet agreed that Chinese labourers could be imported on condition that they were not to be flogged as though they were Africans. Their introduction caused great hostility among the white, mainly English-speaking, miners in the Transvaal, who feared for their jobs. When it was discovered in Britain that the Chinese were being flogged after all, a vote of censure was passed on Milner in the House of Commons and he resigned as High Commissioner. Nonetheless, some of the linguistic seeds he had sown had taken deep root.

When J. D. (Koot) Vorster, brother of the man who became Prime Minister then President, and himself a senior figure in the church, went to the school on their father's farm in the Eastern Cape in 1915, the pupils still had to speak English in the playground.

If you were caught speaking Afrikaans, [he said] you had to carry a placard round your neck bearing the words 'I must not speak Dutch'. When the bell went for school to start again the last man with what was called the Dutch mark, had to write out one thousand times 'I must speak English at school'.

I wrote many thousands of lines on account of that – I even tried to write five lines at once by binding five pencils together.

Every morning they also had to sing the national anthem. Koot Vorster recalls that the boys made it tolerable by altering the words;

> God save our noble King,
> Wash him in paraffin
> And put fire on him.

When John Vorster went to High School in the Eastern Cape, in 1924, there was one English-speaking girl in his age group, 'consequently we had to take our classes, except for Afrikaans, in English, because she could not follow Afrikaans. But they never asked us whether we could follow English, they just took it for granted.'

Years later, the Broederbond made much capital out of language discrimination. They sponsored a film called *Doodkry is Min* – 'They can't keep us down'. One of the best scenes has an English toff, presumably Lord Milner, giving instructions to a senior army officer. 'We have a golden opportunity to make the children of the burghers English-speaking within a few years'.

In a classroom scene, teacher's pet William, reports Pieter for 'an infringement of the rules', for speaking Dutch in the playground. Pieter is hauled out in front of the class and defends himself haltingly in English: 'he hitted me in the face'. But then he raises a huge laugh with an Afrikaner audience when he switches to Afrikaans and threatens to give the sneaky *Rooinek* – 'red neck' – a good hiding.

Carrying the 'Dutch Mark' as a penalty for speaking English. From the Afrikaner film *Doodkry is Min* (They can't keep us down)

Nonetheless, Pieter is told to fetch the 'Dutch mark,' and stand on a chair, ridiculed by the class, with the word 'Donkey' hung on a card around his neck.

In 1937, shortly before the film was made, the youthful South African Broadcasting Corporation introduced its first programmes in Afrikaans. Gideon Roos, the first bilingual announcer, well remembers the letters of complaint from English-speaking listeners. 'Dear Enemy,' began one letter which berated him for 'polluting God's clean air with your Afrikaans.'

Nationalists do not easily forget such slights; nor are they unaware that many English speakers still will not trouble to speak Afrikaans even though it has enjoyed equal status with English since 1925 as one of South Africa's two official languages. Language has thus become one of the focal points of the whole Nationalist creed.

In 1966, five years after South Africa became a Republic, the Afrikaners held a festival in the amphitheatre at the Voortrekker Monument to celebrate the coming of age of their language. Against a huge backdrop of 'I am a Donkey – I speak Dutch', the Prime Minister, Dr Verwoerd, arrived in a horse-drawn coach, folk dancers in Voortrekker costume wove the patterns of the traditional volkspele, children carrying placards saying 'I am a Donkey, I speak Dutch' went in procession across the stage, and an actor boomed his Afrikanerness:

> *'Ek is 'n Afrikaner,*
> *My verhaal is die verhaal van 'n nuwe Volk*
> *Met 'n nuwe Taal*
> *Op nuwe bodem ontstaan.'*

'I am an Afrikaner;'
My story is the story of a new nation
With a new language,
Rooted in a new land'.

Today men like Marius Swart make it their business to see that the status of that language is never again threatened. He is professor of History at the University of Port Elizabeth and also Chairman of the Rapportryers. He regularly goes into shops and hotels in this largely English-speaking port in the Eastern Cape to test the bilingualism of receptionists and counter assistants. In South Africa today, by law, anyone dealing with the public should be able to serve customers in both Afrikaans and English. When Professor Swart finds anyone who does not meet his standard, he reports them. 'As far as I am concerned,' he says, 'if you haven't a knowledge of Arikaans you should be fired. You can go and sweep the streets.' Milnerism has come full circle.

5

'Bring your pipes and matches'

A secret instruction to Afrikaners
at the start of the 1914 Rebellion

While Afrikaners' nationalist sentiments were being fashioned over
the language issue, their political fortunes, in the years after the
English War, had taken a turn for the better. In December 1905 the
Liberals won a General Election in Britain in which Chinese labour in
the South African gold mines was one of the main issues. Milner fell
from favour and his political plans foundered with him.

Jan Smuts took the first boat to London to see the new Prime
Minister, Sir Henry Campbell-Bannerman.

> I put a simple case before him that night in 10 Downing Street, [Smuts wrote]
> It was in substance: Do you want friends or enemies? You can have the Boers
> for friends, and they have proved what quality their friendship may have. I
> pledge the friendship of my colleagues and myself if you wish it. You can
> choose to make them enemies, and possibly have another Ireland on your
> hands. If you do believe in liberty, it is also their faith and their religion.

By the end of the following year the Transvaal and the Free State were
self-governing again. But Milner's worst fears had been realised.
There were nothing like enough new British immigrants to tip the
electoral balance, and in both colonies the Boers were in charge once
more. Balfour, Prime Minister in the previous Tory government
condemned the move as 'the most reckless experiment ever tried in the
development of a great colonial policy'.

Next, the Liberals at Westminster initiated discussions between the
two new Boer governments, and the other two South African colonies
– Natal and the Cape – to consider a new relationship. On 31 May
1910, eight years to the day from the signing of the Peace of Vereeniging, the Union of South Africa came into being.

At its head, as Prime Minister, was Louis Botha, a Boer general
who, those few years before, had been at war with Britain. Two other
Boer generals were in his cabinet, Jan Smuts as Minister of the
Interior, Defence and Mines, and Barry Hertzog as Minister of Jus-

57

tice. There were English-speaking South Africans in the cabinet too, and Leander Starr Jameson, leader of the abortive raid, was on the government benches. This was a government dedicated as Botha put it, to 'the building up of a nation on non-party lines', to reconciliation. Hensoppers, National Scouts and English speakers as well as the Boers who had fought, were all part of Botha's and Smuts' vision of a wider South Africa, part of the great British Empire.

It was a vision that Ernie Malherbe's family was quite willing to share. Even though the family had lost almost everything in the war, Dominee Malherbe did not allow his children to grow up hating the British. 'He taught us,' Ernie Malherbe recalls, 'to hate war, because war is a terrible thing. But in our case, growing up in a family that was widely based and educated, it was never harped on that you must now hate a specific man because he is an Englishman.' Ernie Malherbe, like everyone else, went to a school where English was the medium of instruction. The family was now living at Villiersdorp in the Cape where his father was the minister. He learned English at school, read Dutch at home and the family spoke Afrikaans. But as Malherbe recalled over seventy years later, he did not feel that his Afrikanerness was threatened, or that he was being anglicised.

We just accepted it like the weather. You don't make yourself miserable when it rains or snows' ... Our Afrikanerness, was in our blood. It was like breathing. We didn't need to make a fuss about it and ram it down people's throats. It is very clever of the Nationalists today to use language and identity as a peg to hang all their other paraphernalia. And they certainly get very eloquent about it all, and show what the British have done. The British may have taken our worldly goods but they couldn't kill our sense of personality.

So to Ernie Malherbe the course chosen for the new South Africa by Botha and Smuts was both natural and welcome. To their cause he gave his full allegiance. Years later he was to become one of Smuts' most trusted advisers.

But to Henning Klopper the vision of Botha and Smuts was unthinkable. He believes the British were simply trying to divide the Afrikaners.

There is no better recipe to destroy a people than to divide them. That was an old Roman slogan, 'Divide and rule'. And that is what the British did in South Africa. Small community – divided us and ruled.

Then they did their *pamperlanging* [buttering up] to Botha, idolising him, making him the first Prime Minister of South Africa. And he was an ordinary farmer, a good man, an ordinary farmer. Friend of my people-in-law.

To Klopper it is perfectly clear where the blame lies:

Smuts sold us to the British. He became an Anglophile. He became 'the greatest Empire builder of the day' so the London *Times* said. 'A philosopher, a statesman and a soldier.' He was really a politician. We were under the impression, and we still are of the same conviction, that Smuts misled Botha. Smuts was a very clever, a very cunning man.

Smuts wasn't a man with any feelings. He should not have been born an Afrikaner. He should have been born as an American or a Britisher who had a big force behind him.

The hardline opposition to Botha and Smuts in the Union Cabinet centred on Barry Hertzog, the Minister of Justice, and one of the principal issues was language. Hertzog had always recognised that there were two groups both deeply rooted in South Africa, the English and the Dutch. He accepted them as 'twin streams', equal but separate, and believed that both could be called 'Afrikaners' in the widest sense. He insisted that each group should educate its children in its own language (although each group should also learn the language of the other). In the Free State, where Hertzog had been Minister of Education since 1907, he had turned this precept into law to the alarm of Botha's Union government who were concerned that this Free State firebrand would endanger the good relations they were beginning to establish with the British.

In a speech at Germiston in 1911, Hertzog took his opposition further. Alongside the separate groups of the English and the Dutch, he said, there was a third group, those who had come to South Africa to seek their fortunes at the expense of the others and who really owed their allegiance elsewhere. They were, he said, bastard sheep among the farmer's pure bred flock. But their time was past, and they were worth, 'no more than the dung caked to the wall of the kraal which was washed away by the next rainstorm'.

At de Wildt, a railway halt in Western Transvaal he took up the theme again in December 1912 in a speech which became a landmark in the development of the Nationalists.

'The time has come when South Africa can no longer be ruled by people who do not have the right love for South Africa.' He criticised directly a senior English-speaking politician in the Cape who had announced publicly that he was an Imperialist first and Hertzog's sort of Afrikaner second. He continued, 'Imperialism is only acceptable to me as far as it is of service to South Africa. When it comes into conflict with the interests of South Africa, I am a decided opponent of it. I am prepared to let my future career as a politician rest on this'.

General J. B. Hertzog, Boer War leader, founder of the National Party
and later Prime Minister

Then he turned his attack on Botha and Smuts. 'I am not one of those who always have their mouths full of conciliation and loyalty,' he said, 'for these are vain words that deceive no one. I have always said I do not know what conciliation means. I have no need to conciliate anyone because I have not wronged anyone.' In a clear reference to Botha, who had recently been to London for the Imperial Conference, he added: 'I would rather live with my own people on a dunghill than stay in the palaces of the British Empire'.

Immediately after the speech, nineteen-year-old Henning Klopper, now a railway clerk in his first job, attended a meeting with seven others at Oogies station, where they passed a resolution supporting Hertzog. Klopper was elected secretary and sent off a telegram 'saying we would stand firmly behind him . . . It just came out of your whole being. You couldn't suppress it. You were an Afrikaner and that's all about it'.

Hertzog's inevitable confrontation with Botha came when he was dropped from the cabinet. But in January 1914 he gathered his supporters around him and launched his own party. So the National Party was born. The manifesto set out formally the views Hertzog had been expressing – South African interests to be placed first, mother tongue education to be compulsory, as was also bilingualism in the Public service. In other words, if an Afrikaner went into the Post Office to buy stamps he could expect to be served in his own language.

Even at this stage, Hertzog's split with Botha and Smuts might have been contained but outside events intervened. In August 1914 Britain plunged into war with the Kaiser, dragging South Africa in as well. South Africans were going to have to make up their minds once and for all where their loyalties lay. Westminster had requested South Africa to send troops into German South West Africa and Botha agreed. To Henning Klopper and Hertzog's Nationalists this was nothing short of outrage.

Germany had supported the Boers throughout the two Wars of independence, supplying them with money, arms and artillery – but mostly with sympathy. After the war, Botha himself, with de la Rey and de Wet, had gone to Germany to accept £80,000 the German people had collected for destitute Boers. 'And Botha knelt down before the man who presented the money and he thanked him. Yet he was the man who declared war on the German forces in South West. That made us bitter. How can you do that? How can you be such a hypocrite?' asked Klopper.

On the very day war was declared de la Rey ordered some of his old commando officers to organise a meeting near Lichtenburg in the Transvaal. 'Bring your pipes and matches with you, and see to it that the burghers bring theirs too', was the instruction. It was clear to any nationalist what that meant. For pipes read Mausers. Rebellion was very much in the air. Botha mobilised the Union Defence Forces and called on loyal burghers to support the government. But some Boer War generals like Beyers and Kemp chose to resign rather than fight for the imperialist cause. Colonel Manie Maritz, who commanded training camps in the north west area of the Cape Province, refused to obey an order to move against the Germans in South West Africa. Then he issued a proclamation calling for the restitution of the old Boer republics and naming Beyers, de Wet, Kemp and himself as members of a new provisional government.

Henning's brother Christoffel, who had served on Botha's staff, was offered the rank of General to lead a commando against the rebels but refused. 'He wouldn't fight against his own blood for anybody in the world.'

By this time Ernie Malherbe was a student at the University of Stellenbosch. He was called up along with everyone else and in their new khaki uniforms they had to drill on the University grounds every day. They also went off to short training camps. Some of the students who were against the war refused to wear uniform and made their protest by drilling in flannels and blazers. Malherbe remembers that one of the most respected theological professors, an Afrikaner named Marais, called the students together and told them that, 'the rebellion was the wrong thing; it was anti-Christian, and Anti-Bible'.

That did not stop many of the Stellenbosch students from going to join the rebels, although more stayed where they were. 'We were part of the old régime and we did not feel strongly enough to go against it,' said Malherbe, 'because they were our own people. General Botha and General Smuts were our leaders. We were not going to rebel against them.'

But when General de Wet issued a call to arms in the Free State in October 1914 the rebellion flickered into open war. Botha launched a full scale campaign and in sporadic encounters Afrikaner fought Afrikaner. Some ten thousand rebels against thirty thousand government troops.

In three months it was all over. De la Rey had already been shot in a bizarre accident. Travelling with Beyers just outside Johannesburg, he drove through a road block set up, not for them, but for a gang responsible for a series of murders and robberies around Johannesburg. The police fired and de la Rey was killed by a ricochet. De Wet's forces were defeated at Mushroom Valley in the Free State and de Wet himself captured. Klopper was on his way to join up but it was all over before he arrived. Beyers was trapped near the Vaal River and drowned trying to swim with his horse to safety. Maritz and Kemp took their troops into South West Africa to link up with the Germans, but most eventually surrendered. Maritz fled to Portugal.

Over a hundred rebels had been killed, including de Wet's son; many were dead on the government side. Kemp was sentenced to seven years' imprisonment for treason, de Wet six, though neither served anything like the full sentence.

A young officer named Jopie Fourie was treated less leniently. He had helped suppress the Jameson Raid and had fought the British in the Boer War. He held a commission in the Union Defence Force and like many others defected to the rebels. But he failed to take the precaution of resigning first or even taking off his uniform. After a skirmish in which government troops were killed, he was captured, court martialled for treason and sentenced to death. Jan Smuts, Minister of Defence, confirmed the sentence and on Sunday 20 December 1914, Fourie was executed by a firing squad in Pretoria gaol. To many nationalists he is still the hero and Jan Smuts the traitor.

Left: General Koos de la Rey, one of the Afrikaner leaders killed in the 1914 Rebellion and *right* Captain Jopie Fourie executed for treason

So the rebellion ended with the lines between Afrikaners now clearly drawn. On one side were Botha and Smuts with their wider vision of the role of the Afrikaner. Ernie Malherbe was firmly of their persuasion. On the other side were Hertzog's nationalists and men like Henning Klopper.

Malherbe, after a Bachelor's then a Master's degree at Stellenbosch, went off in 1919 to see something of the wider world. He worked his way twice across the Atlantic, took jobs in London and the Hague and a Ph.D. at the University of Columbia in New York. His thesis on the early history of education in South Africa became, and still is, the standard work on the subject.

Klopper was working his way as a ticket clerk on the railways in Johannesburg. In the narrower world of Afrikaner Nationalism he was now even more opposed to the government of Botha and Smuts with its close ties to imperial Britain. He and his republican friends were soon to found an organisation that would lay even more stress on the competing concepts of Afrikanerdom and eventually put the Nationalists in a more dominant position than they could ever have dreamed was possible.

6

'Naked as kaffirs in Congoland'

Dr D. F. Malan describing the plight of poor
Afrikaners in 1916

When Henning Klopper arrived in Johannesburg in 1911 at the age of sixteen to look for his first job he found himself in a strange new world. He spoke little English and he had never been to a city before, much less a mining boom town like Johannesburg.

'I might as well have gone to Paris or to London, or anywhere else in the world,' he said. 'It was a completely foreign place.'

Johannesburg was virtually an English city. The mines, the railways, the civil service, the police were all run by English-speakers, the Uitlanders. They had poured into the Transvaal when gold was discovered twenty-five years before. In the days of the South African Republic before the English War, old President Kruger had found Johannesburg so distasteful in its ungodliness and its Englishness that he called it *Duiwelstad*, the Devil's Town, and could rarely bring himself to go there.

After the war Milner's take-over of the civil service and the influx of his bright young administrators from Oxford made that Englishness even more conspicuous. The Act of Union may have installed an Afrikaner Prime Minister in Cape Town but it did nothing to reduce English dominance in Johannesburg.

Henning Klopper remembers what it was like to be an Afrikaans speaker on the railways where he was taken on as a trainee clerk. Once when he ventured to speak up in the only language in which he could express himself the response was, 'Don't be a fool man, speak white', meaning English. He also recounts with undiminished outrage a confrontation with his English-speaking boss. 'One of my senior officers said to me one day: "Why do you want to come and work in a community like this? I'll see that you get the sack, you Dutch bastard." That was common language here. And they told me to my face that they preferred blacks to Afrikaners.'

Henning Klopper was just one of many who were moving to the

towns in search of a living. Such an exodus from the land marked a chapter every bit as significant as the Great Trek itself and involved many thousands more. Most of the 'Poor Whites', as they were known, were Afrikaners but they were not the only ones on the move; blacks too were heading for town. It was a double migration coinciding with the country's industrial growth. There were jobs on the railways, in the mines, in the factories; and as they competed for them whites and blacks met head on. For the Afrikaners, particularly, it was a traumatic experience, establishing a position in a world of English dominated industry, competing with people to whom, because of their colour, they felt superior. Many attitudes took root then which go to the heart of South Africa's problems today.

Many of the whites were forced off the land by the disasters of war. In 1900 when the British High Command gave the order to raze crops and homesteads to deny the guerrillas sustenance, they created devastation that no amount of reparation could put right. But there was more to it than that. The Volksraad of the Transvaal had been concerned about the plight of 'poor burghers' back in the 1890s, long before the war. Bad farming methods and social practice were at the root of the Boers' economic battle.

Ernie Malherbe was one of the South Africans who found himself immersed in the problem. As a result of a visit to South Africa in 1927 by its President and Secretary, the Carnegie Corporation of New York sponsored a Commission of Investigation into the whole 'Poor White' question. In 1929 Ernie Malherbe, back from America, was given leave from his teaching post at the University of Cape Town to become one of the five Commissioners. His particular responsibility was educational standards among the thousands of poor whites the Commissioners interviewed as they travelled to every corner of South Africa. In 1932 the Carnegie Commission published its report in five volumes, one of them by Dr Malherbe. In it he traces the history of a phenomenon that had no parallel in the western world.

When the Voortrekkers settled the vast areas of the eastern and northern Cape, the Free State and Transvaal, they took no more care of the land than the blacks they supplanted. South Africa's first two hundred years had bred pioneers whose main economic motive was to open up and to occupy. Land was plentiful and the farms were large. The sons of Boer settlers either lived on the family farm or went further afield to find land of their own. There were few hungry whites in those days – though very few fat ones. The shiftless could always reckon on the hospitality of farmers to provide a livelihood in return

Dr Ernie Malherbe (right) with colleagues of the Carnegie
'Poor White' Commission and the Ford car they drove through
South Africa

for a few odd jobs. Game was plentiful so even those who had no cattle
were never short of meat.

The wealth of the farmer lay in his cattle and in his sheep. With the
Bible as his only instrument of culture, with his gun to shoot game and
protect him against those he regarded as savages the Boer was perfectly
adjusted to his environment. His life was simple, his needs were few.
He was religious, honest, independent and, believed Malherbe, rather
self-satisfied.

But towards the end of the nineteenth century all the best land had
been occupied and change became inevitable. Those with capital,
education or intelligence made the adjustment. Those with no such
advantages were soon adrift. Under the Roman Dutch Law of inheri-
tance a father's property was divided among all his children. After
several generations some ended up with less than a thousandth part of
the family's original farm. There was frequent intermarriage of near
relatives, partly to keep land in the family, partly because the vast

distances kept social life to a minimum; and intermarriage did not help the mental and physical capacities of the offspring.

The descendant of the Voortrekkers who could not adapt found himself in trouble. His little piece of land inherited from his father could not support him. He mortgaged it to tide him over a bad spell but eventually the money went. He did not know a trade. He became a *bywoner*, a squatter on another man's land, grazing his animals where he could. However as the population increased – and poor Afrikaners knew little of birth control – the farmer no longer wanted tenants on his thirsty land. For the farmer himself was in difficulty. Far from the markets, he had been selling his produce to the local store at ridiculously low prices. He had overstocked. He had burned off the grass. He had caused erosion. He knew nothing about revitalising the soil; he kept no books; he had little formal education.

At the Cape, Somerset's policy from 1822 onwards of Anglicising education stood in the way of learning. Dutch-speaking parents kept their children away from school. Education among the rural population was seen as something foreign. So the Afrikaner farmer became a prey to his own ignorance. Rain eroded his soil; drought scorched his crops; his cattle and sheep died of stock disease – east coast fever and gall sickness, redwater and scab disease, rinderpest and horse sickness. And the very independence that had been his ancestor's strength kept him from co-operation with his neighbour. But because he spoke no English, the farmer was still afraid – and so was the squatter – to go to the towns where English was the language of trade and industry.

A few English speakers became 'poor whites' as well but eighty per cent of the rural population were Afrikaners. English farmers were less affected because they did not have the tradition of dividing up the land when the head of the family died. As Dr Malherbe put it: 'Their boys did not all remain on the farm, as was the case generally with the Dutch population, each one with his eyes glued upon the tiny piece of land that he would inherit.' The younger sons of English-speaking families sought occupation in industry and commerce as a matter of course, and the language of the cities held no fears for them.

If poverty now engulfed many Afrikaners, most blacks were even worse off. As the Voortrekkers had moved north through the Free State and the Transvaal, they had taken over the traditional grazing grounds of the native tribes, who were pushed back into pockets of land that came to be known as 'reserves'. White land and black land were hopelessly intermixed.

In the early days of the Great Trek, in the 1830s and 1840s when land was plentiful, farmers allowed blacks some grazing and growing land, sometimes in return for rent, sometimes in return for unpaid work as what was known as labour tenants. But as the demand for white land increased so the meagre plots assigned to the blacks diminished. Nothing was written down, so the blacks had no security. Already there were more blacks available on the land than there were jobs, so many just stayed wherever they could as squatters, eking out a miserable existence.

The situation in the parts of South Africa governed by Britain at the end of the nineteenth century was not much different. When the British annexed Natal from the Boers in 1843, it took them another thirty-six years to subjugate the Zulus. As they did so, they deliberately split up the territory into a patchwork of locations to prevent the Zulus from ever challenging the white man's power again. Some Zulus remained on white farms as labour tenants. A hundred and eighty days work a year was often demanded.

In the Cape Colony white farmers paid no income tax but 'natives' paid twenty or thirty shillings hut tax which meant that they had to work for the white man to raise the money. In 1894 Rhodes introduced a 'labour tax' of ten shillings to be paid by black males unless they could prove that during three months of each year they had been 'in service of employment beyond the borders of the district'. Speaking in the Cape Assembly, Rhodes dressed up the measure in his best philanthropic terms: 'You will remove them [the blacks] from that life of sloth and laziness, you will teach them the dignity of labour and make them contribute to the prosperity of the state . . .'

Until Union in 1910 it was legally possible for blacks to purchase land in all of the provinces except the Orange Free State where it was expressly forbidden by law. Indeed, in the British Cape the ownership of land brought with it, for some blacks, the right to vote on the common roll. But in 1913 that right was threatened when Louis Botha's government introduced the notorious Natives Land Act which entrenched the white man's claim to the land and sought to bring into line differing land tenure practice in the four provinces. The preamble to the Act referred to making 'further provision as to the purchase and leasing of land by natives and other persons' but while the Act defined and guaranteed the areas that were to be set aside as reserves, it also stated that no African should in future own or lease land *outside* those 'Scheduled Native Areas'. They comprised some thirty-five thousand square miles, or 7.3 per cent of South Africa's total area. The rest was to be white man's land where blacks could remain only as labourers. The historian, W. M. Macmillan estimated in 1930 that the land allocated to blacks under the 1913 Act represented approximately one fifth of the area they had formerly occupied.

According to the 1911 census there were about one million blacks living on white-owned land at that time, one in four of the black population. There were a million and a quarter whites and six hundred thousand Coloureds and Indians. So under the 1913 Act, 7.3 per cent of the land was assigned to 67.3 per cent of the population. The Act was successfully challenged in the Supreme Court regarding its application in the Cape because restriction on the purchase of land was adjudged to conflict with the right of the black man to qualify for the franchise, but the effect of the legislation was still devastating. Farmers were enabled to evict surplus natives from their land; tribal chiefs lost traditional grazing ground. A stream of dispossessed black families and squatters left the farms. Many crammed into the already overcrowded reserves, but there was no work, no grazing ground, no room to grow mealies. What land there was had been badly tended, overgrazed or eroded in exactly the same way as much of the land farmed by poor whites. The situation was worse, that is all. Soon after the 1913 Natives Land Act, the government set up a commission with Sir William Beaumont as Chairman, to report on the allocation of reserves. Some of the evidence given to the commission says more about the anguish being suffered by dispossessed blacks than a thousand statistics.

Petition for Land, addressed to the Natives Land Commissioner, Knysna, 30 March 1914:

. . . there is no place where we can make a permanent home; we do not like our children to be homeless wanderers all the days of our life . . . The position is the same for Kaffir, Fingo, Hottentot, Basuto and Zulu. We are equally under one yoke. There is neither first nor last, our grievance is one and the same . . . We earnestly entreat the Government to set apart for us land where we can establish homes. We appeal to the Government which is over black and white alike and should shelter and protect all its subjects as a hen gathers under her wings her little ones without regard to their colour.
Signed: M. K. Mancobo (Pastor)
        J. Ntongwana (Secretary)

Simon Devu from M'Pondo:

I work as a labourer. We want a place where we could be concentrated. There are several little places that we had but it is not sufficient for our requirements. You may be here today and tomorrow you are away. You get shifted against your will. The owner finds that there is something to his advantage and he clears you off. I am speaking for myself. When I left Knysna and I moved to . . . Matthijsbosch, I was not even behind with my rent and I was carrying out all my agreements and I do not think that since I have been here in Knysna I have had a bad reputation but through my being sent away I now have nothing.

Chief Mpefu:

We greet you, but it is with a very sore heart. We are here, as you see, natives, headmen and Chiefs together. We have lived here long before the white man came into this country . . . We are a very large community and the Government collects a very big sum of money from us in taxes. . . we have to pay a £5 tax for dogs although we do nothing with them at all. In my location I am all by myself because little children have been made to pay taxes; they have to go out and work and I have nobody to live with me. My heart is very sore that I cannot get back to my former place where my forefathers used to live.

In 1916 the Beaumont Commission proposed that some seventeen million acres (twenty-seven thousand square miles) of additional land should be set aside for exclusive native settlement, nearly doubling the existing area. It would have increased the black share of South Africa from 7.3 per cent to 13.2 per cent but no bill was passed. Public opinion baulked at returning so much land to the natives. It was another twenty years before any such measure was introduced and then it was not for the full area recommended by the Beaumont Commission.

So, forced off white farming land, unable to find a living in the reserves, thousands of black South Africans headed for the towns. But while the white urban population more than doubled between 1904 and 1936, the black urban population more than trebled. It was the start of that problem of numbers in the cities that still defies resolution and much of it was due to the white man's unwillingness to allow the blacks the land they needed to retain some sort of independence.

The Dutch Reformed Church was particularly concerned about the lot of the poor whites who found themselves in slums on the outskirts of all the major cities, 'living with and like kaffirs', as one letter to the Editor of *Die Burger* put it. In 1916 the church in the Cape called a Volkskongres to discuss the plight of rural Afrikaners in the towns. One of the main speakers was the Editor of *Die Burger*, Dr D. F. Malan, a Dominee himself and also leader of the Cape Nationalist Party. His fear was for what such social contact was doing to the Volk:

I have observed instances in which the children of Afrikaner families were running around as naked as kaffirs in Congoland. We have knowledge today of Afrikaner girls, so poor they work for coolies and Chinese. We know of white men and women who live married and unmarried with Coloureds. They are all our flesh and blood; they carry our names; they are Afrikaners all of them; they are the sons and daughters of the Huguenots and the children of [Afrikaner] martyrs.

It is perhaps no surprise that the man who made that speech was the same man, who, as Prime Minister of South Africa after the Nationalists' election victory in 1948, introduced a ban on mixed marriages as one of the very first pieces of Apartheid legislation.

The poor white problem had been more than a century in the making and was not easily to be solved. In the hundreds of interviews they recorded in 1929, Dr Malherbe and his Carnegie colleagues found themselves facing a situation that extended the length and breadth of South Africa. As they travelled in their two Ford cars they met the 'Trek farmers' of the north western Cape, the *bywoners*, labourers and shepherds of the Karoo, the woodcutters from the coastal districts at Knysna and George, the bushveld farmers of the Transvaal who still lived under pioneer conditions, who hunted for their meat but who were much weakened by malaria and the enervating climate. They went to the diamond diggings of Namaqualand, the mining towns on the Reef and the growing industrial centres like Port Elizabeth where the motor industry was establishing its assembly plants.

From questionnaires sent to almost half of the schools in the Union the Carnegie Commissioners estimated that 17.5 per cent of all the families with children at school were 'very poor', a category which, in Carnegie terms, meant 'those who are largely supported by charity e.g. in cities, or who subsist in dire poverty on farms'. So three hundred thousand of South Africa's white population were effectively living below the poverty line. In the rural areas the Commissioners found many families living in hovels woven from reeds or in mud huts with thatched roofs 'very similar to the ones the Africans lived in'. Invariably there was only one room.

I often asked children where they slept, [recalled Dr Malherbe fifty years later] because I couldn't see enough beds for them to sleep on. Mind you the parents didn't like it when you asked. And one seven-year-old just pointed to a place on the floor, where they put a mat for him. And that was the way many of them slept, especially the children, with probably a bit of straw for a pillow.

The report found that one in three of the homes they inspected were 'unsuitable for civilised life'. There was a high birthrate and much disease due to overcrowding. 'But the high rate of mortality among

A poor white family photographed by Dr Ernie Malherbe in 1929

children must be ascribed largely to insanitary habits and surroundings, often leading to faecal pollution of water and food, which causes
infestation and death, particularly among children'. In his report for
Carnegie, Dr Malherbe described how far some families would go in
order to make a living:

During the visits of a single day I came across a half a dozen homes near the
border of the Rustenburg and Waterburg districts [i.e. west of Pretoria]
where the descendants of those early settlers are today eking out a miserable
existence by going into an adjoining native location and working for the more
prosperous natives during the ploughing season. Their remuneration was in
kind, usually a couple of sheep, a calf, or best of all, a pig.

Many were not even that fortunate. In the schools he visited Dr
Malherbe made a survey of what children ate by asking them to write
down what they had for breakfast, midday meal and supper. 'Most of
them put down P-A-P, pap, that's mealie meal, mealie porridge, that's
all.'

As for simple luxuries, they simply had no part in the lives of the
poor whites Malherbe met: 'I remember a lady who offered us coffee
which she had brewed right there on the floor where she had made a
fire. When she brought the cups she said, "I'm very sorry we haven't

73

A poor white kitchen, visited by Malherbe and the Carnegie Commission

got any sugar in the house, but I'm putting the spoons here so you can dish out the flies with them!"'

Yet still the country poor clung to the farms which could no longer support them. 'This is a clear symptom of a type of mentality', said the Carnegie Report in its general findings, 'that is marked by a narrowness of outlook, by lack of enterprise and by a dread of the strange world outside the farm.' In the schools Malherbe found twenty-seven thousand children whom he categorised as retarded, who were more than two years behind the standard normal for the age group. Over half of the children did not complete primary education. The result was that when finally these poor whites were forced off the land and into the cities, as Malherbe put it starkly, 'They had no prospect of making a living'.

At every turn the parallel with the conditions of poor blacks today in South Africa becomes more striking, and nowhere more than in the Report's general conclusions:

Poverty itself exerts a demoralising influence. It often causes loss of self-respect and a feeling of inferiority. It easily has a detrimental effect on honesty, trustworthiness and morality. If it is long continued the poor white often comes to accept it as inevitable and to bear it with dull and passive

Afrikaner poor whites with the transport that took many to the towns in what was known as 'The Second Great Trek'

resignation. This attitude is further contributed to by the feeling of inferiority that poor whites have.

Change the word 'whites' for 'blacks' and Carnegie could be reporting on South Africa today.

Dr Malherbe was continually struck by the dependence on the state of so many of the householders they studied and the Commission Report was critical that government relief had done nothing to restore a sense of initiative. By subsidising farmers who had used primitive and inefficient methods it certainly kept them on the land. But, said Carnegie, 'It would be hard to find a method more apt to perpetuate an obsolete tradition.'

In other respects, relief hastened the drift towards the towns. In a country area a road or irrigation scheme might be started to provide work. Lured by the wages, white squatters and smallholders would give up their small flocks or herds and go to work for the government. But when the road was finished or the irrigation channel completed, there was not always another project and the farmer on whose land they had lived did not want them back again.

So, [wrote Malherbe] the trek to the city starts. There may be relatives who would not mind sharing their little cottage with them and their many children. In the city, they know, they will not starve because there are at any rate charitable organisations to look after them. The men-folk join the long queue at the Labour Bureau, sitting there day after day, waiting for a job. All they can do is unskilled work. Thus they come into competition with the native, and unless the municipality makes a special effort to employ them they won't find any work to do.

In Johannesburg the municipality fired black cleaners in the early thirties and took on whites. In Port Elizabeth the mayor arranged to collect the wooden crates in which General Motors had shipped cars from Detroit and gave them to whites to build themselves homes. In Bethlehem in the Free State the mayor started a farm on municipal land with school teachers as overseers and the children of poor whites as labourers. The farm was so successful it was able to pay its own way.

Yet despite the need for jobs, many of the poor whites were reluctant at first to take on what they saw as 'kaffir work'. Malherbe remembered his astonishment one day travelling through the Cape when he came across two white men lounging about watching two blacks wielding picks and shovels. The whites were being paid six shillings a day to repair the road but they had simply employed two blacks, paying them three shillings a day each to do it for them. 'The natives were content with the wages. The work was done. The white men 'earned' three shillings each per day. Why should they worry? It was good business.'

He remembered too a school examination in Natal where one of the questions in a science paper called for an explanation of the principles of a lever to shift a rock by using a crowbar. One boy explained how he would adjust the fulcrum so as to get adequate leverage. 'Then,' he added, 'I would get a native at the other end of the bar to lift the rock.'

This was no new attitude. In 1879 the Cape Superintendent General of Education wrote a report on his attempts to include some industrial and agricultural subjects in the curriculum of his district boarding schools. 'I found, however, when the district boarding schools were commenced, a disposition on the part of the farmers to be rather indignant at their children being taught industrially. They did not see why their boys should go into a carpenter's shop or a blacksmith's shop every afternoon.'

In 1925 the Inspector of Agricultural Education in the Transvaal was still encountering the same prejudice.

At nearly every school where the teacher had made an attempt to lay out a garden with the assistance of his pupils, it happened, and still happens, that parents sent messages more or less of the following nature to the school: 'Tell

South African Mine Workers just before the 1922 strike

the teacher that if he wishes to lay out a garden he should engage a Kaffir'. 'My children are not Kaffirs to do the digging and carry water in the hot sun' ... 'I send my children to school to learn, not to work.' Frequently both parents went to the school and called their children from the work in the school garden using unquotable language.

Malherbe believed that such attitudes showed much more than mere laziness.

The prosperous businessman who sits at his office desk and rings the bell for Jim Fish, who is working in the yard, to bring him his spectacles which lie just beyond his reach on the desk; and his wife, who while sewing, drops her thimble and halloes in shrill tones for the little piccanin on the other side of the house to come and pick it up at her feet, are lazy in exactly the same way as the poor white, whom they despise as an indolent scoundrel, is lazy. . . . These illustrations are symptomatic of the energy sapping process that is going on amongst all classes of our white society, due to the fact that we consider ourselves a white aristocracy on a big black foundation of natives. In many cases the native stands, as it were, between the white man and manual labour.[1]

[1] 'Carnegie Commission Report,' Volume III, p. 23.

It is true that the poor white, through economic necessity, gradually moved into work he had previously considered beneath him but it is also true that those attitudes which Dr Malherbe defined fifty years ago are still widespread. A hard day's work in the garden for many a white householder in the working class suburbs of southern Johannesburg often starts off in the car. He will drive to one of the many unmarked yet well-known pick-up points in the suburbs where he will find black mine workers ready to provide a day's labour for a couple of rand. Thus he can sit back and enjoy his Sunday lunch, give the 'garden boy' his bread and jam and tea, take a nap and still the digging is done.

A housewife in Mondeor, one of the up-and-coming Southern Suburbs, told me one Sunday lunchtime how exhausted she was. 'You know we have been flat out all morning. We've had ten coon boys here since eight o'clock working in the garden.'

There is a reminder of this sort of attitude among current stories about van der Merwe, the legendary Afrikaner who is the butt of so many jokes. Van der Merwe, on a visit to London, is intrigued to see so many men employed by the Gas Board just to dig one hole in the road. He stands watching their numerous pauses and tea breaks, until he can contain himself no longer. 'Hell man', he says, turning to his wife, 'but these rooineks are lazy. Just give me half-a-dozen kaffirs and I'd do a simple job like that on my own.'

When the blacks and the poor white van der Merwes came to the cities in search of work there was never any question of their being employed on an equal basis. Where the job brought them together the whites were always the overseers with wages to match. Nowhere were these lines more clearly drawn than in South Africa's major industry, mining. By 1920 the gold mines employed over twenty-one thousand whites, many of them poor Afrikaners from the farms, and nearly one hundred and eighty thousand blacks. The average wage for the whites was nearly £10 a week; for the blacks, fed and housed free in company compounds, it was twelve shillings a week. It was a disparity that was to lead to the biggest industrial upheaval in South Africa's history.

In 1921 the Chamber of Mines announced plans to extend the use of black labour. One of the mining chiefs, Sir Lionel Phillips, stated flatly that the wages paid to European miners put the economic existence of the mines in jeopardy. The price of gold had dropped from over £6 an ounce during the 1914 War to a little over £4. Production costs were rising so the mining houses, entirely English owned and with no great sympathy for their increasingly Afrikaner workforce, proposed to abandon existing agreements with the white unions and open up for black workers some twenty-five semi-skilled jobs previously reserved for whites. The proposals, said the mining houses, would save £1,000,000 a year. In the first phase some two thousand whites would lose their jobs with more to follow.

It was hardly a well-chosen moment. The coal mines had just cut wages by five shillings a week and had sacked eight hundred white miners who had come out on strike. Hertzog's Nationalist party was quick to support the miners and so did the small Labour Party under its very English leader, Colonel Fred Cresswell, himself a former mining engineer. Afrikaner Nationalists and English socialists were united in the defence of the white worker. The miners themselves were an extraordinarily mixed work-force: Welshmen, Cornishmen, Englishmen, Afrikaners; Communists and Nationalists, all marching under the banner, which was actually carried through the streets of Johannesburg, 'Workers of the World Unite and Fight for a White South Africa.'

By early January 1922 twenty thousand white miners were on strike. At first African coalminers had continued to work, bringing up the coal with the help of a few officials but soon the Chamber of Mines started sending black miners back to the reserves to save money; the Witwatersrand came to a virtual standstill. Next the white miners organised themselves into armed commandos, ostensibly to keep order; old soldiers taught them how to throw grenades and unhorse policemen. One of the strike committees set out in a pamphlet why the whites felt they had no choice but to make a stand on this crucial issue of competition with the blacks, and outlined the need for maintaining the colour bar that the mining houses were now trying to repudiate:

With such a system of low-paid labour the European cannot compete, and would not if he could since it must in the end degrade all labour to that level, unless a clear line of demarcation can be drawn and maintained. The aversion of all white races to living and working on a basis of equality with the Negro no doubt enters into the matter; but a part of even that aversion is due to an instinctive perception of the fact that the European worker who accepts equality with the Negro tends to become in the end . . . a Negro ceasing to live up to the standards, traditions and inspirations of the great white race, which can be the heritage of them alone.[1]

----

[1] *The Story of a Crime* published by the Transvaal Strike Legal Defence Committee. 1922.

Smuts, at the head of his South Africa Party Government, tried to mediate but in the end stood by the Chamber of Mines; they rejected a final call from the miners for talks by replying that they would not negotiate with men of 'such mental calibre'. The miners remained convinced that if the strike was broken every one of them would be replaced by 'kaffirs'.

On 29 January the strike unions called on workers and sympathisers to join forces with the National and Labour parties in the struggle to overthrow Smuts and install a government 'calculated to promote the interests of the White Race in South Africa'. A mass meeting of strikers, inspired perhaps by recent events in Russia, proclaimed a People's Republic. Armed groups of miners began roaming the streets, looting and fire raising and attacking native compounds. Smuts responded by proclaiming that commandos were unlawful assemblies. Three miners were shot by the police when a meeting outside the prison at Boksburg refused to disperse. The miners were now beyond recall and prodded less militant unions into proclaiming a General Strike on 7 March. Smuts called up Citizen Force Units of the Army, declared martial law and found himself with a small war on his hands.

On the first day about a hundred and fifty men of the Imperial Light Horse, reporting to Ellis Park Rugby ground in Johannesburg were surprised by a group of strikers who crept up on them as they were collecting equipment. Thirty of them were killed or wounded before the strikers were driven off. At Newlands, to the west of Johannesburg, a police station under siege was relieved only after the Air Force had been called in to bomb the strikers. At Brixton Ridge close by, Smuts ordered artillery to dislodge yet another group. The bombers were used again to attack the headquarters of other strikers in Benoni to the east of Johannesburg but three teenage children and three women were also killed in the raid. At the main strike headquarters at Fordsburg on the edge of Johannesburg city, the miners 'tried' and executed a grocer they accused of being a police spy. They were still holding forty police hostages in Market Buildings four days after the declaration of martial law when the government troops launched the final assault.

It began with a softening up by the artillery's thirteen pounders and ended with a bayonet charge by the Durban Light Infantry. When the soldiers broke down the inner doors they found two of the strike leaders had shot themselves. The insurrection was over, although two days later four more strikers, including three Afrikaans brothers named Hanekom, were killed by the Transvaal Scottish in a rocky valley in the Southern Suburbs. There are still old miners in Johannesburg who will swear they were taken from their homes and summarily executed.

During the fighting, forty-three members of the Defence Forces and twenty-nine policemen had been killed. Thirty-nine miners or 'revolutionaries and suspected revolutionaries' had died and so had forty-two ordinary civilians. About five hundred had been wounded. Some thirty Africans had been killed in indiscriminate acts of racial violence. Nearly five thousand people were arrested and over eight hundred charged. Forty-six were accused of high treason and murder and were tried in special courts. Lawyers from the National party defended the accused; eighteen were sentenced to death although fourteen were reprieved. Four, including one of the best known of the strikers, Taffy Long, leader of the so-called Irish Commando, went to the gallows. He was still singing 'The Red Flag' when the trapdoor opened.

The present leader of the Mine Workers' Union, a fiercely right wing Afrikaner named Arrie Paulus believes the strike marked 'the coming of age' of the urban Afrikaner. Industrial relations in the mining industry have certainly never been the same since. Although the mining houses refused to re-employ all the miners who had taken part in the armed revolt, they had to abandon some of their proposed changes in the categories of work to be done by blacks. White workers had shown they were quite ready to take up arms to defend the colour bar.

Sitting in his office in Braamfontein, not two miles from the old strike headquarters in Fordsburg, Paulus, knows that the Government and the Chamber of Mines are still wary of the power of his union. In 1965 the Chamber of Mines introduced an experiment in job allocation in the gold mines that gave black workers more responsibility; it increased productivity in one mine by fifteen per cent and put handsome bonuses into the pockets of mineworkers, both black and white. But after twelve months the Nationalist government announced the scheme would be abandoned. The white miners, as Paulus will remind visitors, were convinced that such black advancement was a threat to their own jobs; there had been open talk of another 1922.

As for Smuts, the Afrikaner Prime Minister who had ordered Afrikaner soldiers to fire on Afrikaner workers, much as he had done in 1914: 'He is', says Paulus, 'the greatest traitor this country has ever known.' Smuts' ruthless handling of the strike proved a political disaster. In the House of Assembly, Hertzog spoke of the man 'whose footsteps dripped with the blood of his own people'. Smuts' reputation for callousness had not been helped by a decision he had made the year before the strike to send armed police to shift an African settlement near Port Elizabeth. One hundred and sixty-three Africans had been killed and over one hundred wounded.

The National Party was not about to take up the cause of poor blacks but was now clearly established as the champion of the poor whites. The mutual interest with the Labour Party led Hertzog and Cresswell to make a formal pact and in the 1924 General Election Smuts was swept from power. The Nationalists won sixty-three seats and Labour eighteen, giving them a total of eighty-one. The South Africa Party won only fifty-three and Smuts himself lost his seat. General Barry Hertzog became South Africa's first Nationalist Prime Minister.

One of his first measures was known as the 'civilised labour' policy; it meant that the state would employ 'civilised' workers in preference to those called 'uncivilised'. In other words, whites instead of blacks. As a result, large numbers of poor Afrikaners were absorbed into the public sector, particularly the railways; even manual work was reserved for whites, who were naturally paid 'white wages'. Hertzog had made clear his views about the proper scale of wages some years before:

The Europeans must keep to a standard of living which shall meet the demands of white civilisation. Civilisation and standards of living always go hand in hand. Thus a white cannot exist on a native wage scale, because this means that he has to give up his own standard of living and take on the standard of living of the native. In short, the white man becomes a white kaffir.

Between 1924 and 1933 the proportion of unskilled white workers on the railways rose from 9.5 per cent to 39.3 per cent and the proportion of blacks fell from 75 per cent to 48.9 per cent. Put another way, that meant jobs for some thirteen thousand poor whites and the sack for over fifteen thousand blacks.[1]

As far as the Nationalists were concerned every poor Afrikaner trekking to the cities from the platteland now knew what to expect

[1] Figures taken from Lawrence Solomon, 'The Economic Background to the Survival of Afrikaner Nationalism', in Boston University Papers on African History, Boston Univ. Press 1964.

from the English-speaking owners in the mines and factories. The bosses, vilified in the Nationalist press as the cartoon figure of Hoggenheimer, the rapacious Jewish capitalist, cared nothing for them. If Hoggenheimer could employ cheap black labour instead of white, went the party line, he would do it, and gloat over the increased profits. For support in the constant battle for jobs in the cities and succour elsewhere, the poor Afrikaner knew he could depend only on his National Party. But also by now, although he was unaware of its existence, the Afrikaner had another organisation dedicated to his well-being. It was Henning Klopper's secret Broederbond.

As for the black South African, his position was now equally clear. The white farmer had taken most of his traditional grazing land. There was little space for him in the reserves and in the towns, even though the white man could not do without his muscle power, he was to be given no permanency. The Transvaal Local Government Commission, better known as the Stallard Commission, after its chairman, put it frankly in 1922:

It should be a recognised principle of government that natives – men, women and children – should only be permitted within municipal areas in so far and for so long as their presence is demanded by the wants of the white population, . . . [they] should depart therefrom when they cease to minister to the needs of the white man.

As long ago as 1929 Dr Ernie Malherbe had spoken of the problem to come. In a lecture delivered to the British Association for the Advancement of Science in Cape Town in July 1929 about his Carnegie survey of poor whites he added a prophetic postscript:

As I motored through the native areas and noticed the closely-settled land and badly-worked fields of the kaffirs, the thought came to me, that in less than fifty years time the Carnegie Corporation will perhaps feel it incumbent upon them again to appoint a Research Committee, but this time to investigate the causes of the Poor Black Problem – a problem which may prove very black indeed.

Fifty years on, he acknowledges that successive white governments have effectively eliminated the poor white phenomenon. The blacks are another matter. 'It has become such a huge problem, ten times bigger, that we are paralysed.'

7

'Nothing but a cultural society'

Former Prime Minister John Vorster defending the
Broederbond

On the railways in Johannesburg where Henning Klopper started
work he soon found himself among kindred Afrikaner spirits. The fact
that all the senior posts were held by English speakers helped throw
the Afrikaners together. The insults, real or imagined, that they
believed they suffered at the hands of the English were easier to
swallow when there were others who shared the determination that the
sons of the Voortrekkers would not for ever be second-class citizens in
their own land.

From the day the National Party was founded Henning Klopper
and his friends gave their wholehearted support to General Hertzog
but in Klopper's little group in particular there was a feeling that a
mere politician could not give full expression to the range of their
idealism. They spent hours discussing how best to succour the
Afrikaner cause.

There were three of them – Danie du Plessis, H. W. van der Merwe
and Klopper. Du Plessis went on to become the General Manager of
the railways; van der Merwe went into business, one of the first
Afrikaners to do so; while Henning Klopper, after thirty-two years of
railway service, became a Nationalist MP himself and, in due course,
Speaker of the House of Assembly.

They all wanted more than just a victory of their National Party.
They saw many of their fellow Afrikaners giving support to the South
Africa Party led by Botha and Smuts which to them was tainted with
British Imperialism. Somehow they all had to be brought back into the
fold. The three friends had a vision of a united Afrikaner nation, free
from the British, with a vigorous language and culture of its own,
leading the way in Southern Africa. 'We saw party politics as something transitional,' recalled Klopper, 'but ours was a permanent work,
to build up a nation, a virile strong nation.'

Sometimes they met in the house of Dominee Joshua Naudé in

84

Roodepoort, not far from Klopper's lodgings, about ten miles outside Johannesburg. The Dominee was much older than the three young idealists. He had been one of the sixty Boer delegates to the Peace talks at Vereeniging at the end of the War of Freedom in 1902, and more specifically one of the six men who had voted to reject the British terms and go on fighting to the bitter end. To this band of brothers the Dominee brought spiritual reinforcement, encouraging them in the belief that their cause had full support from on high. It is ironic that some fifty years later, Joshua Naudé's own son Beyers, named after the General who was drowned in the Vaal River during the 1914 rebellion and himself a minister of the Dutch church and a highly placed Broeder, would denounce the organisation which his father helped to found.

The events that finally brought the Broederbond into being are now a part of Nationalist folklore. There was a Nationalist Party meeting at the Selborne Hall in President Street, Johannesburg on Saturday 13 April 1918. The main speaker was Dr D. F. Malan, leader of the Nationalists in the Cape and editor of the Afrikaners' own newspaper, *Die Burger* founded three years before in Cape Town. It was an important occasion for the new party; the leader from the southern province had come to express his solidarity with his fellow Nationalists in the Transvaal.

Henning Klopper and his fiancée had arrived early by train from Roodepoort. They walked up Eloff Street from the station as fast as they could to be sure of getting good seats. They were expecting a rousing evening and were not disappointed.

In this British Dominion it would have been normal for the Union Jack to have been displayed in the hall, but just before the meeting, as the official history of the Broederbond puts it, 'a small group of people quietly removed the flag and put it aside'.[1] Another version has it that Klopper's friend, van der Merwe, pulled the flag down and tore it to shreds.

A large crowd of English speakers, having heard about the flag, soon gathered outside the hall singing English patriotic songs and spoiling for a fight. They tried to force their way in but were held back by the police. When the Nationalist audience left there was a free for all in the street, or, as one of their later reports had it, 'the audience dauntlessly went out and a free fight ensued, as the audience had

---

[1] *'Die Afrikaner Broederbond: Eerste 50 Jaar'*, Prof. A. N. Pelzer, 1979, Tafelberg.

An English-speaking mob, hoisting the Union Jack at the National Party Club in Johannesburg, April 1918

decided to do the manly thing and face their antagonists although they were few compared with the English.'

Henning Klopper's fiancée had her glasses smashed, though he maintains that it was in the push from behind from those who 'were trying to get out into the fighting'. They saw an old man attacked, knocked over and kicked. Then the English mob moved up Loveday Street to the unguarded Nationalist Club. Klopper's brother, Christoffel, was one of the club officials. There was nothing any of them could do. The crowd broke in, carried the furniture out into the street and set it alight. Then from the balcony they flew the Union Jack. Later, for good measure, they set fire to the building as well.

Klopper, meanwhile, had taken his fiancée home to Roodepoort but next night he came back to find the fighting had started again. Nationalists had formed a semicircle in front of their damaged headquarters. 'The attackers,' said Klopper, 'were on the other side of the street, throwing bottles and stones and all sorts of things.' Occasionally one man would come forward from the semi-circle and challenge the other side to a straight fight, man for man. There were a few brawls with the mob surging around; and so the night drew on.

The impact of those events never left Henning Klopper. He felt the ignominy of the Afrikaner's secondary position in the land of his birth, the oppressive weight of British Imperialism and what he called 'a sense of shame' that many of his fellow Afrikaners not only tolerated such a situation but actively worked to maintain it. With his friends du Plessis and van der Merwe, he resolved that the time had come to do something about it.

On 5 June 1918 fourteen men met in Danie du Plessis' house at 32 Marathon Street in the modest suburb of Malvern in east Johannesburg, just off what is now the road to Jan Smuts airport. Klopper delivered what was recorded as 'a moving speech' and the group formally pledged themselves to form what they called *Jong Suid Afrika*. As Pelzer's offical history of the Broederbond puts it: 'The fourteen members who came together, quietly, without being aware of it themselves, made a decision that would be of the utmost importance to South Africa. The Afrikaner Broederbond was formed, not in name but in reality.' It was six weeks before they changed the name to the *Afrikaner Broederbond*.

Klopper was elected Chairman, du Plessis was Secretary and Dominee Naudé was President. Their aim, as Klopper put it, was to develop 'an organisation in which Afrikaners could find each other in the midst of great confusion and disunity and be able to work together for the survival of the Afrikaner people in South Africa and the promotion of its interests'. 'This is how the Afrikaner Broederbond originated, out of an urgent need of a people standing on the threshold of permanent extinction', intones the official history.

If it all sounds slightly exaggerated in a country that had recently been given back self-rule under its own Afrikaner Prime Minister, the early activities of the Broeders were hardly those of desperate men faced with extinction. Klopper recalls that the first function they organised was a concert, and musical evenings became a regular part of their programme. Klopper's wife was one of the singers. They also organised lectures, dinner parties and picnics. They started a library with cheap subscriptions for members. They held celebrations to mark what was then called Dingane's Day on 16 December, and Kruger's birthday on 10 October. They also held classes in Dutch and ran a book competition. Those who wished wore dinner jackets to

First Executive Council of the Afrikaner Broederbond, 1918. Standing (l to r): D. H. C. du Plessis (Secretary), J. Combrink, H. le R. Jooste. Sitting: L. J. Erasmus, H. J. Klopper (Chairman), Rev. W. Nicol, J. E. Reeler (Treasurer)

meetings to let their membership be known. They had their own lapel badge, their own tie clip, their own handshake, their own song, and their own flag.

Dominee Naudé was keen for the Broederbond to organise its own football and tennis teams to play at the Wanderers, Johannesburg's prestigious sports club. There was even talk of raising a rugby side to take on all comers, but such a team never materialised.

Klopper rejects the accusation that the Broederbond was founded simply for members to look after one another, and although membership was in theory open he is clear about the sort of Afrikaners they sought; those who could fulfill the demand of the Broeders' motto: '*Wees Sterk*' – 'Be Strong'.

You had to make contact with a person first and judge for yourself whether he was worthy, whether he was a man of stamina, whether he had any guts and potential in himself. If he was an empty shell what would you do with him? So you would see him and judge him and discuss matters with him. You would walk with him. You'd see what he does, what functions he supports.

The idea was not to carry people. We did not want to have weaklings with us to be helped. We wanted people who could help. We didn't want an organisation of people who had to be spoon-fed. We wanted people with sufficient courage to make their own way through life. What we did was to make them study and improve their opportunities for promotion.

What we said to people was: 'Look, wherever you work you must be the best worker in that office, in that area, so that nobody can stop your promotion. And even a man who is of a different political opinion to you should promote you in his own interests.' Then we would build a group of men who would be worthy of carrying a nation.

But within three years, although the idealism was as strong as ever, the bloom of early innocence had faded. On 26 August 1921, at a meeting in the old Carlton Hotel in Johannesburg, the thirty-seven members voted to turn the Broederbond into a secret organisation. Members, particularly civil servants and teachers, claimed they were persecuted because of their open association with the Broederbond. According to one of the members present, L. J. Erasmus, recalling the meeting years later, it was 'a matter of tactics and self-preservation . . . only decided upon under pressure of the crude realities of those post-1918 days'.

Henning Klopper is more defensive about the reasons for becoming a secret organisation: 'Why should it not be secret? Why should they advertise? A Church Council is secret. The Sons of England is secret. The Caledonian Society is secret'.[1]

From 1921 there was less talk of rugby teams and picnics where members brought their wives. Indeed, Broeders were soon enjoined not to tell even their wives they belonged unless, as Pelzer's history allows, it was 'unavoidable'. Members were instructed to reveal nothing that took place at meetings and were not to address one another openly as Broeders. Confidential correspondence was either to be sent back to the secretary or destroyed. Soon postal communication between members was avoided altogether.

Members were more closely vetted but their numbers increased steadily. Two more branches were formed in the Johannesburg area in

---

[1] The 'Sons of England' were founded in 1881 by English-speaking settlers to promote their language and literature and to provide help for needy immigrants. They are now registered as a charity with headquarters in Durban. The 'Caledonian Society' is a similar organisation started in 1876 by Scottish settlers.

Henning Klopper today, founder member and first Chairman of the
Broederbond, later Nationalist MP and Speaker of the House of Assembly

the early 1920s to add to Klopper's founding group. By 1925 there
were eight branches and over a hundred and fifty members; in 1930
there were twenty-three branches and five hundred members. Today
there are eight hundred branches with twelve thousand members.

The strength of the Broederbond lies in the branch, or cell, system.
The members, between five and twenty to a branch, are known only to
each other and to headquarters. Each branch is responsible directly to
the Executive Council and has no formal contact with other branches.
The similarity with the Communist Party cell structure is striking.

In rural areas, the members are drawn from the local Afrikaner
gentry, a headmaster, a dominee of the church, a doctor, a magistrate
and leading farmers. In the towns there are civil servants, youth
leaders, attorneys and the occasional trade unionist as well, all
Afrikaners with influence in the community. By 1944 when there were

some two thousand five hundred members, a third were school teachers, a tenth were civil servants; many were church ministers, many more were farmers.

Meetings are usually held quietly in members' homes. Hosts are encouraged to arrange for their own wives and families to be out for the evening. Alcohol, according to one ex-member, is rarely drunk. If there are refreshments they are likely to be coffee and the Afrikaner favourite, *melktert* (milk tart) served by the host himself. Black servants are considered a security risk and are given the night off.

From their local cell, the Broeders, acting in secret collusion, are in a unique position to exercise influence. In a church or school committee of seven or eight there may be two or three Broeders who know one another but whose Broederbond membership is unsuspected. So they can combine to put forward a particular line of action, to promote a particular candidate.

Each cell sends a delegate to the General Council, the *Bondsraad*, which meets every two years in conditions of maximum security. Each delegate must bring a letter of authorisation from his branch secretary. These meetings used to be held in barns on out of the way farms until the Broederbond bought some two hundred acres of its own at Hartebeespoort Dam, thirty-five miles west of Pretoria, and built a special meeting hall there.[1]

The General Council reviews policy but its principal function is to elect the fifteen members of the *Uitvoerende Raad*, the Executive Council, who control the whole organisation. They are the élite of this élite.

Becoming a member of the Broederbond today involves a series of discreet enquiries about a nominee's suitability that can take up to three years. First a potential candidate is proposed and seconded by two current members who supply extensive details of his background. They must both be convinced that he measures up to an exacting list of standards; that he strives for 'the eternal existence of a separate Afrikaner nation with its own language and culture'; that he gives preference to 'Afrikaners and other well-disposed persons and firms in economic, public and professional life'; that he upholds Afrikaans in his home, in his job and in the community at large; that he is a

---

[1] In October 1978 the Johannesburg *Sunday Times* found out about a General Council meeting at Hartebeesport Dam and caused some consternation by openly monitoring all the arrivals at the gate and putting a photographer in a helicopter overhead to take pictures.

Protestant; that 'nothing in his person, character or behaviour precludes him from brotherhood'; that he is 'principled, faithful and cautious enough to meet the demands of the Bond'; that he is financially sound; and that he is 'able and willing to take part actively, regularly and faithfully in all the functions and activities of the Bond'.[1]

If all the members of the branch agree, the candidate's name is submitted to the Executive Committee who, in turn, circulate it to every other branch in the country. So every single member of this vast organisation has the opportunity to raise an objection. Only after this elaborate procedure is completed is the candidate approached.

Kowie Marais, later to become a judge in the Transvaal and later still to renounce the Broederbond when he joined the Progressive Federal Party opposition, remembered his feelings when he was first invited to become a member of one of the Pretoria branches in 1946. 'I felt very flattered', he said. 'I felt I was being recognised as a true-blue pedigree Afrikaner and of course I accepted.' He was soon to learn what were the failings, in Afrikaner eyes, that would rule out a potential member. A man whose wife was 'of dubious political affiliation' would not be acceptable, nor would a man who did not go to church regularly. Divorce puts an end to any chance of membership and often leads to expulsion. An Afrikaner who sent his children to an English-speaking school would not be considered because, said Kowie Marais, 'this was, and still is, an Afrikaner organisation, exclusively Afrikaans for the promotion of Afrikaner interests against the rest of the world'.[2]

The initiation, said Marais, is usually carried out in a private home. All the members of the branch are present. Candles are lit and placed in such a way that the candidate cannot see anyone's face. A table is

---

[1] These requirements were set out in the findings of a one-man investigation into the Broederbond in 1964 by a Pretoria attorney and church elder, Jan Oelofse. He had been instructed by the Hervormde Church to ascertain whether the Broederbond was exercising undue influence in church decisions. He said he was not himself a member of the Broederbond at the time but told me that he was invited to join soon afterwards.
[2] In a filmed interview in June 1978 for the BBC series 'The White Tribe of Africa', John Vorster, then Prime Minister, maintained that the Broederbond was, 'nothing but a cultural society to promote the cultural interests of Afrikaners' and cited Kowie Marais' membership of the Broederbond while he was at the same time a Member of Parliament for the Progressive opposition to illustrate that it was not an exclusive organisation.
In fact Marais had attended his last Broederbond meeting in October 1976, became an MP for the Progressive Federal Party on 30 November 1977 and was expelled from the Broederbond on 9 January 1978. Vorster himself was still member number 3737.

draped with the South African flag, sometimes with the Union Jack covered as a symbol of the rejection of any British association. Then one member reads out a series of questions: does the candidate swear that he is not a member of any secret organisation; that he will never reveal anything about the Broederbond; that he will strive to promote Afrikaner interests in everything he does; that he will readily subject himself to the brotherly discipline of the organisation.

In the early days the ritual was even more elaborate, culminating in the chilling reminder from the chairman that: 'He who betrays the Bond will be destroyed by the Bond. The Bond never forgets. Its vengeance is swift and sure. Never yet has a traitor escaped his just punishment.'

As membership has increased, so has the range of interests with which the Broederbond concerns itself. From being no more than a semi-religious cultural organisation, it has spread its influence into every walk of life. Nothing which can affect the well-being of the Afrikaners escapes the notice of the Broeders. They are concerned with everything, from birth control to burial clubs; from religion to race relations; from the dangers of Afrikaans children singing English rugby songs to the need for a sympathetic English language newspaper. Education was a key interest from the start. In 1921 the establishment of separate Afrikaans schools was declared as one of the Broederbond's main objectives. The instruction issued to members was 'to fight secretly but with all your might for unilingual medium schools'.

Above all, the Broederbond was concerned about the plight of the poor whites trying to make their way on the land and in the English cities. An organisation called *Helpmekaar* ('Help one another') had been in existence for some years. Its original purpose was to help Afrikaners convicted after the 1914 Rebellion to pay their fines, but now, with Broederbond assistance, the scope was widened. Voluntary donations were used to help Afrikaners buy houses or set up in business, sometimes with disastrous results when, for example, a local Dominee with no head for figures was put in charge of a business project. But it was a start and the forerunner of a considerable effort in the economic field.

Speaking in 1968 at a secret General Council Meeting, the then Chairman, Dr P. J. Meyer, also Chairman of the South African Broadcasting Corporation, recalled the position of the Afrikaners in this early period: 'We were the poor and the poor whites, the Boers without markets and without capital; the lowly paid, unskilled workers in the mines and the factories; we were the civil servants in inferior jobs, on the railways, in the post office, in the police.'

In 1934 the Broederbond started its own bank. Dr Meyer, though never acknowledging that this was a Broederbond venture, recalled that they had little money and less know-how. 'What the man who started it knew about banking was dangerous,' he said. His name was J. J. Bosman and he was an accountant in a Jewish store. Albert Hertzog, son of the General who had founded the National Party, recalled how three of them, including 'Bossie' Bosman – all members of the same 'cultural society' as he delicately put it – drove around the country meeting friends and fellow nationalists to convince them of the necessity of starting an Afrikaner bank. In the 'cultural society' they had long been discussing,

matters affecting our people and we realised more than ever the role that big capital was playing in the development of South Africa, always selecting certain sections of the people and excluding others. We realised how unfriendly – 'hostile' would be a better word – big capital was to the Afrikaner.

They managed to raise pledges of £5,000 of which, said Hertzog, only £615 was paid up but with that launched themselves into business from a first floor office in Pretoria. There was strong opposition from the existing English banks who maintained that they were quite capable of handling all the banking business that was going. Hertzog said that when they went to see the Governor of the Reserve Bank for advice and possible help, he told them that they were a public danger and that he would have to warn the public against them, which he promptly did.

But nonetheless, the Volk brought their savings and their business to The People's Bank. With a little persuasion from the 'cultural society' (although this is always denied) other Afrikaner enterprises, sports clubs and especially churches switched their accounts. Today Volkskas, the Broederbond bank, judging by total assets, deposits and declared profits, is the third largest bank in South Africa. The Board are all members of the Broederbond. For eleven years a former Chairman of the Broederbond, L. J. du Plessis was the bank's chairman.

During all this time the Broederbond had been paying particular attention to what they saw as the need to give the Afrikaner a feeling of identity, a self-confidence in his Afrikanerness that would make the Volk 'stand up' and challenge the English in every sphere of South

African life. In 1929 the Broederbond established the Federasie van Afrikaanse Kultuurvereniging, the Federation of Afrikaans Cultural Organisations, to co-ordinate a whole range of activities. In time, the FAK became the Broederbond's most important public field of operation. But it remained closely tied to the parent organisation which continued to make all the decisions behind the scenes. Dr Piet Koornhof, for example, current Minister for Cooperation and Development (Black Affairs) in the Nationalist Government, was at one time Secretary of the Broederbond but his public title was 'Director of Cultural Information at the FAK'.

A secret circular, sent to all members of the Broederbond on 1 August 1962 announcing Koornhof's appointment, included the following note:

The UR (Executive Council) is thankful that arrangements can be made with the FAK to link the post of our Chief Secretary with the public post as it enables friend Piet Koornhof to carry out our activities tactfully, in the open.

The present Secretary General of the FAK is Dr A. M. van den Berg. He works from an office on the ground floor of the Broederbond headquarters, a large modern building called *Die Eike* (the Oaks) in Auckland Park, Johannesburg. His number is in the telephone book but no number is listed for the Broederbond. He is an affable Afrikaner, happy to give information about the FAK but unwilling to talk about the Broederbond as such. However by sticking to the unwritten rules and using only words like 'cultural society' it is possible to discuss these matters in general terms. For good measure, Dr van den Berg has a habit of producing a tape recorder at interviews: 'It is not that we doubt your integrity but . . .'

There are now over four hundred purely Afrikaner organisations affiliated to the FAK. They range from the Voortrekkers, the Afrikaners' own Boy Scouts, to the *Vrouefederasie*, the Women's Federation: from the *Suid-Afrikaanse Buro vir Rasse-Aangeleenthede*, SABRA for short, the Bureau of Racial Affairs, to the *Afrikaanse Handelsinstituut*, the Afrikaans Institute of Commerce. Often they exist alongside similar organisations for English-speaking people and in direct competition to them. For example, in 1933 Afrikaans students broke away from the existing National Union of Students because of a disagreement over the admission of black students to the union. They set up their own organisation, the *Afrikaanse Studentebond*. The first Chairman was Dr Nico Diederichs, a member of the Broederbond, later Minister of Finance and later still President of South Africa.

When the FAK founded its own First Aid organisation, the *Noodhulpliga*, in 1935, its representatives were soon touring the schools telling Afrikaner children that the Red Cross was ' *'n Engelse organisasie*' and that it was their patriotic duty to join their own Afrikaans-speaking equivalent.

Sport also had its part. The *Jukskeibond* brought together thousands of Afrikaners to play the old Voortrekker game.[1] One year, through the FAK, the annual Jukskei tournament was arranged in Beaufort West in the Cape to coincide with the congress of *Helpmekaar*, the Afrikaner self-help society. Thus were Afrikaners brought together and kept away from outside influence.

In *The Rise of the South African Reich*, a book banned in South Africa, Brian Bunting has analysed the effect of the continual emphasis on Afrikaner exclusivity: 'The Broederbond has thus sponsored a sort of spiritual Great Trek of the Afrikaners in the twentieth century, by which they have removed themselves from "dangerous" contact with other elements of the population and withdrawn into cultural isolation. Once behind the wall, they have become easy victims of the Nationalist virus.'

Henning Klopper played another founding role in one of these exclusive Afrikaner clubs, the Language and Cultural Society of the South African Railways, the *Afrikaanse Taal en Kultuurvereniging*, known as ATKV. There are similar societies for Afrikaner post office workers, policemen, nurses and members of the defence force. But the ATKV is on a much larger scale; the railways were on the way to becoming the biggest employers of white labour in South Africa, and its cultural club came to exercise considerable influence. The ATKV has sponsored documentary films on Afrikaner history; it runs pension schemes and holiday camps, adult education courses and political discussion groups. Its present secretary, an extremely cautious and formal Afrikaner named Horne, naturally enough a member of the Broederbond, was quite shocked that the ATKV might ever be likened to a Working Men's Club in Britain. Drinking, said the secretary, is not encouraged; the emphasis is on the Afrikaners' Christian patriotic duty; gatherings begin and end with prayers. Theirs was not at all the sort of organisation, Mr Horne's committee decided, that would allow a television camera to record some of their activities. Encountering the ATKV today it is easy to see why it was the perfect

---

[1] *Jukskei* is similar to the American game of throwing the horseshoe. The Jukskei, which is used instead, is the wooden pin from an ox-yoke.

ideological base from which, in due course, Henning Klopper was to launch one of the Broederbond's most brilliant successes.

There was obviously much in the early activities of both the Broederbond and what it likes to call 'its considerably bigger son' the FAK, that was entirely innocent and part of an understandable attempt to give the Afrikaner back his self-respect, secure his cultural heritage and promote his new language. But gradually the emphasis changed. The decision to become secret was crucial; other equally important decisions soon followed.

In 1978 two books were published that charted the course of this change within the Broederbond. Both relied on extensive anonymous contacts within the organisation and on a close study of secret documents obtained from them. Hennie Serfontein's book *The Brotherhood of Power* is particularly revealing on the early and middle years while *The Super Afrikaners*, by Hans Strydom and Ivor Wilkins of the Johannesburg *Sunday Times*, remorselessly chronicles the Broederbond's recent activities as its role has shifted from safeguarding Afrikaner interests to conspiring to maintain Afrikaner domination. These books prompted the early publication of the Broederbond's own version of the first fifty years by Professor A. N. Pelzer that had long been in preparation. It paints a completely different picture and attempts to acquit the organisation of any political influence or intent. At the same time the former Chairman of the Broederbond, Professor Gerrit Viljoen, was projected on to SABC television and in an unprecedented but totally bland interview defended the Broederbond's political virginity.

But the evidence suggests that all is not quite as Professor Viljoen would have South Africans believe. In August 1932 the then Chairman, Professor J. C. van Rooy of Potchefstroom University made a clear statement of intent. It came in a secret message to members that was not made known until three years later and then by an unexpected source. Now that the FAK was established, said van Rooy, and 'sufficient vigilant defenders' were taking care of the 'cultural work' there were other demands:

After the cultural and economic needs, the Afrikaner Broederbond will have to devote its attention to the political needs of our people. And here the aim must be a completely independent, genuine Afrikans government for South Africa. A government which, by its embodiment of our own personal Head of State, bone of our bone and flesh of our flesh, will inspire us and bind us together in irresistible unity and strength.

By now the Broederbond numbered among its members Afrikaners

Professor Gerrit Viljoen, Minister of Education and Sport, former Rector of Rand Afrikaans University, Chairman of the Broederbond 1974–1978

well equipped for more than 'cultural' aspirations; men like Dr D. F. Malan, the leader of the Nationalist Party in the Cape, advocate J. G. Strydom and Stellenbosch academic H. F. Verwoerd, all three of whom later became Nationalist Prime Ministers. But the steady change of emphasis in Broederbond activities did not pass unnoticed and soon provoked an attack from what at first sight seemed a surprising direction.

General Barry Hertzog had served his people for more than thirty years. In the Anglo-Boer he had been one of the most successful commando leaders; he was a delegate at Vereeniging and one of the five who negotiated the final terms with Milner. Fearing that union would leave South Africa too much under British Imperialist sway, he founded the National Party; he was the champion of Afrikaner schooling, and of the right of every child to be taught in his own language. But he had always recognised the equal role of English speakers loyal to South Africa. In 1926 he returned from the Imperial Conference in London convinced that, 'the great question of our freedom and independence' had been settled once and for all and that there was 'not the least reason' for English speakers and Afrikaans speakers not to, 'work together in all respects'. So Hertzog agreed in March 1933 to take the Nationalists into a coalition with Smuts' South Africa Party in what was known as the 'Fusion Government'. That led in turn, in December 1934, to a further fusion of the two parties into the 'United South African National Party', known for short as the United Party.

There were other important reasons for reconciliation. South Africa's grave economic position as a result of the Great Depression of 1931–2 had led to calls for a national government. Also, under the constitution, Hertzog needed a two-thirds majority in parliament to push through some of the legislation concerning blacks that most whites favoured.

Hertzog had already erected a formidable industrial colour bar with his 'civilised labour' policy; he had given the government powers to remove blacks 'from any place to any other place in the Union'; he had introduced more stringent pass laws. Now, most controversial of all, he proposed to take blacks in the Cape off the common voters' roll. The eleven thousand Africans who had the franchise were to be grouped into three native electoral sectors, each entitled to elect one white member to the House of Assembly. The new coalition government hardly hesitated and the Representation of Natives Act became law in 1936.[1]

One minister alone in the Fusion cabinet spoke out against the franchise bill. Jan Hofmeyr, Minister of Interior, Education and Public Health, gave a prophetic warning:

By this bill we are sowing the seeds of a far greater potential conflict than is being done by anything in existence today . . . once franchise rights have been given and exercised by a section of the community, then no nation save at the cost of honour and ultimate security should take away those rights without adequate justification.

Nothing, says C. W. de Kiewiet in his *History of South Africa* quite so unambiguously defined the relations between the races: 'To destroy the Cape native franchise was to destroy the most important bridge between the worlds of the two races'.

Dr D. F. Malan and his supporters in the National Party had no objections to any of this legislation but they could not stomach Hert-

---

[1] In return for such legislation Hertzog proposed, under the Native Trust and Land Act of 1936, to make more land available to blacks, bringing their total area up to approximately one eighth of the whole of South Africa. In 1958, 5,686,431 acres, roughly one-third of the additional land designated, had still not been assigned.

zog's association with the Hoggenheimer capitalist elements in the new United Party. They believed the interests of the poor white Afrikaners would be ignored. Nor could they accept working with Smuts who, in their view, had already been cast out by true members of the Volk. Above all they believed Hertzog had lost sight of the Republican aims of true Nationalists. No association with the countrymen of Milner and the mine bosses could give Afrikaners their rights. Only an Afrikaner Republic could do that.

J. G. Strydom announced that the 'National Party must be maintained on a purified foundation'. Malan led the breakaway and the 'Purified' Nationalist Party was established immediately. Its aims coincided exactly with those of the Broederbond. 'Purified nationalism in the Transvaal,' wrote T. Dunbar Moodie in his *Rise of Afrikanerdom*, 'was thus precious little more than the Broederbond writ large.'

Hertzog lost no time in condemning the breakaway and in a famous speech at Smithfield in November 1935 traced the course of both Malan's 'purification', and his antagonism towards the English, to his joining the Broederbond. It was Hertzog who produced the statement by the chairman, Professor van Rooy from the University of Potchefstroom, that the Broederbond should now extend its attention to the political needs of the Afrikaner.

Even as Dr Malan, [continued Hertzog] they have taken an oath secretly to permit no co-operation from the English side with an eye to national unity, and in this way they stand in direct racial conflict with our English fellow Afrikaners, striving by means of Afrikaans-speaking domination to place the foot on the neck of the English-speaking South African.

Then Hertzog produced another Broederbond circular, signed by van Rooy and the Secretary, I. M. Lombard on 16 January 1925 and sent to all members. Hertzog quoted from it at length:

Let us focus our attention on the fact that our chief concern is whether Afrikanerdom will reach its eventual goal of domination in South Africa. Brothers, our solution for South Africa's troubles is not that this or that party shall obtain the upper hand, but that the Afrikaner Broederbond shall rule South Africa.

Hertzog continued in his speech,

Very nice, is it not, flattering to the soul of the Dutch-speaking Afrikaner, like you and me. Only it suffers from the great defect that must necessarily lead to the downfall of Dutch-speaking Afrikanerdom itself, if this kind of Afrikaner-jingo self-glorification is continued. It is being forgotten for instance, that there are also English-speaking Afrikaners in South Africa who are also entitled to a place in the South African sun. When will this foolish, fatal idea cease that some people are the chosen of the gods to rule over others? The English speakers tried it with the Afrikaans speakers and did not succeed. The Afrikaans speakers tried it with the English and they did not succeed either ... The Broederbond had been translated into a secret, purified Nationalist Party which busies itself with secret propaganda work for the advantage of the interests of the purified Broeders and of the purified National Party ... Whatever therefore may have been the cultural aim and striving of the Afrikaner Broederbond in the past ... there can be no doubt that we have today in the Broederbond to deal with a secret political association accessible only to, and consisting only of, Afrikaans-speaking members, the leading political spirits of whom are determined to rule South Africa over the heads of the English-speaking among us.

Then Hertzog went on to give illustrations of how the Broederbond operated in Parliament. His information had come from Broeders who had stayed loyal to his Fusion section of the National Party. He told the story of how this 'cultural society' had tried to influence the passage of a particular bill through Parliament:

While the discussion on the motion was proceeding the Broederbond set to work and secretly, in an organised manner, propaganda was made in the country districts in support of the motion. The Broeders, encouraged by purified Nationalists in Parliament, succeeded in managing to have numbers of telegrams sent to practically every Member of Parliament from the country districts, with the object of bringing pressure to bear on them to force them to vote for the motion. By its secret actions the Bond wanted to give the impression that the Members had to do with a spontaneous expression of feeling by the people in the district concerned.

Of particular concern to Hertzog were the operations of the Broederbond inside the teaching profession. He claimed that parents had come to him complaining of the political influence that was being exercised in the classroom. A woman had confronted him: 'In God's name, General, we mothers make a call on you to do everything in your power to prevent our children in school being so put up against their parents. You have no idea how bad it is.'

Hertzog said he knew that one third of the Broederbond's members were teachers:

I know also that there are few towns and villages in the Free State where the Bond has not made a little nest for itself of five or more brothers, which must serve as a centre for Bond propaganda; and I know that there is pretty well not a single one of these nests where one or more teachers are not sitting hatching.

101

At the end of his speech Hertzog made an appeal to his electorate:

Has the Afrikaner Nation sunk to such hopeless depths that it must seek its salvation in a secret conspiracy for the advancement of race hatred, of national dissension, and of strife among brothers? Is there no higher aspiration for the Sons and Daughters of South Africa, no nobler task than that of racial strife and dissension? Is there no higher ideal for our children to attain than that of racial domination?

There is no doubt that Hertzog's attack on the Broederbond was partly the pique of a politician who feared that the torch of nationalism he had carried for so long was being wrested from him. That is not to say he was the 'broken down renegade' that Malan called him in his reply. In his desire to seek harmony between the 'twin streams' of English and Afrikaans-speaking South Africans, Hertzog was unquestionably sincere. It was this, above all, that had brought him into conflict with the Broederbond.

The Band of Brothers and their 'Purified' colleagues were set on a different course, the path of Afrikaner exclusivism; they were also not averse to instilling the idea that they were really better Afrikaners than those who were non-Broeders. Only seventeen years had passed since Henning Klopper and his friends, with their high ideals, had founded the Broederbond. He complains that Hertzog's attack was misguided. 'Well, Hertzog was a very fine man but he was sometimes . . . too outspoken, too irresponsible. He said some very irresponsible things, Hertzog.' But as he spoke Klopper did permit himself the suggestion of a smile.

8

'A sacred happening'

Henning Klopper's description of the 1938 Anniversary Trek

'I think the whole feeling of the trek throughout was the working not of man, not of me, not of any living being. It was the will and the work of Almighty God.' Forty years after the event Henning Klopper was still slightly incredulous that the simple notion of commemorating the Centenary of the Great Trek turned into a happening that stirred Afrikaner hearts the length and breadth of South Africa. With or without divine assistance, it was a brilliant political event that advanced the cause of the Nationalists more than any of its organisers could have dared to hope.

For years, said Klopper, he had dreamed of retracing the steps of the Voortrekkers in a pilgrimage across South Africa. By 1933 he was suggesting to colleagues in the 'cultural society' his vision of using an ox-wagon to recapture the spirit of the Great Trek. Hertzog's Government was planning to build a memorial to the Voortrekkers just outside Pretoria. It was to be inaugurated on 16 December 1938, the one hundredth anniversary of the Battle of Blood River and its Day of the Covenant. The Broederbond, doing what it did well, co-ordinated the ideas. The Commemorative Trek would follow *Die Pad van Suid-Afrika*, the symbolic road to nationhood taken by the Voortrekkers from the Cape to Pretoria; then continue right to the site of the monument. Klopper, by now Port Superintendent at Mossel Bay in the Cape, would be responsible for the detailed planning through his Society for Afrikaners on the Railways, the ATKV.

Klopper recalls that at one of the first meetings of the ATKV there was some scepticism over how they would ever find the oxen to cover the vast distance. Would enough farmers be prepared to lend their ox-teams for a day or more? 'But then,' he continued, 'two women who hadn't said much at the meeting spoke up. If the men could not provide the oxen, the women would pull the wagons themselves. After that no one said anything against the idea.'

The original plan was to send a single wagon along a commemorative route which Klopper had carefully worked out. At towns or villages on the way the local Dominee, aided by a friendly man or two from the 'cultural society', would organise reception committees, and relays of oxen. The idea brought such response that a second wagon was added. One was to be a travelling post box carrying a hundred thousand messages to the centenary celebrations in Pretoria.

On 8 August 1938, Klopper's two wagons, the 'Piet Retief' and the 'Andries Pretorius', stood at the foot of Jan van Riebeeck's statue in Cape Town. As the ox-teams were harnessed it was as if the emotions of all true Afrikaners were harnessed too. A huge crowd had gathered.

We were astounded [said Klopper]. The reports estimated there were over one hundred thousand people – in Cape Town, an English city. Over one hundred thousand people had gathered to look at ox-wagons that they could see all the time. It was quite unnatural. Why should so many turn out to see the departure of an ox-wagon?

Klopper spoke to the crowd and called on them to remember the Covenant of Sarel Cilliers before the battle of Blood River; he prayed that the symbolic trek they were about to re-enact would bring Afrikaners together again:

We ask the entire Afrikanerdom to take part in the festival celebration in this spirit. We long that nothing shall hinder the Afrikaner people as a whole from taking part. This movement is born from the People; may the People carry it in their hearts all the way to Pretoria and Blood River.

Let us build up a monument for Afrikaner hearts. May this simple trek bind together in love those Afrikaner hearts which do not yet beat together. We dedicate these wagons to our People and to our God.'

Gideon Roos was there for the new Afrikaans service of the SABC to cover the departure of the wagons from Adderley Street. 'The moment you arrived you could feel there was something in the air', he said. Then he went on to Goodwood, eight miles away where the wagons were to stop for the night. There were another twenty thousand people waiting. Two days later he was to have reported from Stellenbosch and then from Worcester; that was meant to have been all until December when the wagons reached Pretoria. In the event Roos stayed with the story for four months, charting the course of the pilgrimage in daily broadcasts. 'You have no idea what emotion it caused. I saw people in tears because of this wave of intense patriot-

Opposite: the symbolic ox-wagon trek of 1938

ism, crystallised around the pride in this romantic page in our history. We never had a symbol before; the ox-wagon became that symbol.'

Towns in all parts of the country vied for the privilege of a visit from one of the wagons. Several other treks besides Henning Klopper's were organised. In the end six more wagons threaded their way to the capital from distant points; four others went to the site of the battle at Blood River for a commemoration service on 16 December.

At every Afrikaner shrine the pilgrims stopped to pay homage: at Slagter's Nek, where the British publicly hanged five Afrikaners for treason; at the grave of Jopie Fourie, cut down by Smuts' firing squad; at the memorial of the 'seventy burghers' murdered by Dingane, including, of course, four of Henning Klopper's own ancestors. At the grave of Sarel Cilliers, Klopper spoke of the 'man who stood between our destruction and the might of God'. Sarel Cilliers had erected the beacon of the first covenant between God and the People, he said. God had saved his people at Blood River but Afrikanerdom had failed to keep its part of the covenant. The only way they would overcome their divisions was to 'return to the God who will honour us'.

Pride in the Afrikaner past swelled in every chest as again and again at every sermon and speech the crowds sang the new Afrikaans anthem *'Die Stem van Suid-Afrika'* – 'We shall live, We shall die, We for Thee, South Africa'. Was it not only the squabbles of the party politicians that were keeping the Volk apart? The spirit of the trek, they said, must be upheld in the same way that the imprint of the wagons, drawn through freshly laid cement at so many halts, was being preserved for all time. Street after street in countless towns and villages was renamed after one or another Voortrekker hero. In Bloemfontein, when the English-speaking town council declined to be caught up in this enthusiasm for Afrikanerising the street names, the organising committee refused to use the oxen the city had provided. 'We pulled the wagons through the town ourselves', said Klopper. 'The children took one, the men another and the wives a third.'

The better to resemble their ancestors, thousands of men grew beards. Gideon Roos was one of them. He had a full Voortrekker uniform made as well, with corduroy breeches and knotted scarf. When he shaved his beard at the end of it all, he said he received much less respect in the office. Not to be outdone many women ran up long Voortrekker dresses and made themselves traditional *kappies* (bonnets). At many stops, couples came forward in their Voortrekker garb to be married; sometimes there were as many as six groups together; others brought their children to be baptised next to the sacred wagons.

Renaming Seventh Street, Boksburg, Transvaal, as 'Sarel Cilliers Street' during the 1938 Centenary Trek

It was indescribable [Klopper marvels still]. Women would come up to the axles of the wagon and smear the grease off with their kappies or their skirts, or with their handkerchiefs, and put it on their faces. Other women came and kissed the wheels, the steel bands on the wheels, until they were shining. They would fall on their knees and thank God for the Ossewatrek.

Klopper, the teetotaller and non-smoker, the man who morning and evening still reads the Bible his mother gave him when he left home, believed then and still does today that the trek was divinely blessed.

Although I organised it and had everything to do with it, I felt it was taken completely out of my hands. The whole feeling of the trek was the working not of man, not of any living being. It was the will and the work of the Almighty God. It was a pilgrimage, a sacred happening.

Not that the Volk did not sometimes need shepherding. At one stop where some forgot their divine calling to the extent of starting to dance, Klopper threatened to in-span the wagons and trek off unless they ceased forthwith. At another, remembered Gideon Roos, Klopper had strong words for the press. It happened shortly after a reporter named Marais Steyn had written something critical about him for *Die Vaderland*, a Johannesburg newspaper. The trek leader was at his outraged best: 'Satan has also sent his reporters with the trek,' he boomed to the assembled pilgrims. Marais Steyn, said Gideon Roos, just doffed his hat.[1]

No opportunity was lost to emphasise the view of the Afrikaner's chosen destiny. At Bloemfontein when a relay of flaming torches arrived, borne all the way from the Cape by young Voortrekkers, old Dominee Kestell, the Boer War chaplain exulted in the symbolism:

We have received a fire from God, that fire is our nationhood. It is wonderful to think that this nationhood is from God, a burning torch which is not extinguished. It has been kept burning all the way from the statue of van Riebeeck to here. By the mercy of God it has burned until now. It must be kept burning.

The Broederbond and Father Kestell had a simple notion for keeping the torch alight. They passed the hat round whenever the wagons stopped. It was the start of what became known as the *Reddingsdaad*, (The Act of Rescue) on behalf of the poor urban Afrikaner. 'Our people must rescue itself,' said Dominee Kestell in Bloemfontein, 'and now is the time.'

In Bloemfontein the crowds moved forward to place their contributions in six chests and over four hundred and fifty pounds was collected.

A year after the Centenary Trek, the Broederbond sponsored a National Economic Conference at which the organisation of the fund was channelled in the *Reddingsdaadbond* (Society for the Act of Rescue). It was to go much further than providing demeaning alms for poor whites. The lessons of Malherbe's Carnegie Commission had been learned. The bulk of the funds would supply capital for Afrikaner businesses. A Broederbond document circulated among members thirty years later, saw the congress as, 'one of the most important milestones in the development of the history of the Afrikaner nation . . . Its greatest value was that it deflected the Afrikaner's eyes from his poverty and made him conscious of his great potential on the economic front.'

The Volk would now begin their invasion of the territory held by Hoggenheimer and the English-speaking capitalists. A subscription of six pence a month bought membership of the Reddingsdaadbond and

---

[1] By 1979 Marais Steyn, for many years a senior member of the United Party, was Minister for Community Development in P. W. Botha's Government, one of the few non-Broeders in the Cabinet. In 1980 he was appointed South African Ambassador in London.

Life and Burial Insurance with the Afrikaner business houses that the swelling fund helped finance. By 1946 the Bond had sixty-five thousand members. In ten years from 1939 the number of Afrikans-owned businesses rose from under four thousand to over thirteen thousand.

The only fly in the financial ointment was the suspicion that while many Broeders were gaining much experience in commerce, some were doing rather better out of it all than was seemly. Indeed, when South Africa's Military Intelligence probed the activities of the Broederbond in World War Two, their report, signed by Colonel Ernie Malherbe, who had temporarily left his academic career to become Smuts' Director of Military Intelligence, was openly critical:

Dr Diederichs, Professor du Plessis, and their associates have involved the Reddingsdaadbond in a complicated financial maze. A terrific fiddling with paper assets is carried on by means of subscriptions, wrung from the poorest of the poor, through monthly extortions of more than three hundred and seventy branches of the Reddingsdaadbond. There is every possibility that a thorough investigation by impartial auditors will reveal grave irregularities and exploitation.[1]

As the wagons rolled towards Pretoria with their ever filling collecting boxes and the exhortations to come forward and help save the Volk, there was another vibrant theme to the speeches and the prayers. 'Everywhere I went,' said Klopper, 'thousands of people asked me: "When will we get the Republic?"'In the Cape, in Natal, everywhere. Their whole idea was, when will we get the Republic?' One English correspondent went so far as to telegraph his office that if Klopper was to proclaim a Republic there and then, they should be ready for the news. But Klopper dismissed all such talk as premature. 'First the people had to be united. Then they would decide where and how.'

Kowie Marais, also covering the trek for the SABC, thought the moment might have come at the climax of the trek in Pretoria. A hundred thousand people had gathered, wrote *Die Burger*, one in ten of all Afrikaners, camping beneath the midsummer skies to await the arrival of the wagons. When the relay of burning torches reached the city they were met by three thousand Voortrekkers each with a torch of his own. They marched in company up the hill to the site of the

---

[1] Du Plessis was a former chairman of the Broederbond and Nico Diederichs was the current chairman. He had given up his post as professor of Political Science and Philosophy at the University College of the Orange Free State to take over additional responsibility for the Reddingsdaadbond. Diederichs later became Minister of Finance in the Vorster cabinet and later still State President.

Monument. A huge bonfire had been prepared and as each Voortrekker filed past he hurled his torch into the flames. Simultaneously fires were lit on the hilltops all round Pretoria.

Finally the wagons appeared but no longer were they drawn by the oxen. No beasts of burden were to defile the sacred hill. Human teams, flanked by lines of outriders, dragged these mobile altars to their place of honour. Three women descendants of Retief, Pretorius and Potgieter laid the foundation stone of the Voortrekker Monument. The crowds sang and prayed, applauded yet more speeches and sang again.

There had been talk around the camp fires that Oswald Pirow, the Minister of Defence in Hertzog's cabinet, a man known to admire Hitler and his methods, might seize the moment, respond to public fervour and declare a Republic. Kowie Marais and his friends were certainly in favour. But no call came and the young men were bitterly disappointed. 'I thought our Nationalist leaders had failed us,' said Marais, 'because they were afraid.' Klopper, on the other hand, felt no such disillusion. He believed the Centenary Trek had achieved all he had hoped for and more. 'We had united the people', he said. 'We had brought them to their senses.'

Even the Malherbe family, who had nothing in common with the ideals of the Broederbond, had been caught up with the Afrikanerness of it all. At Blood River on 15 December, in the shade of one of the wagons, Dr Ernie Malherbe's father-in-law, Dominee Paul Nel, baptised their daughter Betty-Jane with water from the Blood River. It was placed in a copper chalice brought to South Africa by Malherbe's Huguenot ancestor, Gideon Malherbe, in 1688. The next day, the sixteenth, Dominee Nel was called upon to lay the foundation stone of the marble replica of a wagon which still stands on the battlefield at Blood River as a permanent memorial to that day of remembrance.

At Monumentkoppie in Pretoria Alan Paton was one of the huge crowd. He was then principal of an African boys' reformatory at Diepkloof, just outside Johannesburg and still to write *Cry the Beloved Country*. He too had grown a beard and put on Voortrekker dress. Also, to share in this unifying experience, he had trekked the thirty-five miles from Johannesburg by ox-wagon 'flying the Vierkleur flag of the defeated Transvaal Republic.' In a recent essay, he described what awaited him in Pretoria:

We arrived on a hot day, and I went straight to the showers. Here I was greeted by a naked and bearded Afrikaner who said to me, 'Have you seen the great crowds?' I said, 'Yes' (there were a quarter of a million people there). He said to me with the greatest affability: *'Nou gaan ons die Engelse opdonder,'* 'Now we're going to knock hell out of the English'.

The great day was full of speeches, and the theme of every meeting was Afrikanerdoin, its glories, its struggles, its grief, its achievements. The speaker had only to shout *Vryheid* (which is freedom) to set the vast crowd roaring, just as today a black speaker who shouts *Amandla* (power) can set a black crowd roaring. A descendant of the British 1820 settlers who gave Jacobus Uys a Bible when he set out on the Great Trek was shouted down because he gave his greetings in English as his forebear had done.

It was a lonely and terrible occasion for any English-speaking South African who had gone there to rejoice in this Afrikaner festival. . . . After the laying of the stone I left the celebrations and went home. I said to my wife: 'I'm taking off this beard and I'll never wear another.' That was the end of my love affair with Nationalism. I saw it for what it was, self centred, intolerant, exclusive.[1]

Solly Sachs was General Secretary of the Garment Workers' Union at the time of the Centenary Trek. He too came up against this exclusiveness when he asked if a delegation from the union might attend the celebrations in Pretoria. Most of his members were Afrikaner women and they wanted to form what was called a 'Kappie Kommando' in Voortrekker costume to take part in the various processions. Sachs himself was a Jew and had once been a Communist although he had been expelled from the party in 1931. What also offended Nationalists was that his union was non-racial with black and coloured members as well as white. The letter Sachs received in reply from the trek organisers drew attention to 'the mockery of our national traditions your participation in the Centenary Celebrations will mean' and continued:

The Afrikaner nation is busy uniting, to mobilise its forces against you and your sort. The thousands of Afrikaner daughters whom you have in your clutches will settle with you. . . . Our people do not want anything to do with Communists and Jews, the high priests thereof, least of all. The day when we Afrikaners begin to settle with you Jews, you will find out that Germany is a Jewish paradise compared with what South Africa will be. . . . You and Johanna Cornelius [one of the union officials], who all day long organise and address kaffirs, will you dare to bring them also to the celebrations? They are your fellow workers and 'Comrades'. We challenge you to come to the celebrations. . . .[2]

---

[1] *The Afrikaner as I know him*, by Alan Paton, from 'The Afrikaners', Tafelberg, Cape Town 1979.
[2] *Rebel's Daughters* by E. S. Sachs, MacGibbon and Key, London 1957.

In theory there were to have been no political addresses at the final celebrations. The whole Ossewatrek, said the organisers, was above party squabbles. But in the event, while Hertzog was squeezed out of any participation at all and Smuts attended at Monumentkoppie only as a spectator, Dr Malan contrived to deliver the main address at Blood River. There, in what friend and foe agreed was a brilliant speech, the leader of the Purified Nationalists pointed the way ahead for his brand of Afrikanerdom. In the symbolism of Blood River and the battle fought there a century before, he found the inspiration for the century to come. In 1838, he said, thanks to Voortrekker sacrifice and to God's Grace, Afrikanerdom had prevailed. Now Afrikaners faced a trek to a new frontier, to the city.

In that new Blood River black and white meet together in much closer contact and in a much more binding struggle than when one hundred years ago the circle of white-tented wagons protected the laager, the muzzleloader clashed with assegai. Today black and white jostle together in the same labour market.

On this 'Second Trek' to the city the freedom the Afrikaners now sought was more than just the right to rule themselves in a Republic. It was the right which those who had trekked long ago had also claimed.

Their freedom was also, and above all, the freedom to preserve themselves as a White Race. As you could never otherwise have realised, you realise today their task to make South Africa a white man's land is ten times more your task.

As a sign of your national pride you are naming your streets after Voortrekker heroes and demanding that *'Die Stem van Suid-Afrika'* should be recognised as your national anthem. Have you the patriotism and sufficient power in this year of celebration to use this God-given opportunity also to demand something infinitely more important, the assurance that White Civilisation will be assured?

Malan had identified the main issue. In his South Africa the white man must rule. To gain the power to ensure that future Afrikaners must remain united. But the unity envisaged by Malan's Purified Nationalists would exclude the English speakers whom Hertzog had sought to bring into his wider Afrikanerdom. Because of that exclusivity the old Afrikaner hero, Hertzog, rejected them in turn.

But though one hundred thousand in unison had sung the Afrikaner anthem on Monumentkoppie in Pretoria not all were yet in tune with Malan's Nationalism. In the 1938 elections his party had won but twenty-seven seats. The United Party of Hertzog and Smuts, embracing English speakers and Afrikaners alike had taken one hundred and eleven. The Nationalists had yet to turn the undoubted wave of popular support the Centenary Trek had aroused into votes and political power.

Not long after the Centenary Trek, Hertzog wrote to his son Albert, a young advocate in Pretoria, a thrusting member of the Broederbond and staunch supporter of the Purified Nationalists. It was a letter that became famous: 'Allow me . . . in all sincerity and with no other purpose than to be of service to Afrikanerdom, to warn you and your young Afrikaner friends that along the road which you are walking only national destruction is to be found.'

9

'They will bloody well never get us out'

A Mineworkers Union official

The young man pulls the collar of his coat up higher against his neck as he walks round the corner into Kerk Street . . . and stands in front of the building . . . 23 Kerk Street, Trades Hall . . . He has reached his destination.

For a few moments he hesitates in front of the entrance then walks a few yards further and turns round again. . . . Suddenly a car pulls up alongside the pavement in front of the building where Moller Hugo is standing in the half-light . . . For one fleeting moment he looks straight at the man behind the steering wheel . . . then a revolver shot echoes in the twilight quiet of Kerk Street . . .

The young Hugo did not run away. He was not aware of the people who suddenly began to gather around the motor car. He did not see how a couple of men lifted Charles Harris out of the black motorcar and laid him on the pavement . . . He stood there, unmoving and alone, until the police came, took the revolver out of his hand and led him away. His task was accomplished . . .

Thus Louis Naudé, at the beginning of his book *Dr Albert Hertzog, die Nasionale Party en die Mynwerkers* (*Dr Albert Hertzog, the National Party and the Mineworkers*) describes one of the most violent episodes in the Afrikaners' rise to power before the Second World War.

Charles Harris was a Jew and Secretary of the Mineworkers Union. Most of the Afrikaners in the union, and they were the vast majority, believed he was both inefficient and corrupt, working in collusion with the Chamber of Mines against their best interests. Jacob Moller Hugo was a twenty-two-year old Afrikaner from the Cape who had been sacked from the New Modder Mine for sleeping on duty. At the time of the shooting he was out of work, short of cash and persuaded that his plight was all the fault of Harris, the Union Secretary. Witnesses at the trial reported that Hugo had been going around calling Harris 'a Communist Jew taking orders from Russia' and a traitor during the 1922 strike.

Hugo was also known to support the Afrikaner Reform Movement within the union. It had long been agitating for a change in the

114

leadership and there were rumours that two of its officials had put Hugo up to the murder; but the court could find no evidence of conspiracy.

What it did find was that on the night of 15 June 1939, Hugo had been drinking. He had also been taking aspirin and had not eaten for several days. As Harris was about to drive his car out of a garage in Kerk Street close to the union headquarters, Hugo went up to him, and demanded that he resign as union secretary. Harris apparently 'smiled cynically', whereupon Hugo shot him not once but five times.

The court psychiatrist reported that Hugo was unstable and had definite psychopathic tendencies, although he was not certifiable as insane. But the judge did accept that this mental condition constituted an extenuating circumstance; on 12 October 1939 Hugo was sentenced to life imprisonment.

Though an extreme example, the episode certainly drew attention to the feelings aroused in the Afrikaners' continuing battle for survival in the cities. A year after the Centenary Trek, Malan had spoken of the need for 'intensive Afrikaner *Volksorganisasie*' (people's organisation) and nowhere was that activity more intense than in the trade unions.

At the centre of it all was the intriguing figure of Albert Hertzog, the son of the Prime Minister. Physically slight, similar in build to Henning Klopper, and today wearing the same goatee beard, Hertzog shared with Klopper that unshakeable conviction in the destiny of the Volk and an equal determination to dedicate his life to the Afrikaner cause. Untroubled by the wider vision of South Africa of his father, he went on to become a Minister in Verwoerd's cabinet, and later still the founder of the extreme right-wing party, the HNP, the Herstigte Nasionale Party, that still unsettles Nationalist politics today.

In the 1930s Albert Hertzog was an important member of Malan's ideological power house. He had studied law at Oxford, surprising in itself for one so implacably anti-imperialist, and had returned, he said, impressed by the power and potential of the British trade unions, which in 1929 had helped propel a Labour government to power.[1]

[1] At a secret Broederbond Congress in Bloemfontein in 1943, bugged by Ernie Malherbe's Military Intelligence, one speaker, a member of the Senate at the University of Pretoria, warned of the dangers to which Afrikaners were exposed when they studied overseas, particularly in Britain. He warned especially against taking up bursaries like the Rhodes Scholarship. The denationalisation of the youth of a subject country was always the prime aim of such scholarships, he said. Students attended lectures glorifying the British Empire and were introduced to English homes where, if possible, they could be married off to English girls. Their homes would therefore never be without 'a dictator ready to spout British Imperialism at all times'.

Dr Albert Hertzog, who led the Afrikaner bid to take over the trades unions

He found a kindred spirit in Piet Meyer who had been taking a degree in Germany where the way in which Hitler's National Socialists succeeded in arousing the masses had deeply impressed him. In 1934 Hertzog and Meyer had worked together through the Broederbond, raising capital for the new Afrikaner Bank, Volkskas. By 1936 Meyer was full-time assistant Secretary of the FAK. Now they turned their considerable abilities to no less a task than reorganising the trade unions.

What they saw there appalled them. In 1937, out of one hundred and eighteen unions, at least one hundred had non-Afrikaner secretaries. There was a widespread belief that the craft trades were being restricted to English speakers. Hennie Coetzee, for example, now Professor of Anthropology at the University of Potchefstroom, remembers going to the Rand Technical College where his brother applied to become a fitter and turner. There was no vacancy, they were told. While they were still there another man arrived and applied for exactly the same course. He was accepted on the spot. Coetzee believes it was simply because of his English surname. Many an Afrikaner who grew up in the 1930s and 40s has a similar tale.

More important, in the eyes of the 'cultural society' was the danger from the ideas that might rub off on unsophisticated Afrikaners, lately from the platteland, working with English-speaking trade unionists. After all, Communists, Socialists and Afrikaner Nationalists had already marched side by side in the 1922 miners' strike. It was imperative, went the Nationalist argument, to save the urban Afrikaner from the Communism preached by some union officials as well as from the class attitudes that so poisoned society in Britain.

He must be made to see himself as an Afrikaner first and last with more in common with an Afrikaner lawyer or schoolmaster than with an English speaker who worked on the same shop floor. The unions must be turned into strongholds of what Piet Meyer called 'Christian Nationalism', where the ideals of the Volk were dominant; and the unions in their turn would one day help to bring the true Nationalists, Malan's 'purified' Nationalists, to political power.

In October 1936, Meyer and Hertzog with Nico Diederichs and an Afrikaner banker, began by founding the *Nasionale Raad van Trustees*, the National Council of Trustees, to provide the financial base for the move into the trade unions. The Chairman and Secretary of the Broederbond were on the committee and so was Father Kestell. The widow of a rich farmer donated two thousand pounds to start them off.

Since the whole of the country's economy was beginning to revolve

117

around gold, Hertzog said they naturally turned first to the mineworkers. There were already fifteen thousand Afrikaners in the union that Charles Harris ran. If they could control the mineworkers, the rest would follow. So in November 1936, Hertzog and Meyer coolly founded their own union, the *Afrikanerbond van Mynwerkers*, and set about persuading the Afrikaner miners to join it. Louis Naudé described the task they faced:

From one end of the Rand to the other the young men had to work, night after night, from Nigel to Springs, to Krugersdorp and Randfontein, at the shaft heads and in homes. And the time in which such work could be done was short – during the brief hours between the time when the worker returned from the afternoon shift and the time when he crawled early into bed. There were fifty-two mines with one hundred and eighty-nine shafts spread over a distance of eighty miles across the Rand. Thence Dr Hertzog and his fellows had to hasten every evening, winding between endless mine heaps and through thickly populated areas. It was an enormous task.

But the effort was immediately rewarded. Hertzog said they were recruiting about one thousand new members a month; Harris and his official union called a strike on two of the mines in protest at the alienation of their members. Then they contrived a closed shop agreement with the Chamber of Mines. The miners were given a month to rejoin the official union or lose their jobs.

Afrikaner protests mounted; Dutch churchmen condemned this attempt to stop Afrikaners from furthering their religious and cultural concerns through their own trade unions. But Prime Minister Hertzog and his Minister of Justice, Smuts, refused to intervene and the Afrikanerbond van Mynwerkers, having failed to obtain government registration, could no longer operate.

Albert Hertzog's response was simply to change the point of attack. Members of his Afrikanerbond were now encouraged to join Harris's union and support a *Hervormingsorganisasie*, a Reform Movement working from inside. They soon had enough members to try for a move against Harris but, once more, he outwitted them. At a General Council meeting in April 1939 he had himself elected as General Secretary for a further five years and forced through a constitution that gave him even more power. 'Now they will bloody well never get us out,' said Harris's lieutenant, Broderick. 'They can go to hell.'

But within six weeks Harris was dead. What Hertzog's biographer Naudé called 'the hand which guides the fate of men and nations' had struck. Moller Hugo with his pistol had removed this belligerent barrier to Afrikaner advancement once and for all. A much disputed lection for a new Secretary followed, with allegations of ballot rigging coming from the reformers, but before it was resolved World War Two broke out and the government suspended all union activity.

Meanwhile the same process of Afrikanerisation was being applied to other unions, and the garment workers, led by Solly Sachs, were a prime target. Many of the members had been poor whites, Afrikaners from the rural areas, and most of them were women. Sachs, like Harris was a Jew. He also had a strong Communist background. But the greater threat he presented to the purified view of Afrikaner identity was that he presided over a non-racial union.

Unlike Harris, Sachs had proved himself a brilliant union organiser. He had won the loyalty of his Afrikaner girls early in the thirties when he led a series of successful strikes to improve pay and conditions. A dozen of them, including the remarkable Johanna Cornelius, had gone to prison for the garment workers' cause. Shortly after the snub from the Centenary Trek organisers, Sachs challenged a Nationalist rival for his position to a debate before a full meeting of the union in Johannesburg City Hall. Sachs agreed beforehand that if the vote went against him he would resign. But in the event, his Afrikaner members overwhelmingly supported him and the Nationalist candidate was routed.

Now his opponents resorted to strong-arm tactics: gangs broke up his meetings and Sachs always maintained that they were thugs put up to it by Hertzog's *Nasionale Raad van Trustees*. Sachs himself was several times assaulted. Later he was vilified in a new journal called *Die Klerewerkersnuus* (*The Garment Workers' News*) whose owners were a publishing company set up by Hertzog's mineworkers. Sachs, never afraid to take his detractors to court, won substantial damages, and when the magazine failed to pay, the company was liquidated.

By now Sachs was also under assault from another quarter, the Dutch Reformed Church. The Dominees, wrote Sachs:

organised regular visits to the clothing factories, ostensibly to hold prayer meetings, but actually to incite the white workers against the non-Europeans. On almost every occasion when such a prayer meeting was held in a clothing factory, relations between white and non-white workers deteriorated.[1]

It says much for the organisation that Sachs had built up, that his non-racial union was able to withstand all attacks until four years after the Nationalists moved into government. Even then it took a special law, the Suppression of Communism Act, framed, many believe, with

Rebel's Daughters; E. S. Sachs, MacGibbon & Kee, London 1957.

the silencing of union leaders like Sachs as one of the main objectives
to force him to step down from the elected post he had held for
twenty-four years.

While the administration of the unions was slowly being Afrikanerised
the Broederbond was sponsoring yet another movement to fight for
the Afrikaner cause. It was to extend into every corner of the land. Its
members would come from the farms and factories, offices and uni
versities. It was called The *Ossewabrandwag*, literally the Ox-Wagon
Fire Guard, and owed its birth to the fervour of the 1938 ox-wagon
Trek, and to the patriotic spirit and energy that had swelled in so many
breasts in those four months on the road to Pretoria. The OB, as
everyone called it, would be to the masses what the Broederbond was
to the élite. Naturally the leaders of one would often be the members of
the other, although it was not long before the Ossewabrandwag took
on a life of its own and gave a fright, not just to the Broederbond, but
to Malan's National Party as well.

The Ossewabrandwag was launched in the Free State on 6 Febru
ary 1939, less than two months after the laying of the foundation stone
on Monumentkoppie. On its Grand Council were a bevy of Broeders
and a sprinkling of Dominees, but the leader was a farmer and
part-time soldier, Colonel J. C. C. Laas. His stated aims had a familiar
ring: to perpetuate the 'spirit of the Ox-Wagon Trek', to protect and to
further the religious, cultural and material concerns of the Afrikaner
and to bring together all Afrikaners, women as well as men, who
endorsed these principles and were willing to strive for them.

From the start the OB took on a distinctly military flavour. Laas
called himself the Kommandant-Generaal, and organised his sections
throughout the country on a commando basis. The men wore rough
corduroys, jerkins and scarves and kept the beards they had grown for
the Ossewatrek. The women came in their long Voortrekker dresses
and home-made kappies.

Camps, drilling and jukskei brought volunteers in their hundreds
Lectures on South African history fed the nostalgia for the past; the
re-establishment of an Afrikaner Republic was everyone's aim. Regu
lar rifle practice suggested one way of achieving it that fitted in exactly
with the proclivities of many young Nationalists. Hertzog's govern
ment was appalled at these 'cultural' activities, dismissed Laas from
the Defence Force and forbade any serving officer from joining the
new organisation.

120

'They will bloody well never get us out'

hanna Cornelius, President of the Garment Workers' Union, and Solly
chs, General Secretary

But still the OB flourished. Its spiritual headquarters were at
ajuba Hill in Natal, where the Boers' defeat of a large British force
d led to the restoration of the Transvaal Republic in 1881. In
rchlight rallies Afrikaners thrilled to the stories of how
ommandant-Generaal Piet Joubert and his burghers had stormed
e heights to knock the British off their perch.

Events in Europe played an increasing part, with many Afrikaners
awing inspiration from the way National Socialism had united
ermany and brought Hitler to power. The parades, the Hitler

121

Youth, the stress on ethnic purity, all found their echoes in Sout
Africa. No Jew could become a member of the Ossewabrandwag. Th
ubiquitous Piet Meyer was appointed chief information officer. H
studies in Germany meant he knew their methods well. As assista
secretary of the Broederbond, and at the same time a paid official
both the FAK and the Reddingsdaadbond he was a key figure c
ordinating the different strands of Afrikaner activity.

Kowie Marais, not yet a member of the OB but soon to become on
recalls the admiration he and his friends held for Hitler. 'We thoug
he might rejuvenate western civilisation, might put some pep into i
against the communist-socialist trends that were creeping in from th
east. We thought it was the dawn of a new era.'

On 1 September 1939 Hitler's tanks rolled into Poland and a ne
era was indeed at hand. Britain declared war on Sunday, 3 Septemb
but at a weekend cabinet meeting Hertzog's government was split ov
the course South Africa should take. Six ministers, including Hertzc
himself, opted for neutrality, but Smuts and six others insisted that
members of the Commonwealth they could not stand aside. Hertzc
referred the decision to the Assembly, knowing that Malan and h
Nationalists would certainly vote with him for they wanted no part
Britain's war.

The debate was to take place in Cape Town on Monday, 4 Sep
tember. Its outcome was to throw Afrikaners into disarray, to drive
further wedge between the Nationalists and the English and to prop
the fledgeling Ossewabrandwag into the front line of South Afric
politics.

10

'*If I retreat, shoot me*'

Part of the oath of the Afrikaner Stormjaers founded in
opposition to the Allied war effort

When Kowie Marais went to work in Johannesburg on 4 September
1939, he had a pistol in his pocket. It was the day of the crucial vote in
the Cape Town Assembly that would decide whether or not South
Africa would join the war. General Hertzog, the Prime Minister,
would propose neutrality and it was clear that the Nationalists would
back him, but how many of the United Party, born of fusion with
Smuts only five year before, would follow?

Smuts said the only honourable course was to fight for King and
Commonwealth, and that was a persuasive argument not only to
English speakers. But at the South African Broadcasting Corporation,
where Kowie Marais was now Afrikaans programme organiser, there
was talk that even if Hertzog were defeated he might refuse to resign,
might join hands with Malan and proclaim an Afrikaner republic.

If there was any resistance, Kowie Marais for one was ready.

That afternoon, after office hours, all of us, the Afrikaner staff, went back to
the building, first of all to await the news from Cape Town and secondly, if
the word came that the revolution had broken out and the Republic was being
declared, to take over the broadcasting service. It had been arranged that
most of us were carrying arms and we were ready to do the necessary, to take
over and start broadcasting on behalf of the revolution.

But the call never came. In fact telephone communication between
Johannesburg and Cape Town broke down and Marais and his
would-be revolutionaries knew neither the result of the vote nor
whether they had been summoned to serve the cause. In the event,
Hertzog's neutrality motion was defeated by eighty votes to sixty-
seven. He immediately resigned as Prime Minister, recommending
that a general election be held to test the feeling of the electorate. But
the Governor-General declined to follow Hertzog's advice and called
in General Smuts to form a government. South Africa was formally at
war.

The reaction of many Afrikaners was summed up in an editorial i
Besembos the student journal of the university of Potchefstroom:

Parliament made an unjust decision. Indeed, it was decided that South Afric
must wage war against a people which is fighting for its right to life, against
people with which the Afrikaner nation has had no other relationship than or
of friendship. In fact the matter is less simple than that, the decision eve
more unjust, if we regard it in the light of our history. We are not merel
obliged by a bare majority to wage war against a friendly nation, but we hav
to support England in this matter. We have to support our only foreig
enemy!

On the party political front, the declaration of war led to a majo
realignment; as General Hertzog stepped down from the Premiership
Dr Malan offered to step down as leader of the Opposition in hi
favour. The two men shook hands and walked arm in arm to a grea
Nationalist anti-war rally at Monumentkoppie in Pretoria. It wa
8 September 1939.

J. C. van Rooy, a former Chairman of the Broederbond, welcome
them: 'Such unity as we are today experiencing', he said in his speecl
'is unique in the history of our people. This happening stands ou
above all past happenings. We thank you for this but above all w
thank God.' One report said seventy thousand people 'raised thei
hands and promised never again to break away from one another'.

Malan called down the blessings of the sacred past upon the preser
union. 'In spirit I see the figures of Piet Retief, Andries Pretoriu:
Sarel Cilliers, Hendrik Potgeiter and the host of Voortrekkers behin
them, and it is as though I hear them saying: "Even when you wer
divided we loved you, but now that you are one, our love for you i
doubled."'

Hertzog was less effusive. From the very start he was uneasy withi
the narrow confines of the Afrikanerdom proposed by Malan and th
Purified Nationalists. Although he was against England's war, he sti
sought a wide union of English and Afrikaans speakers within Sout
Africa. The differences between the two leaders were too deep fc
their handshake to last, and the Broederbond had not forgotten Her
zog's attack four years before.

The break was not long in coming. In the call for the Afrikan
Republic that was now openly the Nationalists' aim, Hertzog becam
increasingly aware that his own concept of a wider Afrikanerdom ha
little support. In November 1940, believing that the delegates to tl
National Party Congress in the Orange Free State were not eve
prepared to give equal rights to English speakers in their new republi

nd unable to make them change their views, or for that matter, ersuade them to elect him their leader, Hertzog walked out of the ongress and out of public life. It was a tragic end for the founder of the National Party, but the new Nationalists and the Broederbond had wrested his creation from him. He died, a defeated man, two years ater in November 1942.

Meanwhile thousands of non-Nationalist Afrikaners had gone off to ight in the war. There was no conscription but when Smuts called for olunteers roughly one in three Afrikaners of military age joined up longside English speakers. Several thousand coloured and black South Africans served as well although the black soldiers were used mainly in non-combatant roles. Volunteers were further called on to ake the Africa Oath to agree to serve outside South Africa's borders. Those who did so wore distinguishing red flashes on their uniform shoulder tabs and became known to the Nationalists as *Rooi Luisies*, terally 'Red Lice'. Brawls between civilians and red-tabbed servicemen became a regular feature of South Africa's Saturday nights.

But for every Afrikaner who joined up, as many chose the Ossewabrandwag which was rapidly becoming the focus of Nationalist anti-war activity. By the end of 1940 Smuts had one hundred and thirty-seven thousand men under arms; the Ossewabrandwag claimed twice that number, and at one stage, women included, had close on four hundred thousand members. Smuts was concerned enough to ban the private ownership of firearms for the duration of the war and to the overnment's relief thousands of rifles were handed in at appointed ollection points.

Servicemen were regularly beaten up; some were even asked not to ttend their Dutch Reformed Churches in uniform for fear of inflaming the congregation. Some Dominees refused either to marry an Afrikaner who was serving in the armed forces or to baptise his hildren.

For their part, bands of soldiers singled out bearded civilians for iolent treatment. On one celebrated weekend in Johannesburg in anuary 1941, soldiers and members of the Ossewabrandwag fought a wo-day running battle using fists, bottles, clubs and anything that ame to hand. One civilian, without his trousers, was chased up a lamp ost and made to sing 'God Save the King'.

Soldiers damaged the buildings of two anti-war newspapers, *Die Transvaler* and *Die Vaderland*, and after the police had intervened with atons and tear gas, over one hundred and fifty combatants needed ospital treatment. Often, in these engagements, the very presence of

125

the police was inflammatory; everyone knew who among them was for
Smuts and who was not, for the police too were called on to take the
Africa Oath, and those who did wore the revealing red tabs.

At a Commission of Inquiry after the weekend riot, a Military
Police officer testified that when the fighting between soldiers and
civilians was at its height the police had openly joined in, kicking and
batoning soldiers lying on the ground. Other police were alleged to
have secretly supplied the OB with tear gas bombs to use against the
soldiers.

The divisions among Afrikaners reached right into families. Riaan
Kriel's father left their home in Cape Town and went with the 'Red
Lice' to North Africa. But if his mother and the children were out in
the streets when the noon-day gun from Signal Hill was fired, the
moment for many to pause in prayer for those who had gone to war
she refused to let any of them stop, so strongly was she against this
Englishman's war.

South West Africa, the former German colony, administered by
South Africa since 1920, threw up even more curious family differences. Gerry Muller, later Chief Executive of Nedbank, was captured
in North Africa and spent some time in a prisoner-of-war camp with a
'South-Wester' whose brother was in the Luftwaffe. He recalls that it
was not unusual for them to be guarded by Germans from South West
Africa, serving in Rommel's Afrika Korps, who regularly slipped
extra rations to Afrikaner prisoners.

As the fortunes of the British zeroed, so the Ossewabrandwag
zenithed. A German station, Radio Zeesen, helped to stir up feelings
pouring out classical music and classic propaganda to anyone eager to
hear ill of the Empire. The chief presenter was an Afrikaner Lord Haw
Haw, Erik Holm, a former Natal headmaster and, according to Military Intelligence, a member of the Broederbond. He specialised in
stories of British atrocities in the Anglo-Boer War and a recital of the
evils that Jewish capitalists had wrought on the Afrikaner working
man.[1]

In the Assembly in Cape Town, shortly before the Battle of Britain
a Nationalist member said he thought it was right that the people of
Britain should have their homes burned so they could realise what

---

[1] In September 1946, Erik Holm was sentenced to ten years' imprisonment for
treason. He was released in 1948 immediately the Nationalists came to power and was
eventually given a job in the Ministry of Education Library. Two Dutch Reformed
Ministers organised a rehabilitation fund to bring his wife and six children back from
Germany.

'If I retreat, shoot me'

Erik Holm, Afrikaner broadcaster from the German wartime
propaganda station, Radio Zeesen

Afrikaners had suffered in the War of Independence. A few months later another MP, B. J. Schoeman, who became Minister of Labour in 1948, said at a National Party Congress: 'The whole future of Afrikanerdom is dependent upon a German victory . . . If Germany wins the war we shall be able to negotiate with her, and in that way ensure the establishment of an independent republic in South Africa.'

The Ossewabrandwag had already begun to work actively towards that victory. Laas had been replaced as Kommandant-General by Hans van Rensburg, who resigned from a senior position as Administrator of the Free State to take over the post. At the swearing-in ceremony on the slopes of Majuba early in 1941, the Chairman of the Broederbond himself officiated.

In his address, van Rensburg let it be known that he would not necessarily be sticking to democratic methods:

With democracy in its academic sense I have no special quarrel. In any case one should not speak evil of the dead. But I wish to add that a democracy or any other -ocracy is not an end in itself but merely a means to the end. The end is the nation. If I can serve my nation better by democratic action, I will do so, but if I have to choose between Afrikanerdom and democracy, then there is no choice. Then I am not the least concerned about the system.

Hans van Rensburg, Kommandant-Generaal of the Ossewabrandwag; taken from 8mm film shot by a member at a wartime meeting on Majuba Hill

Iis gesture at the end of such speeches looked uncommonly like the
Iazi 'Heil Hitler' salute.

A man of action who confessed himself irritated by the plodding
ace of politics, van Rensburg said he 'immediately felt at home' with
n élite group among the Ossewabrandwag who called themselves
'tormjaers (Stormtroopers). They had devised for themselves a some-
vhat melodramatic oath not unlike that of the IRA. It was taken with
ne hand on the Bible, with a pistol pointing at the chest and another at
he back:

> If I advance, follow me.
> If I retreat, shoot me.
> If I die, avenge me.
> So help me God.

Thus braced, the Stormjaers planned to sabotage the war effort and
eed Germany with intelligence information. They cut telephone
vires, blew up pylons, power lines and railway tracks. They also
imed their blast at post offices, shops and banks. Two Stormjaers,
ulian Visser and Hendrik van Blerk, were sentenced to death in July
942 for causing an explosion at Benoni Post Office which killed an
nnocent bystander, but after a campaign by the National Party their
entences were commuted to life imprisonment.

The police were increasingly implicated in this anti-war activity and
arly in 1942 no less than three hundred and fourteen members of the
orce, and fifty-nine railway policemen, were relieved of their duties
nd placed under arrest. A plan to sink a ship in the entrance to
)urban harbour was pre-empted and fifty-eight men, defended by
\lbert Hertzog, appeared before the courts. Several Stormjaers,
ncluding a policeman, were shot trying to evade arrest. At least two
vould-be saboteurs suffered from what the British army in Ulster call
own goals' – blowing themselves up with their own explosives. After
uch deaths, Ossewabrandwag funerals with parades and armbands,
vith uniform hats on the coffin, and volleys over the grave, had an
Jlster flavour that would have stirred many an Irish Republican heart.

Radio Zeesen lauded van Rensburg as the real leader of the
\frikaner people, and in a bizarre episode Germany sent reinforce-
nents in the burly shape of a former Springbok heavyweight boxer
namd Robey Leibbrandt. He had once fought for South Africa in
Germany, had stayed on and joined the German army.

Leibbrandt was landed from a yacht on the coast of the North
Western Cape with ten thousand dollars, a radio transmitter and

J. F. (Kowie) Marais, Progressive Federal Party MP, former Judge
and member of the Broederbond and the Ossewabrandwag

instructions to make contact with van Rensburg. But he never got on with the OB, and initiated his own band of near fanatics which he called National Socialist Rebels. Their war was shortlived. Two blew themselves up at Denneboom near Pretoria, and a matter of days later on Christmas Eve 1941, Leibbrandt was arrested. He was sentenced to death for treason but again the sentence was commuted to life imprisonment by Prime Minister Smuts who had fought in the Boer War with Leibbrandt's father. Smuts was reputed to have said that he would not be responsible for the death of the son of such a brave man.

By September 1940 Kowie Marais had left the SABC and was an active member of the Stormjaers. He was building radio transmitters in one of five secret workshops set up around Johannesburg and Pretoria. Using mainly stolen parts, the transmitters were to provide a communications network – 'if there were to be a rebellion against the government'.

'It was doubtful if the National Party would be able to come into power', Marais recalled. 'It was unthinkable that they would do so as early as 1948, so we believed that maybe a violent overthrow of the government or at least a marshalling of the Afrikaner forces would be necessary.' They were certain that Hitler was going to win the war and that a German invasion of England would give them their chance.

Marais had no problems of conscience over the acts of sabotage. The object, he said, was not to cause bloodshed. 'We were told over and over again that we were not to waste lives and, as things happened, less than a handful died. Our objective was sabotage which would keep troops in South Africa and away from the war.'

Surprisingly perhaps, it was not until almost 1945 that his views about Hitler changed. 'It was the greatest disaster in my spiritual life to realise suddenly that the people I had thought to be the heroes of a new era in western civilisation should in fact turn out to be just a band of murderers and nothing else.'

Hennie Serfontein, author of one of the recent investigations into the Broederbond, remembers his near adulation for Hitler when he was a small boy growing up during the war in a strongly Nationalist family. The day they heard the news that Hitler was dead he cried.

Kowie Marais's active role on behalf of the cause did not last long. One of the technicians building radio transmitters wanted to drill some holes, so he took a transmitter to the radio workshop where he normally worked. Someone grew suspicious and informed the police.

The garage from where the group was operating at Sydenham wa raided and they were all arrested. Under Smuts's emergency wartim provisions Marais was interned at a former old people's home that ha been turned into a detention centre.

On 11 October 1941, not a day he is likely to forget, Marais was fre again. A group of internees had spent six months digging a tunne under the wire; they had escaped and were on the run. They split u and friends in the Ossewabrandwag and the Stormjaers looked afte them. Before long, Marais, disguised with a moustache and glasse and calling himself Roussouw, found himself a job as a shop assistan at Heilbron in the Free State. Later still he worked in an attorney' office in Vredefort and it was there in July 1942, after almost nin months of freedom, that he was re-arrested. He had received a tip of from Johannesburg that the police were on his track but had no thought the danger was very great. This time he was interned, agair without the formality of a trial, at Koffiefontein, an old diamon mining town in the Free State.

In Koffiefontein Marais gave lectures on law to his fellow internee at what was called the *Boere Universiteit* that they themselves ha organised. Before long another lawyer arrived, and joined the volun teer teachers. It was the beginning of Kowie Marais's long associatior with John Vorster. Internee number 2229/42, Vorster was, a twenty-seven, the youngest *Hoof-Generaal*, Chief General in the Ossewabrandwag, in charge of the Port Elizabeth district where he was working. He had been detained without trial for nearly three months and had led a three-day hunger strike in protest before bein transferred to Koffiefontein. It was an experience which Vorstei exploited to brilliant advantage years later when he became Minister o Justice; he simply turned opposition questions in Parliament abou prison conditions for blacks and the government's sweeping powers o arrest and detention into reminiscences about his own days in solitary confinement:

Those people are living in a palace compared to the place where we had to live. The privileges they have cannot even be compared to the privileges we had . . . I had six weeks of solitary confinement when I was not let out of my cell for one single second. The Honourable Member asks about doctors. During those three months I never saw a doctor or one of the people with whom I had been detained.

The Honourable Member talks about legal representation for these people. He asks further why the Minister does not have the names of the detainees published to let people know. When I was arrested my wife wanted to inform my mother and she went to the post office to send her a telegram. On the instructions of the Honourable Member's Government [i.e. United Party], the post office refused to accept the telegram . . .[1]

Vorster's bitterness over the reasons for his internment has not been dissipated by time. He says he was informed that, 'the authorities are in possession of information that you harboured interned fugitives' and that he was anti-British. He is very precise about this detail: 'I was not told that I was anti-South African or pro-German: the official reason was that I was anti-British.' He has always denied being involved in sabotage, and indeed there was little violence in the Eastern Cape. But Vorster's aim, just like that of van Rensburg and of Kowie Marais, was an Afrikaner Republic. 'Our attitude was whichever way it came it was acceptable to us,' said Vorster. 'Whether it came out of the chaos of war or no, we would have welcomed it.'

Vorster's commitment to the Ossewabrandwag antagonised not just the government; it put him into conflict with the National Party as well. In 1941 Malan, concerned at the way he believed van Rensburg's OB was trying to usurp the position of the Party, demanded that all nationalists choose between the two organisations. He was particularly incensed at van Rensburg's habit of declaring at public rallies that his was the only organisation which could save the Volk and the only one which could achieve a Republic. Vorster told the National Party in Port Elizabeth that since both organisations were for Afrikaners he was loyal to both and would resign from neither. The party made the choice for him and threw him out.

Vorster's older brother Koot pursued an even more militant line. In 1938 he had taken up a ministry in the Dutch Reformed Church in Cape Town where he too became a General in the Ossewabrandwag. In a speech to the Afrikaner Students' Organisation in September 1940, he suggested that Germany could show South Africa the way. 'Hitler gave the Germans a calling. He gave them a fanaticism which causes them to stand back for no one. We must follow his example because only by such holy fanaticism can the Afrikaner nation achieve its calling.' Almost forty years later he explained what he meant:

Unless we have a great and fervent patriotism, whether you call it fanaticism or not, that's beside the point; but unless you believe in your calling as a nation here, unless you believe in being a separate race and a separate people here, you'll never achieve anything. No nation has ever achieved anything without believing in itself, without fanatically adhering to its ideals and to its calling in that country.

[1] House of Assembly debate, 16 May 1960.

133

Dominee Vorster maintains that he was not pro-German in the war and that had the Germans ever been in a position to dominate South Africa as the English had tried to he would have opposed them too. Nonetheless, in February 1941 he was sentenced to three years' hard labour for contravening the Official Secrets Act and obtaining information about naval gun positions at the Simonstown Base on the Cape Peninsula. Vorster maintains that it was a trumped-up charge, but with a disarming candour admits that he knew exactly what he was doing in the Ossewabrandwag and expected the Government to move against him sooner or later. He spent the first eight months of his sentence in hospital in Cape Town suffering from a serious liver complaint and the remainder in Pretoria gaol.

Henning Klopper enjoyed a rather less dramatic war. With his keen memory for such slights he recalls the way women would stop young men in the streets and call them cowards for not joining up: 'Here's a white feather for you. You're no good. You're despicable, loafing here while our menfolk are fighting your war overseas.'

He was now a senior administrator on the railways in South West Africa and, like virtually every other Nationalist, joined the Ossewabrandwag. But in the elections of 1943 he presented himself as the National Party candidate for Vredefort his father's former seat in the Orange Free State, and became a Member of Parliament at his first attempt. With his strong Broederbond connections he was much more at home following the Malan democratic line than with the irregulars of the Ossewabrandwag.

In that wartime election the Nationalists won forty-three seats, sixteen more than in 1938 but the Smuts government was still riding the crest of the patriotic wave, its leader a world figure now adding his status and experience to Churchill's wartime Cabinet.

By now Colonel Ernie Malherbe was a senior member of Smuts's staff. Just before the war he had been appointed South Africa's Director of Census and Statistics, and had slipped easily from there to the Army Information and Education Services of which he became Director. They began by training young men to lecture recruits about conditions in South Africa, about Hitler, and why they were going to war.

'It was a new thing in the army', Malherbe recalled. 'At first we called them Education Officers, but several of the Commanders and Generals wanted to know what the hell they had to do with education, so we changed it to Information Officers.' Eventually Malherbe commanded over three hundred officers, some with the training

Dr Ernie Malherbe

battalions, but many more with the fighting units in North Africa.

Their concern, above all, was for the troops' morale and, as Malherbe put it,

how to protect them from the subversive propaganda that was often sent up from South Africa. My men would find a soldier not eating and thoroughly miserable and they would press him to find out what was the matter and finally he would confess.

Later we found out that the Broederbond was behind it, but it was mostly Nationalists and the Ossewabrandwag that did it. They'd send an anonymous letter to a man saying that his wife was unfaithful; they would even go so far as to write to a man and tell him that his child had died. There was enough authenticity attached to it that the man believed it and became utterly miserable. They deliberately poisoned the men's minds.

So I got my men to intercept the letters, and that is how we started censorship. We interrupted these letters and got a pretty good insight into this undermining of morale that was going on from the Union.

And then Smuts had an idea, and he said: 'Why not merge this with the Intelligence section?' So my men became Intelligence Officers as well as Army Information Officers. It was a wonderful adaptation which he made. And a little earlier Smuts had said to me, 'Look, seeing you have your finger in parts of this thing you had better take the whole intelligence over.'

135

So Malherbe became Smuts' Director of Military Intelligence for the rest of the war.

Another immediate concern was how to combat the Ossewabrandwag. Because of the risk of sabotage it was important to keep troop movements secret, particularly after the incident in December 1941 when two Stormjaers 'General' D. K. Theron and 'Doors' Erasmus tried to blow up a train carrying troops near Pretoria.

They went under a bridge [said Malherbe] and they had their dynamite there to blow up the bridge just before the train came. But – and I wouldn't say unfortunately – they blew themselves up. Had they succeeded they would not have blown up the troop train but the train of the families who were going to Durban to say goodbye.

Malherbe recalls that the Stormjaers had a particularly dramatic method of testing whether a recruit had the determination to commit an act of sabotage. They would pretend to find a traitor and present him to the recruit.

'He betrayed us', they'd say. 'Here's a revolver. You must shoot him! And this recruit would be given a revolver with blank cartridges. Naturally he would be frightened. He'd say, 'I can't do it, I am not a murderer.' So they would taunt him and tell him he was a coward. Eventually they taunted one fellow so much that he snatched a loaded revolver from one of the others and said, 'All right, I'll do it.' And they just caught him in time before he shot this chap who was only acting as a dummy.

There was also the problem of violence against men in uniform. Hitch-hiking soldiers going home on weekend passes were favourite targets to be stripped and beaten up.

This happened quite frequently, so much so that in Pretoria the troops threatened to burn Pretoria University because so many university students were involved. Also van Rensburg had a farm just outside Pretoria which he kept like a huge defended fort. Many of the soldiers wanted to attack that and take him prisoner but General Smuts was very much against it. He did not want bloodshed on any account. That is why he did not take violent action against saboteurs and why we rather interned them.

Malherbe still believes that Smuts was right not to have taken more stringent action against the Ossewabrandwag. Smuts was very afraid of a civil war, he said. Above all Smuts remembered the bitterness caused by the execution of Jopie Fourie that he himself had ordered after the 1914 rebellion, and the heavy loss of life when he had brought in troops to put down the 1922 miners' strike. Also, as the prospect of a victory for Hitler receded, so support for the Ossewa-brandwag waned. Many Republican Afrikaners were dismayed by the increasingly strident tones of van Rensburg and the violence of the Stormjaers. The OB with its political presumptuousness had affronted both the National Party and the Broederbond by publishing its own constitution for a future Afrikaner Republic that appeared to have no room for either the English or the Jews and would allow citizenship only for a narrowly determined elect of 'pure white descent'. The cry of *Die Kies is uitgedien* – 'the vote is useless' – heard at many rallies now began to frighten as many Nationalists as it attracted.

For Malherbe's Military Intelligence the real enemy was not so much the Ossewabrandwag as the organisation that lay behind it. In March 1944 Malherbe submitted a twenty-five page intelligence report to Smuts on the Broederbond and its activities. His conclusions did not mince matters:

1. The Afrikaner Broederbond, with its fanatical racial aims and with its offspring, the Ossewabrandwag as action front, has become a formidable subversive force.
2. The parent is much more dangerous than the child. The Ossewabrandwag, which sprang up in the night like a toadstool, could do so only because the soil had been prepared for it by the Broederbond. Its leaders had been in close contact with the Nazis and had copied their methods wholesale.

   The Ossewabrandwag has waxed with the rise of Nazi power; it will wane with it. The Broederbond will outlive both, because its policy is much more patient and insidious . . . the Broederbond is a malignant cancer in our body politic and only the knife can remove it.

The Broederbond was active during the war years on many fronts. They provided financial assistance for the families of men who had been interned; they worked steadily at Albert Hertzog's plan to Afrikanerise the trade union movement. The minutes of a wartime UR (Executive Committee) meeting authorised Hertzog 'to establish secret reform organisations inside the trade unions. He is instructed to work out a scheme to do this and to submit it to the UR for its approval and support'.

By now the Broederbond had perfected the technique for exercising influence on government decisions, which General Hertzog had criticised but which still impressed Malherbe both with its simplicity and its effectiveness.

A secret instruction would go out from Broederbond headquarters to each cell to send a telegram to a certain minister protesting about a certain thing or recommending a certain thing. The minister would suddenly find two or three thousand telegrams on his desk and he would take that as being *vox populi*, the voice of the people. And he could be very much influenced by that, even though it all emanated from the centre and not from the people at all.

At one of the Broederbond's full council meetings in October 1940, Nico Diederichs, who was by now chairman, had spelled out the role he believed the Broederbond should play.

It should live in the closest contact with everybody, see to it that they give the necessary leadership. And only when those leaders fail in their duty, leading to a situation dangerous for the Volk, must the Bond intervene. In a certain sense the Afrikaner Broederbond must be the axle round which turn the different aspects of the Volk; or rather the authority that stands above them, which co-ordinates them with a view to a unity of direction and action.

In one area where the broeders tried to exercise this self-appointed authority they achieved little success; that was in the attempt to heal the breach between the National Party and the Ossewabrandwag. They invited van Rensburg to attend meetings of the Executive Council and extended a similar invitation to Malan. They set up a Unity Committee under a senior member and former chairman of the Broederbond, Wikus du Plessis. He had been the first Chairman of the National Party in the Transvaal and was the current chairman of the board of Volkskas. His committee held regular meetings but the differences between the two sides were beyond the Broederbond's healing balm. Malan, with supporters like his new MP, Henning Klopper, was committed to the parliamentary route to the Republic; van Rensburg and his still large popular movement backed by the Vorsters and Kowie Marais, though all three were now behind bars, were committedly careless of the democratic process.

The split troubled the Broederbond itself. Piet Meyer, propaganda chief of the Ossewabrandwag, Secretary of the FAK and Deputy Secretary of the Broederbond, was called upon to make a choice between his conflicting loyalties and eventually opted for the Ossewabrandwag, presumably still convinced that the National Socialism he had come to admire in Germany still had a future in South Africa. Worse still, Wikus du Plessis, the very man who was trying to bring the warring elements together, threw in his lot with van Rensburg and became the movement's policy chief.

But while the tactics of the three main Afrikaner Nationalist groups may have varied, and while the Broederbond 'axle' was temporarily somewhat off centre, the Nationalist wagon was still rolling steadily towards its republican objective. Colonel Ernie Malherbe, Director of Military Intelligence, had been gathering yet more striking evidence of the lengths to which the Broederbond would go to see that *Die Pad van Suid Afrika*, the symbolic path that lay ahead, was neither blocked nor obscured.

11

'The Broederbond must be destroyed'

Director of Military Intelligence, Colonel E. G. Malherbe, in a
report to General Smuts, 29 March 1944

Early on the summer morning of 13 December 1943 a small group
slipped unnoticed into the Afrikaans Teachers Training College in
Bloemfontein in the Orange Free State. They were officers from
Colonel Ernie Malherbe's Military Intelligence. They hid a micro-
phone close to the stage in the main hall, ran a cable down into the
basement, connected up a set of ear-phones and waited.

Military Intelligence had discovered that the Broederbond were to
hold a secret Council meeting in the hall to mark their twenty-fifth
anniversary. It coincided with a large congress of Afrikaner
educationalists at the Bloemfontein City Hall, thus providing the
perfect cover for three hundred leading Broeders from all over South
Africa to gather without arousing suspicion.

Outside the hall another of Malherbe's men drove up in his car and
staged a breakdown just as the delegates were starting to arrive. He
noted the names of many that he recognised and took the numbers of
all the cars parked around the college. When they checked the owners,
said Malherbe, they found that a large proportion of the Broederbond
delegates were Dutch Reformed Church Ministers or school teachers.
Among the leading lights were Albert Hertzog, Nico Diederichs,
Hendrik Verwoerd, the Editor of *Die Transvaler* and later Prime
Minister and, naturally, Henning Klopper.

Under the stage an officer took down all the main speeches in
shorthand; Malherbe's only regret was that they could not pick up the
interventions from the floor. Nonetheless they ended the day with a
unique record of Broederbond views and plans. Much of it Malherbe
himself retailed over thirty years later in a comprehensive section on
the Broederbond in the second volume of his *Education in South
Africa*.

At this secret anniversary meeting I. M. Lombard, the Chief Secretary, began with a long address in which he outlined the history and

140

the achievements of the Broederbond during its twenty-five years. He boasted that the Broederbond had succeeded in getting its members into controlling positions in almost every sphere of South African life. He regretted that it had not quite succeeded to the extent it wished in the political field. The solemn undertaking for Afrikaner unity given in 1939 at the Voortrekker Monument had turned to ashes; sharp divisions had arisen between the Party and the Ossewabrandwag. He deplored the unbrotherly acts that had been perpetrated in this struggle. Nevertheless the Broederbond had weathered even this storm, the worst and most dangerous in its history. Then it was the turn of Dr Verwoerd who launched into a lengthy attack on the Jews; he pointed out the menace they presented to Afrikanerdom because of the important positions they obtained in the professions. He drew attention to the un-Afrikaans conduct of some Brothers who had sold property to non-Europeans; he outlined the tasks which still lay ahead for the Broederbond: 'The Afrikaner Broederbond must gain control of everything it can lay its hands on in every walk of life in South Africa.'

Henning Klopper spoke in a similar tone. He denounced all the enemies of Afrikanerdom with special reference to the English and the Jews. He called for the greatest possible activity by the Broederbond in the fields of industry and commerce and extolled the achievements of Volkskas and other Afrikaner business houses. He recounted 'with pride', said Malherbe, what the FAK had achieved in the cultural field and dwelt on particular successes in the Broederbond's fight for separate facilities for Afrikaners in universities and schools.

Education had become a major issue in that year of the Broederbond Silver Jubilee, particularly in the elections for the four Provincial Councils that in South Africa each administer their own school system. The United Party, enjoying the support of many Afrikaners as well as the English speakers, had embarked on a policy of trying to bring the children of both groups closer together.

Under what was called the 'dual medium' system, Smuts proposed that all children would receive their elementary education in their mother tongue, English or Afrikaans; gradually the other language would be introduced and would eventually become, in secondary school, not just a second language but a medium of instruction as well. In other words, Afrikaans-speaking children would eventually find themselves taking, for example, mathematics or chemistry lessons part of the time in English. English children would do the same in Afrikaans. The groups would be in separate classes in the same school but in the playground and on the sports field everyone would mix.

That way each would naturally come to pick up the other's language and everyone, hoped Smuts, would develop a common loyalty to South Africa. Eventually separate single-medium schools would be abolished.

The government had been encouraged to introduce such a policy by what Malherbe and his Intelligence officers pointed out was clearly happening among the troops fighting in North Africa. Despite the differences and antagonisms between many English- and Afrikaans-speakers back home, in the desert, faced with a common enemy, Malherbe saw evidence among the soldiers of a real unity.

In the midsts of strange surroundings, strange customs and usages, strange languages, [wrote Malherbe,] they turned to the familiar South African things for comfort. They discovered that Afrikaans songs, speech and literature, for instance, interpreted better than anything else the sights, sounds and backgrounds which for them spelled home, South Africa. Soon it was found that English-speaking soldiers were singing, speaking and even reading Afrikaans with natural enthusiasm and confidence . . . In fact in many cases it was regarded as 'good form' to speak Afrikaans in the messes . . .[1]

Malherbe carried out a survey among seven thousand English and Afrikaans-speaking soldiers from over two hundred units. Ninety-three per cent of them agreed that there would be more national unity if English and Afrikaans children went to the same schools and eighty-one per cent further agreed that while children should be taught mainly through the medium of their home language, it was a 'good thing' for them to learn some subjects through the medium of the other language. In the Provincial elections back home in 1943 the results showed similar feelings among the electorate. The United Party's educational policies were accepted by large majorities in three of the four provinces, the Cape, Transvaal and Natal while even in the Free State, a Nationalist stronghold, the United Party gained four seats. In due course, Parliament also endorsed Smuts' educational plans.

To the Broederbond and their Nationalist allies such a policy was anathema. It ran totally against all they had fought for during twenty-five years. If Afrikaans-speaking children were to be brought up as true members of the Volk they must be educated separately away from damaging outside influences. The response of the Brothers was to go to the lengths of trying to organise a strike to thwart the government's plans. In October 1943, an instruction, signed by M. C. Botha,

---

[1] *Education in South Africa*, Volume 2, E. G. Malherbe, p. 42.

secretary of a special Broederbond educational committee, was prepared for all members.

The churches were to encourage parents to refuse to send their children to schools where the government policy had been introduced: 'where a minister is unsympathetic, a strong personality in the church council or congregation should take the lead'; each member of a school committee should undertake responsibility for ten or so parents and children and persuade them to be ready to strike at a given moment; 'sympathetic principals and teachers can co-operate covertly'; members of Parliament and provincial council members were to be co-opted; the FAK was to launch a press campaign 'to intimidate the government'; finally, 'the strike had to last long enough to bring the government to its senses.' But the strike never happened; Malherbe's Military Intelligence intercepted the Broederbond circulars and the plan was exposed before it could be put into practice.

Thirty-three years later, the Nationalist government faced a strike of its own over education; black students were protesting against the compulsory teaching of certain subjects in Afrikaans. It was the issue which sparked the Soweto riots in 1976 in which nearly six hundred black South Africans were killed. The minister responsible for black education at that time was the same M. C. Botha, the Broederbond strike organiser. Thus the wheel, with its Broederbond axle, had turned full circle.

In December 1943 two months after the strike incident Malherbe was involved in another episode that was equally revealing of the Broederbond's wartime thinking. Although many Afrikaners were now fighting for the Allied cause, few ministers of the Dutch Reformed Church went with them. So when two senior churchmen, Dominee William Nicol, the Moderator of the Transvaal, and Dominee A. J. van der Merwe, Moderator of the Cape, requested to visit the troops in North Africa, permission was given although Malherbe had some misgivings because of their Broederbond affiliations.

Of Nicol, Malherbe wrote: 'He went under the guise of ministering to the spiritual needs of the Afrikaans-speaking troops'. But when he started preaching the Broederbond doctrine of separate medium schools 'he ran into quite a storm of indignation from his audiences'. Nicol also complained about the presence of non-whites among the troops and said that at the appropriate time voices from the church would be heard against their recruitment.

In North Africa, Nicol and van der Merwe wrote two reports. One, full of warm statements about the friendly treatment they had received, was made public. The other was sent home secretly via Jerusalem. It was nonetheless intercepted by Military Intelligence. The report spoke of the fears of the two predikants that Afrikaner soldiers were being converted to other churches and anglicised. It urged that more ministers be sent to the front. But, as Colonel Malherbe wrote to the General in charge of Administration in North Africa,

> they stress particularly that no general call among the predikants of the three Dutch churches should be made, but that instead certain predikants should be approached directly and personally asked to volunteer . . . This can only be in order that these new recruits will be trusted Broeders.

Throughout this wartime period the Broederbond infiltration of the Civil Service continued. Malherbe, as an educationalist himself, became increasingly concerned at what was happening in the schools. He estimated that about nine hundred of the Broederbond's two thousand seven hundred members were teachers and that fifty per cent of all members were in a position to influence schools or children, either as teachers themselves or through serving on school boards or committees.

He discovered that the political views of teachers were being checked before they were given a job. Those who supported the government were not promoted. Children were coming home from school parroting the anti-Smuts sentiments they heard in the classroom. By January 1944 Malherbe reported to Smuts that unless something was done 'it is plain that the approved policy in education will not be carried out'. In March the same year Malherbe set out his fears in detail:

> The Broederbond has obtained a stranglehold on education which will enable it, in sober truth, to govern South Africa within a few decades . . . Some thousands of servants of the State, more especially teachers, are bound by inclination and by oath to carry out the subversive plans of the Broederbond . . . As this policy of Afrikaner dominance creeps into the various spheres of employment, and particularly into the higher professional and state services, those who are not that particular brand of '*ware Afrikaner*' [true Afrikaner], required by the Broederbond, will be more and more pushed into the background to posts of secondary importance . . . Today, with the bitter experience of the Broederbond's evil influence on the war effort, and its stranglehold on South African public life, the need for action is more urgent. If we are to live together in peace and amity in South Africa, the Broederbond must be destroyed.

In December, nine months later, Smuts finally acted. He banned members of the Broederbond from working in the public service, giving them the alternative of resigning from one or other. One thousand and ninety-four resigned from the Broederbond though a small group of prominent Broeders chose, with some ostentation, to give up their jobs in the Civil Service rather than leave their secret society. The story provided the Nationalist press with copy for weeks. Some said Smuts was foolish to forgo the services of such able men. In January 1945 Smuts denounced the Broederbond in Parliament, calling it 'a dangerous, cunning, political Fascist organisation of which no civil servant, if he was to retain his loyalty to the State and the Administration, could be allowed to be a member.'

Malherbe, expecting Smuts to list the names of prominent Broeders, had tipped off the Press. But the Prime Minister drew back.

He was afraid, [says Malherbe,] because such a big proportion of them were Dutch Reformed Church Dominees, that it would harm the church. He always seemed to have such a soft spot for the church. But I am still sorry today that he did not publish the names openly because it would have just emasculated the whole affair, there and then.

People would have known how certain things happened in their own communities which they couldn't otherwise explain. Because it wasn't as if everything just happened at the top. It happened in the schools, in the church councils, in the local shops, in the offices, even in the organisation of rugby. That's why I was keen to blow the whole thing open.

Stung by Smuts' actions, the Broederbond, for the first time in its history, came out in public with a statement of policy. A series of five articles appeared in both the English and Afrikaans press, signed by the Chairman, Professor J. C. van Rooy and the secretary I. M. Lombard. They denied the 'absurd, uninformed and also shamelessly false accusations', explained that the Broederbond was 'born out of the deep conviction that the Afrikaner nation was planted in this country by the hand of God', and regretted that General Smuts 'in his ignorance or driven by those of his followers imbued with a spirit of persecution, has found himself called upon to stone the Bond'. Their protestations of innocence notwithstanding, the Broederbond continued to throw their own stones at the government's educational policy, obstructing wherever they could the development of Smuts' dual medium schools. Elsewhere, at every turn, they continued to insert their Nationalist spokes into the wheels of the trades union movement.

Field-Marshal Jan Smuts

Nowhere was that activity more intense than in the Mineworkers Union. Backed by the White Workers' Protection Society, recently formed by the Broederbond, supported by funds from the Reddingsdaadbond, Albert Hertzog's Reform Movement was now ready to take on the union administrators once more. After the murder of Harris and the uncompleted elections to find his successor, Harris' deputy Broderick had assumed the secretary's role until normal union activities were resumed after the war.

By 1946 there had still been no new elections and the financial affairs of the union, according to Hertzog, were in chaos. Subscriptions were going astray and there had been a number of cases of wrongful prosecution for alleged non-payment. As a protest, one of the leaders of Hertzog's Reformers, a miner named Hattingh, refused to pay any further subscriptions. When the union cancelled his membership, Hattingh was sacked since the mines were still operating under a closed shop.

It was the signal the Reformers wanted, the crucial test of strength with what Louis Naudé called 'the corrupt clique in control of the Union'. On 14 March 1946, six hundred and fifty miners refused to go underground at three shafts on the West Rand. By next day three thousand men stopped work. In a week sixteen thousand were on strike and every mine on the Reef was affected. For nine days South Africa virtually dug no gold. The government had no other course but to intervene, setting up a commission of enquiry into the running of the union and ordering new elections.

There was no question this time of using force to break the strike. The lessons of 1922 had been learned, although it could not be said that the same rules applied to everyone. Five months after the white stoppage, sixty thousand black miners came out on strike in support of a minimum wage claim of 14s 6d a week, but were literally batoned back underground again by police. Six black workers at least were killed. Smuts' government said that the strike was not caused by real grievance but was the work of agitators.

Meanwhile the enquiry into the affairs of the white mineworkers dragged on. Broderick was eventually removed for what the commission called 'wrongful conduct' and the Reformers gradually assumed control of the Mineworker's General Council. By 1947 they were strong enough to take the union out of the Trades and Labour Council, the South African equivalent of the Trades Union Congress. They had argued that it was 'dominated by communistic influences and . . . comprised a record number of Coloured and

147

native delegates'. By 1949 the Reformers were in complete control of the Mineworkers Union, with their own nominee, Daan Ellis, as General Secretary. It was the reward for thirteen years of dedication to the cause by Albert Hertzog. In recognition the union made him an 'honorary mineworker'.

But the year before that local success, miners and Nationalists everywhere had been celebrating a far greater triumph. 1948 was election year, and the chance for the party and its Broederbond backers to test themselves once more against Smuts' United Party. The wartime divisions among the Volk were healing. With the defeat of Nazi Germany the Ossewabrandwag was on the decline. Most of its members were back in the Nationalist fold, although the more extreme, led by van Rensburg, had joined the splinter Afrikaner Party under N. C. Havenga. But all of them effectively fought on the same ticket once a pre-election coalition had been agreed and Malan had assigned to Havenga some safe Nationalist seats.

In the Transvaal, Hertzog's miners brought organisation and impetus to the National Party campaigns in several marginal United Party seats. The Nationalists had already made important gains in local government. Helped again by Hertzog's staff work they now controlled Pretoria City Council; for the first time too they held seats on the Bloemfontein Council in the Free State. In the Cape the Nationalists had built up solid local organisation thanks partly to the efforts of full-time party officials such as a thirty-two-year-old Assistant Secretary, named P. W. Botha. As recognition of his ability as an organiser he was promoted to national publicity secretary for the 1948 campaign.

Botha himself was standing as a candidate at George. Henning Klopper was up for election again in the Free State and Hertzog for the first time in the Transvaal. John Vorster was nominated by the Afrikaner Party to stand in Brakpan, a gold mining town on the East Rand, but Malan refused to accept him as a candidate because of his militant Ossewabrandwag background. Then the National Party in Brakpan nominated Vorster as their candidate too. There was a fierce internal party row, but the Brakpan Nationalists refused to back down and Vorster's name eventually went forward. But the delay cost him two crucial weeks of campaigning.

The issues in the election were largely dictated by the National Party. Separate schools was one and the so-called communist threat was another, centred on Solly Sachs' multi-racial activities in the Garment Workers' Union. The fact that the United Party declined to take a stand on mixed unions gave Nationalists the chance to accuse them of going soft on communism. What is more, it was argued, Smuts had recently fought a war as an ally of the communist, Stalin, another example of his un-Afrikaner tendencies.

For the moment, the Nationalists played down the Republican issue, aware that many floating voters still cherished the ties with King and Commonwealth. When King George VI, the Queen and the two Princesses had visited South Africa in 1947 huge crowds had greeted them everywhere, although *Die Transvaler*, edited by Verwoerd, had virtually ignored the event.

Above all, on their election platforms the Nationalists attacked the United Party for their ambivalence on the quintessential question: black and white relations. For ten years Nationalists had been making capital out of the United Party's refusal to ban mixed marriages and out of the fears of widespread miscegenation. The presence on the government benches of Jan Hofmeyr, Smuts' Deputy Prime Minister and possible successor, drew regular Nationalist barbs. Hofmeyr had stood out against General Hertzog's successful bid to take qualified blacks off the common voters roll in 1936 and the Nationalists never let anyone forget it.

Johannes Strydom in particular, who was to succeed Malan as Prime Minister, sneered at Hofmeyr's views on race. What was the 'trusteeship', the 'leadership' of which he and his party spoke, demanded Strydom in the Assembly in January 1948. 'Either you are *baas* (boss), the equal, or the inferior. One of the three. If you are not baas, you must be a man's equal . . . It is so clear and logical. If you say that you do not want to dominate the Native it simply means that you stand for a policy of equality.'

There is no doubt that Hofmeyr's stand on matters of race set him apart from many members of his own party. In 1945 Malherbe had gone so far as to urge Smuts to drop him. Malherbe had proposed a pact with Havenga's Afrikaner Party to try to win the middle ground. With a keen eye for the political facts of life in South Africa, Malherbe had written to Smuts: 'Hofmeyr will be an embarrassment in any effort to unite the great majority of the United Party with the moderate elements which Mr Havenga will bring with him from the Nationalist Party ranks. However much we deplore it, we cannot get away from the fact that Mr Hofmeyr will be an indigestible lump in the make-up of such a group.' It was perhaps a measure of the extreme conservatism of most whites that such a letter was ever written.

The Nationalists, for their part, presented a racial policy that offered the voter a clear path for the future: separation between the races. In Afrikaans they called it *Apartheid*. The reserves would become the separate and proper homelands of the black population; education would be separate for all groups at all levels; in the towns all races would live separately, travel separately, work in tasks separately reserved for them. The mixed population, the Coloureds, would henceforth have their separateness revealed to them as well, and it would be enforced. Black trade unions would no longer be necessary as the State would be the guardian of the workers' interests. Native representation in the House of Assembly – by three whites – would be abolished as it would in the Cape Provincial Council.

For fifteen years or more the Afrikaner intellectuals in the Broederbond had been debating and defining the Nationalist views on race, among them Diederichs, Albert Hertzog, Meyer, Verwoerd and the professor of sociology at Pretoria University, Dr Geoff Cronje. In 1944 a special FAK congress had justified Apartheid on the grounds of centuries of Afrikaner experience, scientific proof and biblical witness. Professor Cronje had presented evidence which demonstrated irrefutably, he claimed, that miscegenation led to racial decline. The poet and theologian, J. D. du Toit, known as Totius, had addressed the meeting on the religious basis of Apartheid. Because racial differences were grounded in the ordinances of creation, he had argued, racial integration was not only foolish but sinful. Apartheid was thus justified because God had called the Afrikaner to implement it for the well-being of black and white alike. Racial separation was thus not only a Boer tradition, it represented the Divine Will.

A Party commission under the chairmanship of a Nationalist MP, Paul Sauer, further refined the policy shortly before the elections. Equality between blacks and whites would lead to 'national suicide of the white race', whereas the policy of Apartheid would protect and make safe the future of every race with full opportunities for development in its own area. One group would not be a threat to the other.

Arguing the rightness of their cause, backed by considerable local organisation, the Nationalists approached election day on Wednesday 26 May 1948. Few thought they could topple Smuts. At the dissolution, in a House of one hundred and fifty-three seats, the United Party held eighty-nine and the Nationalists forty-nine. The other fifteen were all anti-Nationalist, six of them Labour and three held by whites representing Natives. To gain a majority the Nationalists had to take twenty-eight new seats, a swing unparalleled in South Africa's history.

Smuts, however, was an old man of seventy-nine, tired from the war. And, as Malherbe and others have since recalled, he had been so much involved with world war politics that he was more at home with the broader international issues than he was with the bread and Broeder politics at home.

Joel Mervis, an Assistant Editor on the *Rand Daily Mail*, interviewed Smuts five days before the election. He was planning to write a story for the first of June, the fiftieth anniversary of Smuts' entry into public life as State Attorney of President Kruger's Transvaal Republic on 1 June 1898. He asked Smuts what he thought of his prospects in the election, less than a week away.

'My boy,' said Smuts. 'I anticipate victory in the election. My only fear is a mechanical difficulty'.

'Do you mean, General, that your party does not have enough transport to bring voters to the polls?'

'No, I do not mean that. Many of the constituency boundary lines have been redrawn. I fear, for instance, that a voter formerly registered in Parktown may not know that he is now in Johannesburg North. He will go to the Parktown polling station, he will find he is not on the roll there and he won't know where to go. The result is we will have a lot of people milling around. Maybe they will just go home without voting.'

For years the Cabinet had been urging Smuts to change an electoral provision he himself had agreed to in 1909 that allowed urban constituencies to be overloaded by fifteen per cent and rural constituencies to be underloaded by the same amount. But nothing had been done so it took far fewer votes to win a seat in the country than in the towns. In the event the franchise loaded in favour of country seats cost Smuts dear. He took fifty per cent of the poll against forty per cent by Malan and Havenga and still lost the election. The Nationalists and the Afrikaner Party won seventy-nine seats against the United Party's sixty-five. When all the returns were in, Malan and his ally had an overall majority of five. Six of the National Party's new seats were in the gold towns of the Witwatersrand where Hertzog's miners and their organisation had played a vital role.

Hertzog himself was returned as the member for Ermelo in the Eastern Transvaal. Klopper was in and so were Diederichs and P. W. Botha. Vorster was defeated by two votes in Brakpan. On a recount the margin rose to four. Smuts himself lost his seat at Standerton, beaten ironically by Wentzel du Plessis, one of the civil servants who had resigned rather than quit the Broederbond. 'To think', said Smuts in the first moment of anguish, 'that I have been beaten by the Broederbond.' Malan, the new Prime Minister, was naturally triumphant:

Dr Daniel F. Malan, Nationalist Prime Minister 1948–54

'Today,' he said, 'South Africa belongs to us once more. For the first time since Union, South Africa is our own. May God grant that it will always remain so.'

Colin Legum, then General Secretary of the Labour Party, met a lift attendant who put it more bluntly. 'From now on,' he said, 'a kaffir is a kaffir again'.[1]

Malherbe remembers his dismay at the result.

I was very much upset at losing that election because I knew the kind of people that would get into power and what they would do, particularly in the educational field. That is what upset me most, because I knew what their aims were, from what I knew of the Broederbond. Unfortunately my fears were realised.

I did not have the foresight to know they would stay in power for thirty years. But knowing the type of people who got in, they were no fools. They were able people, abler in many respects than some of the people Smuts had kept on in the United Party. That I also knew.

[1] Just how much this basic attitude has changed in over thirty years of Nationalist rule is a matter for endless debate. In 1978 one of my own South African relatives said to me: 'The trouble in South Africa these days is that you don't know where you stand. We used to call them Kaffirs. Then we were told they were Bantu. Now they say we must call them Africans. But to me a Coon is a Coon!'

152

Encouraged by Smuts, Malherbe had already taken over as Principal and Vice Chancellor of the University of Natal. His successor as Director of Military Intelligence was his wartime deputy Colonel Charles Powell. In July 1948, two months after the election, F. C. Erasmus, the new Minister of Defence, walked into Powell's office and dismissed him with twenty-four hours' notice. He then proceeded to remove what Malherbe described as 'two lorry loads' of secret files including 'a lot of the intercepted stuff on what the Broederbond and Nationalists and others had done to sabotage the war effort.'

'Though two detectives were present,' wrote Malherbe later in his *Education in South Africa*, 'the Minister of Justice was in no way concerned.'

Malherbe was still Chairman of the Prime Minister's War Histories Advisory Board and he complained in person to Dr Malan at this rape of the official War Archives, but Malan said Erasmus was within his rights to deal with official documents. He would give no undertaking that they would be returned and they have never been seen since. As Malherbe added, 'That is why people like Vorster can so easily say today: "Can you prove it?"'

12
'Nothing less than a miracle'
Verwoerd on the establishment of the Republic

With Parliament at last in their hands, the Nationalists now set about making their position unassailable. For the first time in the history of the Union every member of the Cabinet was an Afrikaner. For the first time since its humble beginnings in 1918 the Broederbond had one of its own as Prime Minister. All but two of Malan's Cabinet were Broeders as well.

From this new power base, the Nationalists dispensed patronage in a style hitherto unknown in South Africa, rewarding those of like mind, removing those whose politics offended them. Robey Leibbrandt and Erik Holm, serving sentences for wartime treason, were both released. A wartime hero, Major General Evered Poole, who had commanded the Sixth South African Armoured Division fighting with the allies, found himself posted to Germany and his position as Deputy Chief of the General Staff abolished. Poole had been widely expected to take over as Chief of Staff but the promotion went instead to an Afrikaner general brought out of retirement.

By insisting, not unreasonably, on bilingualism in the civil service the Nationalists had every excuse to promote Afrikaners. English speakers who had never deigned to learn Afrikaans were squeezed out and there were plenty of bilingual Broeders to take their places. Although it was not known at the time, eight hundred and seventy civil servants who had resigned from the Broederbond in 1945, when Smuts forced them to choose between their jobs and their membership, now quietly rejoined their secret society.

On the railways the English-speaking General Manager, Marshall Clark, was given a golden handshake of seventy thousand pounds and replaced by an Afrikaner named Heckroodt. In 1953, he in turn was replaced by Danie du Plessis, one of that first band of brothers who, with Henning Klopper, had founded the Broederbond thirty-five years before.

The Nationalist Cabinet in 1948. Back row (l to r): E. H. Louw; Dr T. E. Donges; F. C. Erasmus; B. J. Schoeman; J. F. Naude; Sen H. Verwoerd; J. H. Viljoen; Dr K. Bremer. Front row: S. P. le Roux; J. C. Strydom; Dr D. F. Malan; Dr E. G. Jansen; N. C. Havenga; C. R. Swart and P. O. Sauer

Even the courts were not exempt; over the coming years a host of Afrikaner magistrates were appointed and a few judges too. Never again would an Afrikaner complain that his case could not be heard in his own language. Whether all those promoted to the bench deserved the preferment was another matter.

In Parliament one of the Nationalists' first acts was to suspend a plan that had been proposed by Smuts to recruit British immigrants. A bill passed in 1949 made it more difficult for those who were already there to qualify for citizenship and the vote. At the same time by reducing the voting age from twenty-one to eighteen, the Nationalists increased their own potential electoral strength since Afrikaners already outnumbered English speakers and, according to a survey in

155

1951, had a higher birth rate. Another Smuts enactment that would have given some representation to Indians in the white Assembly was reversed, while the Electoral Laws Amendment Act made it much harder for Coloured voters in the Cape to register for their qualified franchise on the common roll. Previously an applicant had simply filled in a form and sent it to an electoral officer. Under the Nationalist proposals the application had to be completed in the presence of the electoral officer himself, or before a magistrate or police officer. 'If this amendment is carried,' said the United Party's former Minister of Justice in the Assembly, 'it will in practice make it virtually impossible for any qualified Coloured person to be registered.' In 1948 the number of coloured voters was 46,051; ten years later that number was almost halved.

In their handling of their own slim parliamentary majority the Nationalists showed themselves to be even more ingenious. When he surveyed the government benches in 1948 Dr Malan could command an overall majority of only five; after he had appointed the Speaker it was down to four. But with brilliant sleight of hand Malan simply produced another six seats – from South West Africa. South Africa had administered the former German Territory under a League of Nations mandate since 1919. Resisting continuing demands that the territory be handed back to the United Nations, Malan proposed instead that South West Africa should be represented in the Union parliament by six elected members and four senators, one of whom should be nominated by the government for his knowledge of the area.

The timing was particularly astute. Since General Smuts had also defied the United Nations on this issue Malan was certain of the support of much of the United Party. The white electorate in South West Africa came to no more than twenty-four thousand. In South Africa, where constituencies were usually between nine and twelve thousand voters, they would have been entitled to three seats at most. Malan assigned twice that number as well as the four senators, and in due course ten new Nationalists took their seats in Cape Town.

With his majority thus stiffened Malan now embarked on an even more intricate constitutional exercise. Having already made it more difficult for Coloured voters to register, the Nationalists now proposed to remove them from the common roll altogether. For almost one hundred years Coloureds had gone to the polls alongside whites in all of the fifty-five Cape constituencies. Their vote was considered significant in about half of the seats and decisive in perhaps seven even though so few had qualified and registered. But it had not escaped the

156

notice of the National Party organisers that those who did vote invariably supported the opposition.

Indeed in 1949, in the Provincial elections in the Cape, the United Party had won back two seats at Paarl and Bredasdorp with the help, so Nationalists calculated, of Coloured voters. So the government proposed to remove this troublesome influence altogether. From now on, the Coloureds would vote on a separate roll returning four white members to represent them in the House of Assembly and two in the Provincial Council. Thus at a stroke, the ideology of separation would be promoted and the strength of the opposition depleted.

For justification, the Nationalists argued then, and still do today, that the Coloureds were being exploited by whites without gaining any advantage for themselves and would therefore be much better off on a separate roll. By June 1951, the Separate Representation of Voters Bill had gone through all stages in both the Assembly and the Senate, and awaited the Governor General's assent. But four Coloured voters contested the legislation on the grounds that their franchise rights were entrenched in the constitution and could therefore be changed only by a two-thirds majority of the two houses of Parliament sitting together. The Appeal Court supported them and the Bill was thrown out.

But the government was not to be thwarted. In 1952 Malan proposed that Parliament should itself become the High Court to adjudicate on the validity of the laws it passed. The new 'High Court' solemnly sat and reinstated the Separate Voters Bill only for the Appeal Court to throw it out again and, for good measure, to declare the 'High Court of Parliament' itself invalid.

In 1953, the argument over the sovereignty of Parliament became one of the issues in the general election and helped the Nationalists to an increased majority. But when Malan presented his Coloured voters bill to a joint session he still failed to muster the necessary two-thirds margin. So the issue dragged on. In 1954 at the age of eighty, Malan resigned and was replaced by J. G. Strydom who quickly devised a way through the impasse. He enlarged the Appeal Court and appointed five new judges to fill the vacancies. He increased the size of the Senate from forty-eight to eighty-nine members and changed the basis of election in such a way that the National Party provided most of the new senators. Having thus assured the parliamentary arithmetic, Strydom put the Coloured voters issue before another joint session of the Assembly and the Senate, in February 1956. To no one's surprise, but to the dismay of many, he won the day by well over the necessary two-thirds majority. The Appeal Court made the appropriate endorsement and after a five year struggle the Coloureds were finally off the common roll. In 1960 the Nationalists completed an astonishing cycle by putting through another bill to reduce the Senate to fifty-four members.

Afrikanerdom did not emerge unscathed. Every stage of the constitutional battle was marked by vast public protests from an organisation called the War Veterans' Torch Commando, established in 1951 explicitly to oppose the government's Coloured policy. Alongside them stood members of the Women's Defence of the Constitution League, draped in black mourning sashes pledged 'to dog the movements of Cabinet Ministers to remind the country continuously of the wrong and dishonour perpetrated.' The Torch Commando, for all its popular support, did not last long, but the Black Sash remains, ever faithful to that early promise. Another protest came from thirteen Afrikaner academics, led by Professor Willem Kleynhans of the University of Pretoria. Unanimously they rejected their Nationalist affiliations and condemned the packing of the Senate as a cynical piece of political gerrymandering. Kleynhans had once been chairman of the junior Nationalists in the Transvaal and his defection was marked by poison pen letters, abusive telephone calls and even threats of lynching.

The most lasting damage had been done to the relationship between Afrikaners and their Coloured cousins. No population group was closer to the Afrikaners than the million or more South Africans of mixed race. Since the days of the Hottentots they had worked and lived alongside the Boers, learning their customs, sharing their blood. They spoke the Afrikaner's language which they had enriched with their own idiom. They worshipped in their own branch of the Afrikaners' Dutch Reformed Church. Yet now Afrikanerdom was rejecting them. It is true that later, with protestations of good intent, the Nationalist government would offer them their own Coloured Representative Council where, under the theory of Separate Development, they were to make their own laws. But the people called Coloured were given no territory of their own. Their Council had no real powers; and when, in the very first election in 1969, most Coloured voters supported anti-Apartheid candidates, the Nationalists simply nominated enough members to give the pro-Apartheid party the majority. At the same time they installed as leader the man whom the voters had rejected. Naturally, under Nationalist logic, the establishment of the Council meant the Coloureds had no need for represen-

Torch Commando rally, Johannesburg 1951, protesting against Nationalist government attempts to remove Coloured voters from the common roll

tation in the white Assembly and their four seats were abolished in 1968.

This cynical disregard of their aspirations has turned many Coloureds into bitter opponents of the government. An increasing number no longer acknowledge the ties that once linked them to the white man. Some now refuse to speak Afrikaans. More and more are aligning themselves alongside black South Africans. So in their determination to consolidate their own position the Nationalists steadily alienated the one group whom they might have recruited to their own side.

However, in those first years after 1948 no such considerations seemed to trouble Afrikaner Nationalists. Their eyes were still set on a distant goal, the goal of the republic. Such a vision had set their forbears on the trek to freedom; such a vision had provoked the Wars of Liberation against the British and inspired the leaders of the Party and the Broederbond. Only a republic could ensure the independence to run their sort of South Africa in the way they chose. Only in a republic outside the Commonwealth would Nationalists be assured that never again would the Volk be inveigled into a British war. Only in a republic would Afrikaners feel that they were finally free. As the Chairman of the Broederbond, Piet Meyer, told his members in 1971, 'The Republican road was not a road of abstract constitutional freedom, but of embracing spiritual freedom in which the Afrikaner could always be himself.'

On 20 January 1960 Prime Minister Hendrik Verwoerd announced to an astonished House of Assembly that he proposed to hold a referendum later in the year on whether or not South Africa should take the step and become that republic. Verwoerd had been in office for only sixteen months. His predecessors Malan and Strijdom had steadily increased the Nationalists' parliamentary majority in two elections but neither had felt strong enough to face the electorate with such a controversial issue. In the 1958 election, the Nationalists had won a hundred and three seats to the United Party's fifty-three but an analysis of voting figures suggested that the opposition was still supported by a majority of the electorate. It was the farming seats of the country districts that continued to give the Nationalists their disproportionate majority. A nationwide survey conducted by party officials on Verwoerd's instructions at the end of 1959 had suggested that if ninety per cent of the electorate were to participate in a referendum on the issue of a republic, the vote would go against by a margin of between sixty and seventy thousand votes.

Nonetheless Verwoerd had determined that the moment had come. Before going to Parliament he had told the party caucus of his plan for a referendum. Henning Klopper MP could hardly believe it: 'We were astounded. We didn't know what to say. There was such division in the caucus.' Undeterred, Verwoerd set about organising his lieutenants. Meyer was not yet Chairman of the Broederbond but the previous August had been appointed Chairman of the South African Broadcasting Corporation. He received a summons from the Prime Minister. 'All you cultural chaps', said Meyer, using the Broeder's favourite euphemism as he recalled Verwoerd's instructions, 'have been pestering me about the Republic. Now we are going to hold a referendum and stick with the decision. We have only a fifty per cent chance of winning. You cultural people must help us. But if we fail this time, that's it. We can't keep on about it.'

Judging from his wartime statements Verwoerd would have preferred a republic as far outside the Commonwealth as possible and so too would the Broederbond. But in order not to inflame the antirepublican vote Verwoerd promised to maintain the Commonwealth link. The monarch as head of state would simply be replaced by a

160

president, who unlike the presidents of the Boer republics, would have no executive power. Thus, again, Verwoerd was doing his best to meet the objections of those still opposed to the idea of a republic. The voters he needed to attract to win the referendum were the Afrikaners who still supported Smuts' United Party. *'Slim Jannie'* (clever Jannie), had been dead for ten years. Perhaps many of his old supporters, without going as far as espousing Nationalism, could still be warmed to the republican cause. After all, that was what every burgher had fought for at the turn of the century.

The party organisers with their Broederbond back-up set about their campaign. Naturally only whites would vote. The Coloureds were now safely off the common roll and had no say in the proceedings. But as 1960 progressed a number of events played an unexpected part in the final decision.

First, the British Prime Minister, Harold Macmillan, arrived in South Africa at the end of an extensive tour of Africa. On 2 February he made his famous 'Wind of Change' speech before the combined Houses of Parliament that were still digesting the prospect of an end to close links with Westminster. To them Macmillan spoke of the emerging nationalism of the African continent. But he spoke also of a vision that the white nationalists certainly did not share:

The most striking of all the impressions I have formed since I left London a month ago is the strength of this African National consciousness. In different places it may take different forms, but it is happening everywhere. The wind of change is blowing through the continent. Whether we like it or not, this growth of political consciousness is a political fact. We must all accept it as a fact. Our national policies must take account of it. Of course, you understand this as well as anyone. You are sprung from Europe, the home of nationalism. And here in Africa you have yourselves created a full nation – a new nation. Indeed, in the history of our times yours will be recorded as the first of the African nationalisms.

Macmillan stressed that it had been British colonial policy,

not only to raise the material standards of living but to create a society in which men are given the opportunity to grow to their full stature, and that must in our view include the opportunity to have an increasing share in political power and responsibility; a society in which individual merit, and individual merit alone, is the criterion for man's advancement whether political or economic.

British aims were not South African aims; for this reason the Nationalists policy of Apartheid could expect no aid and comfort from the United Kingdom:

161

Dr Hendrik Verwoerd, welcoming British Prime Minister, Harold
Macmillan, to South Africa, 1960

As a fellow member of the Commonwealth, it is our earnest desire to give South Africa our support and encouragement, but I hope you won't mind my saying frankly that there are some aspects of your policies which make it impossible for us to do this without being false to our own deep convictions about the political destinies of free men, to which in our territories we are trying to give effect.

Macmillan's speech caused a sensation, both in South Africa and Britain. Many English-speaking South Africans, as well as Afrikaners were affronted that the British government seemed to accord the white man no place of his own in Africa. Britain, for its own national interest, was getting out of Africa. The white men who remained could expect no help from Westminster. Verwoerd exploited the moment brilliantly. A month after Macmillan's speech he spoke to the Assembly:

It was not the Republic of South Africa that was told, 'We are not going to support you in this respect.' Those words were addressed to the monarchy of South Africa, and yet we have the same monarch as this person from Britain who addressed these words to us. It was a warning that was given to all of us, English-speaking and Afrikaans-speaking, republican and anti-republican. It was clear to all of us that as far as these matters are concerned, we shall have to stand on our own feet.

No one could dispute that Verwoerd had made a valid point.

On 21 March came the second event to cast its dark influence over not just the republican debate but over the whole decade: the Sharpeville shootings. As part of a protest against the pass laws, the newly formed Pan Africanist Congress had called for a nationwide day of protest. Throughout the country members and supporters left their reference books at home and presented themselves to the police for arrest. At Sharpeville, a township outside Vereeniging in the Transvaal, a crowd of some fifteen to twenty thousand had gathered outside the police station. As the number of Africans increased their mood became more aggressive. At Cato Manor near Durban the previous January, four white and five black policemen had been killed by a black mob. Perhaps that was uppermost in the minds of the police at Sharpeville. One of them opened fire without orders. His colleagues took it as the command to do so as well. When the shooting stopped sixty-seven Africans were dead and a hundred and seventy-eight wounded. Many had been shot in the back. There were more shootings at Langa in Cape Town where a crowd rioted and burned cars and buildings.

The government acted immediately, banning all public meetings in the main centres. Within a week Verwoerd had introduced legislation

163

making both the Pan Africanist Congress and the African National Congress illegal. On 30 March a state of emergency was declared. Twelve-thousand, mainly blacks, were detained in pre-dawn arrests. Eventually more than eighteen thousand were held. Many were released after screening but over five thousand were convicted and sentenced for various offences. Thirty thousand blacks marched on Cape Town but dispersed when their leader announced he had been granted an interview with Erasmus, the Minister of Justice. Instead of meeting him, Erasmus had him arrested.

The outside world was scandalised. The American government publicly regretted 'the tragic loss of life'. Press condemnation was universal; the front pages were full of the pictures of the dead and dying. *The Times* wrote of the 'wicked myth of Apartheid' and the 'blind obstinacy of Verwoerd'. The London *Sunday Times* called the pass laws 'an affront to humanity'. A protest meeting outside the South African Embassy in Trafalgar Square drew over ten thousand people; the South African consulate in New York was picketed; the Security Council in the United Nations demanded that Apartheid be abolished. Foreign investors began to withdraw their money; gold shares slumped.[1]

While the United Party opposition was loud in its condemnation of the government many Nationalists simply could not understand what all the fuss was about. They believed the reaction of the outside world was both hysterical and hypocritical. Verwoerd said in the Assembly that the troubles were a symptom of the times, 'a result of all sorts of ideas expressed in the world and inspired in other parts of the world'. They could in no way be described as a reaction against the government's Apartheid policies. The disturbances were periodic events 'which came in cycles as a result of incitement in regard to some or other matter of law.' By implication Macmillan's 'Wind of Change' was partly to blame. Albert Hertzog, Verwoerd's Minister of Posts and Telegraphs was quite specific; in the Assembly he called Macmillan's speech 'a message of death'.

Verwoerd pointed out that recent troubles in Nyasaland, the Cameroons and the Congo had been far worse. When over fifty blacks had been killed in various incidents during the Smuts regime no one

---

[1] Between 1957 and 1960 there was a net outflow of capital from South Africa of R20 million. In eighteen months between January 1960 and June 1961 a total of R248 million left the country. One by-product was that many Afrikaners were able to buy their way cheaply into business and industry, extending Afrikaner interests in an area still dominated by English-speakers.

had reacted so strongly. At a huge gathering at Meyerton ten miles from Vereeniging, Verwoerd made his first public appearance since the shootings. It was his opening speech in the republican campaign and he spoke exactly the words the whites wanted to hear: Nobody should be at all upset. Nobody should think that law and order could not be maintained.

The black masses of South Africa – and I know Bantu in all parts of the country – are orderly and peace-loving. They are loyal to the government and administration of the country . . . The groups of people seeking their own gain are small and they make use of mass psychology at mass gatherings, and by threats and other means are sometimes the cause of the trouble . . . We do not intend to be perturbed about what is done and said in the outside world in all ignorance.

The critics overseas were the *skollies* (teddy-boys) of the political world. They were playing into the hands of the Communists.

Not for the last time a Nationalist Prime Minister turned overseas' criticism to his own advantage. Foreigners did not understand South Africa, went the argument; they simply condemned every effort the government made, however well-meaning. South Africans should be aware that they stood alone in the world. It was splendid grist to the republican mill and did no harm to Verwoerd's image as the father figure in whom all whites could have confidence. He exuded it himself. In April when the Prime Minister survived an assassination attempt by a deranged white farmer, he became even more of a hero.

In the Congo, the mayhem following Belgian withdrawal provided more material for the republican campaign: *Ons republiek nou, om Suid-Afrika blank te hou* (Our republic now, to keep South Africa white) became a popular slogan. As *The Rand Daily Mail* reported: 'The whole republican referendum is reduced to the simple question of whether you want your daughter to marry an African, or, more to the point, be ravished by a Congolese soldier.'

On 5 October 1960, ninety per cent of eligible voters queued up to cast a simple 'yes' or 'no' vote to the question of whether they wanted a republic. 850,458 voted in favour, 775,878 against. Verwoerd declared himself delighted with the majority of 74,580; the pro-republicans represented just over fifty-two per cent of the poll.[1]

[1] One of the main arguments of the anti-republicans was that the establishment of a republic would lead to economic disaster through the end of preferential trade agreements with the Commonwealth. No such fears were realised. In the ten years from 1960 to 1970 the South African economy grew at an average annual rate of six per cent. Trade flourished; foreign capital, withdrawn after Sharpeville, returned to contribute to the greatest economic boom in South African history.

Natal had voted against; in the Cape the republicans had a majority of fewer than two thousand from over half a million votes cast. But the Afrikaner strongholds, the Free State and the Transvaal had swung the victory. What Verwoerd would have done had the majority gone the other way is not clear; with his parliamentary majority he could still have put a republican bill through the Assembly. But the issue did not arise. The gamble had paid off. As Henning Klopper put it; 'We had got the republic without firing a shot.' 31 May 1961 was appointed as the birthday, the anniversary of defeat by the British and the Treaty of Vereeniging fifty-nine years before.

There was still the issue of South Africa's position in the Commonwealth but that too resolved itself. In March Verwoerd flew to London for the Commonwealth Prime Ministers' Conference. He had promised to do everything in his power to retain South Africa's membership although not at the price of allowing interference in her domestic policies. But the assembled Prime Ministers were determined to voice their disapproval of Apartheid. Verwoerd's urbanity and benign appearance may have impressed British television audiences but both they and the Commonwealth Ministers remained unimpressed at his attempts to explain Apartheid as a policy of 'good neighbourliness'. Nehru of India and Nkrumah of Ghana wanted South Africa out of the Commonwealth. Diefenbaker of Canada joined the condemnation. Macmillan did his best to achieve a compromise in the form of a communiqué confirming South Africa's membership while recording the strong feelings of some of the leaders about Apartheid. But it was not enough for the anti-South Africa lobby.

On 15 March 1961 Verwoerd informed the Conference that he was withdrawing South Africa's application to remain a member of the Commonwealth. 'I am sure', he said in a statement, 'that the great majority of the people of my country will in the circumstances appreciate that no other course was open to us . . . I must admit that I was amazed and shocked by the spirit of hostility, and, at the last meeting, even of vindictiveness towards South Africa shown in the discussions.' Thus saying, Verwoerd cancelled scheduled visits to Bonn and Paris and flew home. It was 20 March, a day short of the first anniversary of the Sharpeville shootings.

We have been thrown out of the Commonwealth, out of the group of the most tolerant, the most civilised, the most fair-minded peoples in the world [wrote the *Cape Times*]. And we have been thrown out because of the narrow-minded, inflexible doctrines of racism which began the sabotage of South Africa in 1948 and came to their climax under the direction of Dr Verwoerd.

The Johannesburg *Star* also blamed no one but Verwoerd. 'He has been a disastrous failure and it would be in the interests of the country if he could be persuaded to resign.'

But for Afrikaners Verwoerd's achievement was nothing short of miraculous. Henry Kenney summed up that view in his biography of Verwoerd, *Architect of Apartheid*.

A republic within the Commonwealth would have been a regrettable compromise, accepted only in the interest of white unity and because it would be preferable to no republic at all. It would never have had the same emotional appeal as a republic which had broken all constitutional ties with the historic enemy. Verwoerd had now achieved the historic ideal and returned home a hero of the first magnitude.

At Johannesburg airport a great crowd turned out to greet him. 'What has happened in London was not a defeat but a victory,' announced the Prime Minister. 'We have freed ourselves from the Afro-Asian states.' That same evening he addressed another cheering crowd in Cape Town: 'What happened is nothing less than a miracle. So many nations have had to get their complete freedom by armed struggle . . . but here we have reached something which we never expected.' For John Vorster, ex-General in the Ossewabrandwag soon to become Verwoerd's Minister of Justice, it was 'the fulfilment of a lifetime's ambition. To become a Republic; that's what you fought for, that's what you hoped for, that's what you prayed for.'

Piet Meyer, now Chairman of the Broederbond that had worked so hard in the referendum campaign, remembered his elation but also a feeling of anti-climax; the impetus had gone with the achievement of the goal. He did not even attend the celebrations in Pretoria on 31 May when, in the pouring rain, one of his fellow Broeders, C. R. Swart, the former Minister of Justice, was sworn in as the first President of the Republic of South Africa. The government had taken precautions against any other sort of disruption by arresting between eight and ten thousand blacks in the days before the event.

Henning Klopper experienced no such feelings of anti-climax. He still had a vision for his band of brothers, a vision he later spelt out at the secret fiftieth anniversary conference held in October 1968:

A question of great importance has been raised: has the Broederbond then not achieved its goal in the formation of the Republic? Has not the time perhaps come when we can dissolve and outspan and let the cause run its natural course? If that is so Brothers, we will have to ask ourselves who will give us the government of the land? Who will give us our future Prime Ministers? Who will form them?

Dare anyone then still ask the question: Has the Broederbond outserved its time? He may not ask such a question. No Brother dare ask such a question. Take the Afrikaner Broederbond out of the life of Afrikanerdom and what is left? Take Afrikanerdom out of the bosom of Africa and what is left over for the Kingdom of God? Who will carry the cause on the bosom of Africa if the Afrikaners are not here? Just ask the people of Rhodesia: We know that the Republic stands behind us. And who is the Republic? It is the Afrikaner Broederbond's Brothers.

13

'Good fences make good neighbours'

Dominee Koot Vorster on the Group Areas Act

With the establishment of the Republic, one Nationalist goal had been achieved. There remained another, yet more alluring, and that was the resolution once and for all of the problem of racial harmony in South Africa. The Nationalists were sure of the route to salvation; it lay through separation and Apartheid. From the moment of their election victory in 1948 they had set about turning principles into practice, fancy into fact.

'The National Party was going to build a new heaven and a new earth, which one day would command the wonder of the world', wrote Alan Paton in an essay on the Afrikaners.[1] 'The calling of this small nation', said Verwoerd's Minister of Bantu Administration and Development, Daan de Wet Nel, in the Assembly in 1959, 'is to give the world the basis and pattern on which different races can live in peace and safety in the future, each within its national circle. That is the prescription for the solution of the racial problem not only in Africa but throughout the world.'

Thus from their first days in power the Nationalists had launched a project of social engineering the like of which the world had never seen. South Africa was to be restructured. Every citizen would be classified into his race or group; groups would become 'nations', their people moved around like so many different sets of chessmen on the same giant board. Each 'nation' was to be separate; they were to live separately, make love separately, go to separate schools, vote in separate parliaments. South Africa itself, as the policy reached fruition, would be divided into separate 'states' although the whites would retain possession of all the best squares and control the whole checkerboard.

[1] 'The Afrikaner as I know him' taken from *The Afrikaners*, edited by Edwin S. Munger, Tafelberg, Cape Town 1979.

Blacks were not asked if they agreed with the course the Nationalists had chosen for them. The Afrikaners, from their position of power, made no such concession. They were the winners and South Africa was the prize.

Apartheid was to ensure that their winnings were never wrested from them and that the white tribe was preserved for ever. 'Let me be very clear about this,' Verwoerd told the Transvaal Nationalist Congress soon after Republic Day in 1961, 'when I talk of the nation of South Africa, I talk of the white people of South Africa. I do not say that in disparagement of any other racial group in South Africa. I do not see us as one multi-racial state descending from various groups.'

The early legislation, in the first years after 1948, was straightforward even crude. Its aim was simply to enforce separation in every sphere of life, from buses to bed. The Nationalists put it more delicately; their aim was to 'eliminate points of friction between the races'. In one of their first measures, in 1949, marriage between whites and those who skins were of a different colour was prohibited although there were but a hundred such unions in a year. Then the Immorality Amendment Act made sexual intercourse a serious offence if indulged in across racial frontiers, extending a law that General Hertzog had introduced in 1927 that had applied only to whites and blacks.

To Dominee Koot Vorster, back with his congregation in Cape Town after his wartime prison adventure, such measures were fundamental to maintaining the Afrikaner identity. 'That legislation helped immensely', he said, 'to keep people to their own grounds'. He remembered particularly his early pastoral days in Cape Town before the war when he had come across a young Afrikaner girl living in the chicken shed of a house owned by an Indian. 'We had poor white women even selling their bodies to non-whites', he recalled.

It was the memory of this sort of traffic plus the conviction of the difference between races that allowed the Dutch Reformed Church to give the new legislation its full support.

We felt very strongly that we had to preserve our identity, [said Vorster] because that is a God-given right that every man has, the black man, the coloured and the white. God created us differently, and it is to the honour of God that we must preserve that difference. We felt so strongly that we pointed out to people that God gave mankind Ten Commandments and one of them said 'Honour thy father and thy mother'. That means it is not just a matter of being obedient to your parents. You must also honour your parents and preserve their identity too.

To the church therefore the next piece in the jigsaw of Apartheid

Dominee J. D. (Koot) Vorster, former Moderator of the Cape Synod of the Dutch Reformed Church

legislation was equally Christian and equally necessary. It was the Group Areas Act, passed by Malan's government in 1950, providing different residential areas for every section of the population. The fact that the Act cut across all traditional property rights and led to the eviction of thousands of blacks, Indians and Coloureds from their homes was acceptable under the Apartheid logic because it contributed to the common good. Indeed Dominee Vorster believed the Church should take credit for its long advocacy of that very Act. 'That was the idea of the church, to have separate residential areas. It was very pointed and very clear that the church wanted separate areas because we believed what the Americans say, 'Good fences make good neighbours'.

By one of those great South African ironies, almost the first to stray across the fence and be found guilty under the Immorality Act was one of Vorster's clerical brethren, a Dominee of the Dutch Reformed Church. At Barkly East in the Cape a minister was caught *in flagrante delicto* in the garage built by his parishioners next to his house. Although the Dominee was given only a suspended sentence his irate parishioners bulldozed the offending garage to the ground.

At the University of Natal, where Dr Ernie Malherbe was Principal, the case evoked much interest and some lines of verse which pointed up the difficulty of trying to prevent by legislation what Afrikaners and everyone else had been enjoying for a long time. Malherbe himself disclaimed authorship:

> In Barkly East as I heard tell
> A Dominee there chanced to dwell.
> Black was his suit and black his vest,
> Black was the colour that he liked best.
> And 'neath the black of his clerical breeches,
> Dwelt some black uncontrollable itches.
>
> Early one morn he chanced to spy
> Eggy Mpele passing by.
> He paused, transfixed, quite taken aback
> At such an intriguing shade of black.
> Hers was the beauty that never fades
> For she was as black as the Ace of Spades.
>
> A wink, a nod, a hurried question,
> And Eggy o.k.'d his suggestion.
> Into the garage slipped the pair.
> Opinions differ as to what happened there.
> Whether or not it was copulation
> Appears a matter for speculation.
>
> I swear it's true, you can have it in writing,
> The Judge said: 'No, he was just inciting,
> And since he truly shows repentance,
> He only gets a suspended sentence.'
> For justice may be harsh or lenient,
> Whichever is the most convenient.

Since 1950 it is estimated that there have been over ten thousand convictions under the Immorality Act; and prosecution has trailed in its wake social disgrace, family break-up and many cases of suicide. Probably no one item of legislation has brought down upon the Nationalists more contumely. Thirty years on there is now widespread discussion in Afrikaner circles about abolishing both it and the Mixed Marriages Act, but the fact remains that the two acts together are at the very foundation of Apartheid. If the Mixed Marriages Act were abolished, where could mixed couples live if the Group Areas Act were not amended also? And to which population group would the children of such unions belong? For since 1950, every South African has been assigned to a particular ethnic group under the Population Registration Act that was another of Malan's basic articles of legislation. After all, if the races were to be separated it was necessary to be quite sure to which one each person belonged. Ultimately everyone would have to carry an identity card which would have his race classification clearly marked.

From the very start the attempts at definition in a population as diverse as South Africa's proved extremely difficult. As any casual visitor knows, there are South Africans of every skin colour, from white to black and many hues between. The criteria used were to be 'appearance', 'general acceptance' and 'repute' but some of the early classification procedures were crude in the extreme.

White officials were occasionally known to use what was known as 'the pencil in the hair' technique. If a pencil pushed into the hair of the applicant stayed there because the hair was crinkly, then he was put down as 'African'; if it fell out because the hair was straighter, then he was 'Coloured'. Families found themselves inexplicably divided. Couples of different race groups who had married before such unions were declared illegal, could find their children assigned indiscriminately to one or other group. Parents classified black could be told their children were coloured and must therefore live in a separate area. It was not unknown for brothers and sisters of the same parents to be given different classifications.

By 1966 there were still approximately one hundred and fifty thousand borderline cases to be settled, but the Nationalist Minister of the Interior stuck doggedly to his text. In Parliament in September that year he said: 'I cannot accept that there will be borderline cases for all time. If that is so, then the position is in reality so complicated that this legislation is not workable.' Just to make matters even more complicated, the classification 'Coloured' had by then been broken down into seven further categories: Cape Coloured, Cape Malay, Griqua, Indian, Chinese, 'Other Asiatic' and 'Other Coloured'.

But still the legislation comes back to haunt those who invented it. In Parliament in February 1980, Alwyn Schlebusch, P. W. Botha's Minister of the Interior, answered a question on the previous year's reclassifications:

A total of one hundred and one Coloured people became white; one Chinese became white; two whites received Coloured classification; six whites became Chinese; two whites became Indians; ten Coloured people became Indians; ten Malays became Indians; eleven Indians became Coloured; four Indians became Malays; three Coloured people became Chinese while two Chinese were reclassified as Coloured people.

Of all the many stories of individual anguish concealed by such bald statements there is probably none more typical than the experience of a Belgian born white South African named Raymond du Proft. In 1950, just after the government introduced its Immorality Act and its new rules for race registration, he was serving in the police force as a member of the Governor General's mounted escort. He was twenty when he met a waitress named Diane Bassick working in a Cape Town restaurant. They fell in love, but since she was classified Coloured – her mother was white and she never knew her father – they could meet only in secret.

Du Proft remembered how scared they were that they would be found out. 'If they so much as saw you talking to somebody in the street you were liable to be picked up.' As a policeman himself his position was particularly vulnerable. But before long they took a chance and started to live together. When their first son was born six years later they found a house in an Afrikaans-speaking district and passed themselves off without difficulty as a white married couple. Eventually they had five children, all of whom were classified Coloured. Under the Nationalist law they should have gone to a school for Coloureds in a different district, but to maintain the pretence of being white the du Profts kept the children at home and educated them as best they could. Regularly they applied for Diane and the children to be reclassified white and just as regularly they were refused. So marriage remained out of the question. When their eldest son Graham was nineteen he started going out with an Afrikaans-speaking girl and she became pregnant. But again because he was classified coloured and she was white they could not marry. Graham's response, in a moment of despair, was to throw himself under a train. He died instantly.

A few weeks later the du Proft's four other children were reclassified as white. 'If my son had not committed suicide,' said du Proft, 'they might not have done anything.' But still no word of explanation came from white officialdom and still no reason was given why Diane Bassick's classification could not also be changed. While the family now lived in open disregard of the law, the grief of this couple who only wanted to get married did not diminish:

'The thing is,' said Diane Bassick, 'I know that if I am not reclassified I can never marry unless we go to another country. That is the

Raymond du Proft and Diane Bassick, one couple prevented from marrying by the Mixed Marriages Act of 1949

only thing that worries me. I am not worried because they won't reclassify me. I'm worried because I am not married. I mean to put it straight, people can come up to my children and say "You are bastards" and there is nothing I can do about it.' And if she could be neither reclassified nor married? 'I think I might take the same way out as my son, that's how I feel.'

At the end of 1980 there seemed at last the prospect of a happy ending to the story. Diane Bassick's case had attracted a good deal of attention. She had followed the rules of officialdom, swallowed her pride and collected a clutch of affidavits from white friends saying she was 'acceptable' to them as a white person. Her son, Dean, was fighting for South Africa on the border. A hysterectomy operation meant she would not be having any more children. After her fifth application she was informed that she might now be eligible for reclassification.

Meanwhile the Nationalist machine had been moving on. By the end of the fifties segregation affected every aspect of life. Stations, post offices, park benches, buses, lavatories, lifts and libraries all bore the apartheid signs that to the outside world now typified South Africa. Entertainers played to separate audiences whether they had come, as one historian put it 'to watch boxing or listen to Brahms'.[1]

Black protest against the growing ledger of Apartheid laws was continuous and briefly spectacular. In a two-year Defiance Campaign starting in 1952, thousands of Africans deliberately ignored 'Whites Only' entrances in stations and post offices and disregarded the curfews and permits that had come to dominate their lives. All refused to pay fines and went to gaol instead. At the end of the campaign over eight thousand people, including a handful of whites had been imprisoned. But the violence, provoked or not, which interspersed the campaign, lost what little white support there was and enabled the government to bring in further measures to combat unrest.

The motor and the motivator behind the apartheid legislation in both the Malan and Strijdom governments was future Prime Minister Dr Hendrik Verwoerd. As a former professor at Stellenbosch and wartime editor of the Nationalist Party newspaper, *Die Transvaler*, as well as a member of the Broederbond think-tank, he had long been involved in working out the theories for future race relations. In the election that swept Malan to power, Verwoerd had been narrowly defeated at Alberton in the Transvaal but was immediately appointed to the Senate to lead the Nationalists in the Upper House. It was not until Malan made him Minister of Native Affairs in 1950 that the Apartheid juggernaut really began to roll.

Verwoerd was not a pure Afrikaner; he was born in Holland; his parents emigrated to the Cape in 1901 when he was three months old. But no native South African adopted Nationalist ideology with more fervour than this son of a missionary. Helen Suzman, after almost three decades facing Nationalist politicians from the opposition benches, often said he was the only man who had really frightened her. Harry Oppenheimer, later head of the giant Anglo American Corporation, but in 1958 still a United Party member of parliament, called Verwoerd 'an impractical fanatic'.

By the time Verwoerd became Prime Minister in 1958 on the death of Strydom, much of the crude work of separation had been done. Gradually now a new phase emerged. Verwoerd began to clothe the raw bones of Apartheid with a philosophic covering that eased the consciences of whites and inspired some to believe that the Nationalists were not just intent on keeping the blacks as second class citizens for ever. Piet Meyer ascribed full credit to the man at the top: 'Verwoerd gave us our direction. He said Apartheid must end. Now it is

[1] T. R. H. Davenport *South Africa, a Modern History* Macmillan South Africa, 1977; page 275.

going to be Separate Development. We have got to give them full freedom and independence. It took a lot of selling. I had doubts myself.'

By 1959 Verwoerd's, Minister for Native Affairs, de Wet Nel was putting forward a bill that gave substance to this so-called 'positive' Apartheid. Under the Promotion of Bantu Self-Government Act the meagre African reserves were to become self-governing Bantustans. In Parliament de Wet Nel said he was now offering the Bantu 'the possibility of bringing to fullest fruition his personal and national ideals within his own ethnic sphere . . . We grant to the Bantu,' he said, 'what we demand for ourselves.' In the flood of the new idealism it hardly seemed to matter to whites that the same bill finally abolished all black representation in Parliament by removing the three seats, albeit held by whites, that had been their only means of access to government since 1936.

Kowie Marais, for one, was seized by what he called 'the Verwoerdian vision'. 'I really thought it might work, that we could have happy, satisfied, prosperous Homelands, developing into independent republics; that most of the blacks would be sheltered there and find an income there while we, the Whites, in the rest of South Africa might be able to manage our own affairs.'

Yet the gulf between what was proposed and what actually happened grew ever wider. Soon after the Nationalists had come to power Malan had set up a ten-man commission under Professor F. R. Tomlinson to 'devise a scheme for the rehabilitation of the native areas with a view to developing within them a social structure in keeping with the culture of the native based on effective socio-economic planning'. Or, in plain language, to see if Apartheid could really be made to work. The Commission spent five years examining evidence, investigating every aspect of African life. By October 1954 they had seventeen volumes ready to present to Dr Verwoerd, the Minister of Native Affairs. Their findings were awaited as the solution to the country's most insoluble problem.

The report was very matter-of-fact. For Separate Development to become a practical realisation, and that was the course the Commission recommended by a nine to one majority, the Bantu areas had to be fully developed. At the time they comprised two hundred and sixty-four scattered sections which were over-populated and underproductive. Because of bad farming methods and the migration of male workers to the white towns the agricultural yield was declining. Even assuming a very low annual income per family, Tomlinson estimated that there was enough land in the present reserves to support only half the total black population as it stood at the time of the 1951 census. Money should therefore urgently be spent in providing alternative jobs and improving agriculture. Industry should be set up both inside the Bantu areas and on the borders.

More land was necessary: six million acres that had been set aside at the time of the Native Trust and Land Act of 1936 had still to be acquired. The reserves should be consolidated into seven main divisions or Bantustans. Three of them should eventually be incorporated into the British Protectorates of Bechuanaland, Swaziland and Basutoland. In this way the total area assigned to blacks would be equal to roughly half of what might be called 'Greater South Africa'.

The Commission suggested that £104 million would be required for the first ten-year programme. Fifty thousand jobs should be created each year. If this tempo of development were maintained, said the report, the Bantu Areas could support a population of nine million by 1981, two million of whom would be living on the earnings of migrant workers. Under the figures for the projected population this would still leave six million blacks living in white South Africa, some on the farms and the rest in the towns. But at least they would hardly outnumber the ruling white population.

Tomlinson's tonic proved too strong for the Verwoerdian vision. In a White Paper in April 1956 on the Commission's recommendations, the government accepted the principle of the Bantustans but could not commit itself to detailed boundaries at that time. The government agreed that it was essential to spend large sums in the development of the Bantu Areas but did not 'deem it desirable' to fix, at that stage, the amounts needed for the various projects. The government rejected outright the investment of private white capital in black areas on the basis that it would be unfair to expect inexperienced blacks to compete with that form of white imperialism. Whites would invest only through the Bantu Investment Corporation under government control.

It was soon clear that Verwoerd was hardly going to speed up the economic development of the homelands at all. In the six years immediately following the celebrated Promotion of Bantu Self-Government Act, only thirty-five industries were established. Government assistance had amounted to R1,100,000 (about £650,000). A total of thirty-seven whites and nine hundred and forty-five blacks had been offered employment. It is true there had been more substantial investment in what were called 'Border Industries', factories set up in white areas close to black reserves. The government was offering incentives in the form of tax concessions, subsidised transport costs and exemption from minimum wage agreements to industrialists who were willing to move there. Up to the end of March 1967 ninety-eight new industries had been established and sixty-one existing firms extended. Government assistance to white industrialists involved £26 million while a further £36 million had been spent providing power, water, housing, transport, and other related services. Even so, the estimated number of people employed in these Border Industries was only 4,600 whites and 36,000 blacks. By June 1978 the Official Year Book of South Africa stated that 78,731 job opportunities had been created for black workers in Border Industries after government assistance to private industrialists.

It had not escaped the notice of those who lived in the future 'independent homelands' that while black wages brought some money into the reserves, the control of the Border Industries, and the profits, stayed in white hands. The suspicion that the Bantustans were really little more than pools of cheap labour was not removed. After 1969 some of the restrictions on private white capital in the homelands were removed. Industrialists who were prepared to operate on an agency basis for fixed periods, without owning the sites they developed, were allowed access and were given similar concessions to those offered to industrialists moving to the border areas. But by March 1978 the total number of black employees in all agency industries, excluding the Transkei which was no longer included in government statistics, was still only 16,430. It was a figure that even when taken with the numbers employed in the Border Industries fell ludicrously short of Tomlinson's estimated requirement of fifty thousand jobs a year.

As for the much vexed question of homeland consolidation, progress there has been equally revealing of the white man's reluctance to make any real concessions. In 1936 the Native Trust and Land Act theoretically added a further fifteen million acres to the black reserves. When Tomlinson reported in 1954 six million acres had still not been assigned. Since 1960, four homelands have accepted Pretoria's brand of 'independence', even though one of them, BophuthaTswana, was still in six pieces. But while in 1980, Prime Minister P. W. Botha talked for the first time of adding land beyond the provisions of that forty-year-old Act, his Minister for black affairs, Dr Piet Koornhof, was still obliged to let it be known in Parliament that at the beginning of that year some one million two hundred thousand acres from that 1936 settlement had still not been acquired for black use.

Dr Werner Eiselen, a leading Broederbond theorist and Verwoerd's Secretary of Native Affairs, resigned his post in 1960 and became High Commissioner for BophuthaTswana. Some said it was because of his general disillusionment that so little had been done to promote genuine separate development. Some time later he gave an interview to a French journalist who wanted to know why the government had not practised what it had preached.

My dear sir, you can't imagine the bitterness of our internal political struggles. The opposition criticises us when we put into practice what they demand in theory, that is to say, when we improve the lot of the Bantu. The farmers lose sight of our aim, they do not think ahead. When the state purchases land for the Bantu they say: 'Perhaps it is my farm they are going to buy up tomorrow.' Our people . . . only think of their daily comfort. They accept the theory. But at the same 'time they want comfort. Obviously a generous theory and unchallenged comfort are incompatible.

Professor Frederik Tomlinson is today a cattle farmer at Hammans-kraal, north of Pretoria. He is cautious about embroiling himself in politics but nothing can disguise his disappointment at the way his commission was treated. Rather than talk indiscreetly he offers visitors a copy of a speech he made twenty years after the report was completed. It was the first time he had spoken out on an issue that still concerned him greatly.

The essence of the problem of developing the homelands, he said in that speech in 1974, had been speed. Bearing in mind the numbers involved, no small-scale programme would have been adequate. What was required were 'economic weapons applied with inspiration, with sacrifice and with force'. It was crucial to build up an economy in the 'home areas' that did not depend solely on agriculture. Border area development was not enough. The government's refusal to use white capital had lost 'fifteen valuable years'. By opting instead for government development corporations to help Africans launch their own businesses and industrial enterprises it had meant that 'virtually no development at secondary level would take place, and total development would move at snail's pace.' Because of the failure to change traditional methods, agricultural yield had turned out to be one fifth of what it could have been and there were actually many more black mouths to feed than the Commission had allowed. 'Our prediction of population growth was considerably short'.[1]

[1] Using the 1950 Census as a basis, Tomlinson had predicted a total African population of 21 million by the year 2000. After the 1980 Census, projections suggested 35 million was more likely.

So, bearing in mind the huge numbers of blacks who had now left the homelands to seek work in white man's land, could the Bantustans ever become the independent black states that Verwoerd had promised? Tomlinson today shrugs his shoulders and will not answer. But his meaning is clear.

14

'The police burned our homes down'

One Zulu boy's experience of the government's
policy of resettlement

In 1953, while Tomlinson was completing his original commission, a
South African Rhodes scholar at Hertford College, Oxford, handed in
a thesis on the subject of migrant labour in South Africa. It contained a
sad picture of what Verwoerd called 'homelands'.

An enquiry into the living conditions of the Reserves reveals strikingly that its
[sic] inhabitants find it impossible to supply even the bare necessities for
living on a subsistence level . . . Opportunities for gainful employment are
almost non-existent. There is evidence of malnutrition. Disease is rife in
many areas.

The author of that thesis was an Afrikaner graduate named Piet
Koornhof; just over twenty-five years later, as Minister for Cooperation and Development in P. W. Botha's government, he would himself
have the responsibility for those same black areas. From Oxford he
outlined what he saw as a fundamental reason why the white man had
never seen fit to develop them:

The easier the living in the Reserves, the less the labour is available for outside
employment. The temptation for European employer-legislators not to
improve the living has, therefore, always been strong and it has been the
economic force, represented by the demand for labour, which has usually
decided the issue.

Yet for those blacks who were thus forced to seek work in the white
man's cities, Verwoerd had no better conditions in store. The
Nationalists, like all white governments before them, saw black
workers only as passing guests. As Blaar Coetzee, a member of John
Vorster's cabinet, once pointed out, conditions for the 'urban black'
must not be made too comfortable either; otherwise he would want to
stay. The black worker was to be left forever on the migratory round-
about.

It is accepted government policy that the Bantu are only temporarily resident in European areas of the Republic for as long as they offer their labour there, [said a government circular in 1967, a year after Verwoerd's death]. As soon as they become, for some reason or another, no longer fit for work or superfluous in the labour market, they are expected to return to their country of origin or the territory of the national unit where they fit in ethnically if they were not born and bred in the homeland.[1]

Verwoerd's officials and policemen, backed by a battery of bills, had been zealously enforcing such a policy for years. 'Endorsed out', in other words banished from white areas to the reserves, became part of the language and experience of hundreds upon hundreds of blacks whose only offence was to be regarded as superfluous. Many of the able-bodied found themselves in penal work colonies supplying labour for white farmers. 'The aged, the unfit, widows, women with dependent children', were, according to Circular number 25, 'normally regarded as non-productive and as such have to be re-settled in the homelands.' In their administrative enthusiasm white officials were seen not to shirk from open harassment. Families were sometimes evicted when they were late with the rent or when the male breadwinner died. There was at least one case where officials arrived with an eviction order before the body had been buried. Once out of the house the family had to leave the municipal area as well.

Verwoerd introduced tighter controls on the flow of blacks into the cities by more rigorous use of the labour bureaux in the homelands where all work-seekers were supposed to register. Movement was further restricted by rigid application of laws which allowed black visitors without residential qualifications no more than seventy-two hours in the urban areas. The hated pass book, the 'dompas' now had to be carried by women as well as men.[2]

It provided all the information officialdom needed on who was entitled to be where: fingerprints, photograph, identity number, details of birthplace, tribal origin, 'permanent' address, plus dates and places of employment. Regular sweeps by the police mopped up hundreds of pass offenders every day; blacks found in white areas after the evening curfew produced scores more. The whole process was known in the bureaucratic jargon as 'influx control'.

[1] General Circular No 25, 1967, from the Secretary for Bantu Administration and Development, Pretoria; 'Settling of non-productive Bantu resident in European areas, in the Homelands'.
[2] The Bill, which in 1952 extended the carrying of passes to women and other blacks previously exempt, was known, in a fine example of van-der-Merwe-speak, as the 'Natives (Abolition of Passes and Co-ordination of Documents) Act'.

Bulldozing the homes of the Batloung tribe at Putfontein, Western Transvaal, November 1977. Five hundred and sixty families were moved from land redesignated 'white' and resettled one hundred miles away

It was no new system; the first laws restricting Hottentots to their own districts were introduced by the British. Rhodes took similar controls for granted and so did every Prime Minister after Union. Verwoerd's contribution was to refine the laws into a sophisticated means of regulating every aspect of a black man's life.

Pass offenders and superfluous blacks were not the only unfortunates on the move in Verwoerd's new world. Under the Group Areas Act thousands more were being shifted as the map of South Africa was being redrawn. For example, when the central area of Cape Town, known as District Six, was proclaimed white in 1965, hundreds of Coloureds whose ancestors had lived there for generations were shunted off to new townships on the Cape Flats. Better houses, miles from town, did not assuage all the anger; nor did the fact that some of the bulldozed spaces, where their homes had once stood, were still bare of development sixteen years later.

Compensation was paid to families forced to move but rarely at the market price. Many of the areas proclaimed white were in spreading city suburbs. Fortunes were made by white speculators offering slightly more than the government rate. When the area had been cleared of dark skins, plots were sold off again for desirable white

Tents providing temporary accommodation for black families in a resettlement village

residence. Unsavoury tales were widespread of civil servants with advance knowledge of areas to be proclaimed, sharing in the bonanza. Families who had been evicted often found their compensation was not enough to buy again in the areas allocated to them out of town.

The Coloured and Indian communities bore much of the burden of the Group Areas Act. Seventy-three thousand families had been moved by the end of 1972 with thirty-eight thousand to go. In the same period only fifteen hundred white households were affected.

Elsewhere scores of African residential areas, in towns both large and small, were simply abolished and their occupants moved to one or other of the homelands. Areas known as 'black spots' where Africans had enjoyed property rights since the 1913 Natives Land Act (see page 69) were cleared. As Verwoerd sought to bring an end to the system of labour tenancy on white farms, surplus black labourers and their families were removed. On other farms, the squatters who had been a feature of agricultural life since the whites had helped themselves to great chunks of land, were evicted as well.

Over two million Africans had been resettled by the end of the seventies with another million still scheduled for removal. As one scheme which involved moving complete townships in the Potchefstroom area got under way, *Die Transvaler* reported that 'enthusiasm for the plan is running very high among the Tswanas of the western Transvaal'; but elsewhere a hundred other testimonies spoke of the misery of families uprooted from their homes. A fourteen-year-old Zulu boy named Mboma Dladla told one such a story:

One day the farmer said we must move off his farm at the end of the month. He said we must live on the other side of the Tugela river. We could not move as we had no homes to go to. The farmer was angry and the police burned our homes down. They forced us to move across the river. We made shelters from leaves and branches. Later we made new huts.[1]

Such removals were basic to the whole separate development plan. As Helen Suzman put it, 'they are part of the tidying-up process of the racial checkerboard'. Part of Verwoerd's final solution was that many more Africans should commute to their jobs from the homelands, sometimes up to seventy or eighty miles a day. Others who lived further away would leave their families and stay in bachelor hostels, going home whenever they could. Migrant labour had been a feature of the South African industrial practice for generations. Now it would be extended by reducing still further the number of blacks living in white areas. The family life of Africans was of no great concern to Nationalist governments; after all as Dr Connie Mulder, Minister of Plural Relations, told us in 1978: 'You'd be surprised how many of these blacks prefer migratory work. I think you should learn to know the soul of the black man. In many of these cases they prefer to be away from home for a certain period.'[2]

Many black families, moved by government decree, found themselves in what were called 'closer settlements'. They were closely packed resettlement areas where there was not enough space for tenants to grow crops or keep animals. New arrivals were supplied with a small plot and a tin hut and left to their own devices. Sometimes there was water supplied from communal taps; often there were no lavatories, no shops, no medical facilities, no schools, no jobs nor any prospect of any.[3] General Circular Number 25 sets out

---

[1] 'Mboma' by Mboma Dladla, as told to Kathy Bond, translated by her from the Zulu and published by the SA Institute of Race Relations.
[2] 'The White Tribe of Africa' Part Three, BBC-TV January 1979.
[3] An English-born priest, Father Cosmas Desmond spent six months visiting resettlement villages during 1969 and in *The Discarded People* drew attention to the appalling conditions he found. The names Limehill, Klipgat and Stinkwater were thrust into the national consciousness. Cosmas Desmond was silenced through banning and his book could no longer be distributed in South Africa.

Nondweni, a 'Closer Settlement' in Natal, known locally as 'Tin Town'

the standards that local authorities were supposed to observe:

Normally only a rudimentary lay-out on the basis of agricultural residential areas is undertaken . . . as the premises are not offered for sale. A common source of water where the inhabitants can fetch their water, either a borehole(s) equipped with a pump(s), a fountain, river or dam, is a pre-requisite. The inhabitants are also expected to install their own cesspit latrines together with the dwellings (traditional or otherwise). These settlements offer a refuge for squatters from European farms, black spots and missionary farms, to whom plots are allocated on which they may erect their own dwellings. A rental of R1.00 per annum is payable in accordance with Proclamation 92 of 1949.

Nondweni, in the Nqutu district of Northern Natal, is just such a resettlement village. It stands on what used to be white farmland bought up by the government and now administered by the office of the senior white civil servant in Natal, the Chief Commissioner. In due course it will be handed over to the homeland administration of Kwazulu. For the moment the responsibility for what happens there is in white hands; white officials give, or withhold permission to visit.

187

The first dispossessed Africans started to arrive on government trucks in 1976; there was not room aboard to bring all their belongings; nor were they allowed to bring livestock larger than fowls. Those who had been moved from white farms had often sold their cattle to the owners at knock-down prices or left them with relatives hoping to reclaim them one day. The families were installed on plots about twenty by thirty-five metres in the standard single-room tin huts; sometimes ten people shared a room. The huts were allocated initially for three months during which time families were expected to build their own mud huts. Wood was available at Nqutu twenty kilometres away but it was a long time before permission was given to cut it. Thatching grass had to be carried from farms far to the south.

Taps were installed but the pump supplying the reservoir broke down and was out of action for months. The villagers took what water they could from a *donga* (gulley) below the camp. In the first year of settlement the Chief Health Inspector of Dundee (a white town seventy kilometres to the west) reported that the new pit latrines were half full of water, and could soon overfill and pollute the water supply. There was a plan to install a bucket system but late in 1979 the original latrines were still in use and were still flooding. There was no refuse removal service.

Two cases of typhoid were diagnosed at the hospital of Nqutu in 1976 and doctors began vaccinating the whole population of what had become known as 'Tin Town'. They also requested the authorities to halt the resettlements there. But five thousand vaccinations later, doctors reported that new families were still arriving every day. Cases of typhoid continued to occur and so too, with increasing frequency, did the diseases relating to malnutrition.

With room to grow only a meagre plant or two, with no cattle to provide meat and milk, the Zulus of Nondweni inevitably declined. Apart from employment in constructing the village itself there was virtually no work. The hospital at Nqutu was the biggest employer in the district but there was no industry. So the able-bodied men had no choice but to leave and seek work elsewhere. For some families the only money coming in was the pension of a grandparent although the first arrivals in Nondweni had had to wait a year for their grants to be transferred.

At the Black Sash advice office in Johannesburg the Director, Sheena Duncan, explained the importance of the old age pension:

I heard of a nurse in a clinic and a grandmother who came in with three or four very small children in tow. The nurse gave the milk ration to the grandmother and made her drink it there and then. A person who was visiting this clinic said: 'But surely the milk should go to the children?' And the nurse turned round and said to her: 'In our situation you must understand. We have to keep that grandmother alive, because those four children are entirely dependent on her.'

At the Charles Johnson Memorial Hospital in Nqutu the doctors charted the steady growth of the population in the district and the decline in health. Tomlinson, in his report in 1954, had recommended that the area could support about thirteen thousand people. That would have meant absorbing some five thousand families elsewhere. But no such emigration occurred. By 1979 the doctors estimated the Nqutu district, including Nondweni, was supporting two hundred thousand. By 1980, Dr Bitty Muller, in charge of the children's ward, reported that half of all the children they admitted were under weight. Diseases directly attributable to poor diet, like marasmus and kwashiorkor were commonplace. In 1980 more than fifty children died from malnutrition, half of all the child deaths in the hospital. Nationally it was believed that fifty thousand children were liable to die from malnutrition in that year. The true figures may never be known; but all this was happening in a country which claimed that its per capita income was five times that of the rest of Africa.[1]

Nondweni meanwhile has shown some development. It can now boast a bottle store (owned by a member of the Kwazulu Legislative Assembly), a general store and a clinic. A school has been started in some of the buildings of the former white village. According to the authorities 'Tin Town' is a 'popular' place and people 'flock' there. Certainly the nominal R1 rents have attracted some. But residents in a nearby squatter settlement, under constant threat of removal, are not among them. Perhaps many of the applicants for plots were 'volunteers' in the government's sense. For, as M. C. Botha, John Vorster's Minister of Bantu Administration once put it in a fine example of van-der-Merwe-speak: 'On occasion we do have to use a good deal of persuasion to get them to move – but they are all volunteers.'[2]

Petrus Ndlovu, an old Zulu, recently arrived in Nondweni, surveyed his possessions piled up behind him in his one tin room, and expressed it another way: 'It is helpless to say whether we like it or not. If the government says go, then you go.'

[1] *Official Yearbook for South Africa*; 1978. Page 113.
[2] Johannesburg *Star* 21/11/69.

15

'*What is the use of teaching a Bantu child mathematics?*'

Hendrik Verwoerd addressing the Senate, June 1954
about government policy on black education

As the Nationalists erected their apparatus of Apartheid it was vital to prepare future generations for their role in the Grand Design. The white man's superiority must never be doubted, the Afrikaners' right to re-structure the whole of South African society must be unquestioned and men of colour must be taught to accept the position assigned to them. For all this, education was the key.

Most black schooling, and virtually all black teacher training was in the hands of the mission schools. For many whites, and not only Nationalists, the results were far from satisfactory. Dangerous 'liberal' ideas were being fed by outsiders into untrained minds, they said. A government commission, set up by the Nationalists in 1949, found the missions had 'achieved nothing but the destruction of Bantu culture . . . nothing beyond succeeding in making the native an imitation Westerner'. Even a fairly progressive journal, *The Forum*, wrote in 1953 that the 'academically educated non-European, with no roots in reality and his head full of book learning' could be 'a social misfit and a political danger'.

Verwoerd changed all that. His Bantu Education Act of 1953 removed control of black education from the provinces to the central government, although it was not the Ministry of Education that assumed responsibility but Verwoerd's own Department of Native Affairs. By reducing government aid to the mission schools, then stopping it altogether, Verwoerd forced most of them into the state system. Of some forty denominations of church school only the Roman Catholics could raise enough funds to maintain their independence; and all schools were required to register and follow the syllabus set by Pretoria. Next the government announced that it was taking over the training of black teachers, for, as Verwoerd explained to the Assembly in 1953, 'Good race relations cannot exist when education is given under the control of people who create wrong expectations on ıe part of the Native himself.'

The mission training colleges were given the choice of renting or
elling their premises to the government or giving up teacher training
nd starting primary or secondary schools instead. The government
llowed that the missions could go on training teachers entirely at their
wn expense but as Verwoerd made clear in parliament 'we shall not
ecessarily employ persons who have been trained at such private
:hools'. Those who were being transferred to the government pay-
ɔll were warned not to have too heady expectations. 'The Bantu
:acher serves the Bantu community and his salary must be fixed
ccordingly.' And Verwoerd let it be known that the new salary scales
ould 'possibly be less favourable than the existing scales.' A qualified
lack teacher in 1953 started at just over £2 a week and a university
raduate at just over £4, rising to £7 a week after thirteen years.

The immediate result of Verwoerd's measures was that the number
f black teachers in training dropped: from 8,817 in 1954 to 5,908 in
961. In 1953 the pupil-teacher ratio in black schools was 40 to 1: by
960 it had risen to 50 to 1. Correspondingly, examination results
eteriorated. In 1953, 259 blacks passed matriculation; in 1961 the
ɔtal was down to 115.

Not that such statistics were of great concern to the Nationalist
overnment. Dr Verwoerd measured black achievement by com-
letely different standards, as he explained in the Senate debate on his
ßantu Education Act:

he school must equip the Bantu to meet the demands which the economic
fe of South Africa will impose on him . . . There is no place for him in the
uropean community above the level of certain forms of labour. Within his
wn community, however, all doors are open . . . Until now he has been
ubject to a school system which drew him away from his own community
nd misled him by showing him the green pastures of European society in
ɹhich he is not allowed to graze . . . What is the use of teaching a Bantu child
ıathematics when it cannot use it in practice? . . . That is absurd. Education
; not, after all, something that hangs in the air. Education must train and
:ach people in accordance with their opportunities in life . . . It is therefore
ecessary that native education should be controlled in such a way that it
hould be in accordance with the policy of the State.

Ϲhat policy was by now all too clear and nowhere more so than in the
ɪoney allocated to Verwoerd's new Department of Bantu Education.
Vhile the number of black children at school doubled between 1954
nd 1965, government spending showed no corresponding increase.
n his *History of Education in South Africa*, Malherbe calculated that

191

during that same period, the expenditure in real terms on each black pupil dropped from R8.7 to R4.9. At the same time spending on white child rose from approximately R50 to R75.

The legacy of these years of calculated neglect is not easily erased By 1975, although government funding had hugely increased, nearly half of black children aged between six and nineteen were not in school, and of the four and a half million who were, one in four was being taught through double sessions because of the shortage of schools and staff. That involved dividing each age group into two sections, one attending in the morning, the other in the afternoon using the same classrooms and the same weary teachers. As far as the qualifications of black teachers were concerned, by 1977 only one in fifty had a university degree and only one in nine had passed matric.[1]

The effects of such poor learning conditions are now widespread according to Dr Chris Cresswell, the head of the Department of Botany at the University of Witwatersrand. 'Most of the able black men around today', he said, 'were brought up pre-Bantu Education Men like Gatsha Buthelezi and Nthatho Motlana. But today the product of black schools is disastrous.'

Michael Corke, headmaster of St Barnabas College, a private school in Johannesburg, says Bantu Education:

produces young blacks who suffer from lack of confidence in dealing with privileged whites, and whose skills in communication and understanding are poorly developed. Their command of English, even as a second language, is unsatisfactory and they show a marked neglect of the early development of conceptual thought.

Black educational aspirations were further affected by another government measure put forward in 1957 under the relentless logic of Apartheid. The Minister of Education, J. H. Viljoen, proposed to put an end to integrated education at university level. Until then black students had been allowed to enrol for degree courses at white universities, usually the three main English language universities Witwatersrand, Cape Town and Natal. From now on blacks were to be provided with their own 'ethnic' universities. There was to be one for Zulus, another for Sothos, Tswanas and the northern tribes, one for the Indians and another for the Coloureds. It was important said the Minister, that the future leader should remain 'in close touch with

---

[1] Comparative figures for white teachers were 29.6% with a degree, 64.9% with matric; from *Education in South Africa*, Vol. 2, by Dr E. G. Malherbe, and 'Conflict and Progress in Education' by the same author from *Fifty Years of Race Relations in S.A.*; Macmillan SA Ltd, 1979.

the habits, ways of life and views of his population group.'

The existing university college of Fort Hare, that was affiliated to Rhodes university, had long drawn students from all over Africa. But it was now to be reduced to a Xhosa tribal college. The tradition which helped form Nelson Mandela, Gatsha Buthelezi, Robert Mugabe and Charles Njonjo, the Attorney General of Kenya was to be set aside. In the eyes of the Minister, Fort Hare was nothing but an English University for non-whites and he said as much in parliament. What the Xhosa needed, he said, was an institution of their own, expressing their own culture and rooted in their own community. Knocking a final nail into the coffin of academic freedom the Minister also announced that it would be a punishable offence (a fine of R200 or six months' imprisonment) for a black to register at a white univerity without his permission.

Once more the protests swelled. The University of the Witwatersrand pledged itself 'to uphold the principle that a university is a place where men and women, without regard to race and colour are welcome to join in the acquisition and advancement of knowledge.' In Cape Town three thousand demonstrated outside Parliament when the Bill came up, among them a recently retired Chief Justice of South Africa, the Chancellor of the University of Cape Town, his Principal, and vice-Principal, many of his teaching staff and most of the students. Inside, the Minister told members that 'the only possible inference is that this agitation is taking place under the influence of a leftist movement in our country.'

At Malherbe's university, Natal, there were nine hundred black, Indian and Coloured students, most of them in the separate Medical School for blacks that was, nonetheless, part of the university. It had been set up during the Smuts' government and had opened only in 1951. When the Nationalists proposed that it should be placed under the direct control of Pretoria, the entire staff of the Medical School, whites, blacks and Indians, threatened to resign. 'The argument lasted for two years', Malherbe recalled. 'We received support from all over South Africa, and we attacked on every front.' In the end the government gave way and the black Medical School survives to this day. By 1980 its one thousandth graduate doctor was already in practice.

In the hope of winning a reprieve for the other faculties as well, Malherbe invited the acting Minister of Education, John Vorster, to Durban, and spent three hours showing him round the university. He remembered Vorster's total refusal to accept his arguments, that to restrict black students to the confines of strictly tribal colleges was the very negation of university education, that the huge sums the government was allocating to establish these separate institutions would be far better spent extending courses at existing universities.

The University of Natal was far from integrated, as Malherbe acknowledges. Lectures for blacks were separate although the staff was the same; blacks ate and slept in their own hostels. But even that was too much for the man from Pretoria. 'Vorster's mind was closed' said Malherbe. 'He just kept saying that it was government policy to educate blacks and whites separately and that was that.'

By 1959 the extraordinarily named '*Extension of University Education Act*' was law and the battle was lost. Students who had already registered were allowed to complete their courses but for many others it meant the end of academic hopes. 'The Zulus, who had had their homes in Durban for many generations,' said Malherbe, 'and who had "earned while they learned" as part-time students, were told that if they still wanted to have a university education, they could either get it by correspondence or go to the new college for Zulus about a hundred miles away at Ngoya. The Indian students were not so seriously affected because their college was to be established at Westville, just outside Durban. The Coloureds, of whom there were a considerable number in Natal, were forbidden access not only to our university but also to the Indian University. If they wanted a university education they had to travel twelve hundred miles to the College for Coloureds at the Cape. Hardly any of them ever went because of the expense and also because the medium of instruction was Afrikaans which was quite strange to them.'

The government exercised rigid control over the staff of the five tribal colleges. At Fort Hare, which had been teaching blacks, Coloureds and Indians since 1923, the Principal was sacked as were eight other senior members of his multi-racial staff. In the Assembly the Minister said, 'I disposed of their services because I will not permit a penny of any funds over which I have control to be paid to any persons who are known to be destroying the government's policy of Apartheid.' The Vice-Principal and four other members of staff resigned. The men appointed to replace them and the ones to take the key posts at the four new colleges were usually Afrikaners, and invariably members of the Broederbond as well.

The courses offered by the tribal colleges were limited mainly to arts and humanities with little science and no engineering. Should subjects not be available, blacks could apply to study at white universities but permission was not readily granted by the government. In 1960 the Minister reported that he had received one hundred and ninety applications from Africans to enrol at white universities but had approved only four. Seven applicants who wished to study engineering at the University of Witwatersrand had been refused permission because, in the Minister's opinion, there were as yet 'no prospects of employment for qualified Bantu engineers'.

Malherbe, trying to build on the exemption that had been granted to his Medical School, applied to found a veterinary college for blacks in Natal. Improved animal husbandry in the overcrowded homelands was desperately needed. The government's own Tomlinson report had highlighted the problem. Malherbe had already been offered the free use of a plot of land by a Zulu chief and some funds were available. But the request was categorically refused. Malherbe is convinced that ideological reasons were the cause. In South Africa, veterinary surgeons are a step higher up the professional ladder than dip inspectors and often give them instructions. But dip inspectors at that time were white; and blacks in South Africa rarely give orders to whites. In 1980 there were still no black vets.

In *The Rise of the South African Reich*, Brian Bunting recalls the case of Reginald Boleu, a black student at the University of the North, who wanted to study atomic physics. There were no facilities at any of the tribal colleges and he was unable to gain admission to the white universities where such courses were available. When he won a scholarship to Uppsala University in Sweden the Anglo-American Corporation arranged to pay his expenses. But after a delay of a year, Reginald Boleu's application for a passport to enable him to take up his scholarship was refused by the government. He was compelled to apply for an exit permit which meant that he would be unable to return to the country and would automatically be deprived of his citizenship. The exit permit was granted within a few weeks.

In 1979, adding an ironic postscript to the story, the President of the South African Atomic Energy Board, Dr Ampie Roux, drew attention to a shortfall of seventeen thousand engineering technicians at all levels in the Republic. The annual output of three thousand technically trained people, he said, was far short of the demand. 'Widespread efforts to attract suitable technicians from overseas have borne little fruit,' he went on, 'and it is evident that South Africa will increasingly have to rely on its own resources . . . One solution to the shortfall is to train blacks as technicians.' In 1980, Professor Gideon Jacobs, director of the Graduate School of Business Administration

195

at the University of Witwatersrand, estimated that one hundred thousand jobs remained unfilled and described the lack of skills as the most serious problem industry faced.

So the ethnic chickens have come home to roost. What opponents of Apartheid have been pointing out for thirty years has now become apparent to Nationalists as well; that by refusing to develop the potential of its black citizens South Africa has stultified its own growth. Nor is that the only consequence of Apartheid in education. The government's systematic attempts to produce generations of docile, unambitious blacks have now rebounded in its face.

Malherbe recalls that after John Vorster, the Acting Minister of Education, had completed his visit to the University of Natal, he had accompanied him to the airport. When Malherbe reached home, still seething with the frustration of his attempts to change the mind of a Nationalist politician, he sat down and started to write a pamphlet in Afrikaans called 'The Autonomy of our Universities and Apartheid'. It was published in 1957, and forecasts with remarkable prescience what was to befall the tribal universities.

These isolated institutions in the Native areas may easily become centres of political disaffection, for, no matter how strict the supervision may be, it is impossible to isolate non-European students from outside influences. They read newspapers and will undoubtedly be exposed to expressions of discontent with the various disabilities under which their people suffer. This will not be avoided by placing the institution in the native rural areas. A little yeast of discontent will soon leaven the whole lump. In an isolated group of this kind there is a strong tendency for a grievance to be cherished, so that sooner or later, there is an outbreak that may have disastrous results.

Or, to put it more bluntly, as Malherbe did to the future Prime Minister of South Africa. 'They'll hate your bush colleges so much that I bet you they burn the bloody places down.'

Nearly twenty years later, on 16 June 1976, Malherbe's prediction began to come tragically true. A protest about the enforced teaching of various subjects in Afrikaans in the black schools of Soweto developed into a full scale confrontation. The government had been warned for months that young blacks were no longer prepared to accept the system imposed from Pretoria but answered protest only with force. In the riots which spread across South Africa six hundred people died.

At the University of Zululand students burned down the library and administrative buildings and the university was closed for the rest of the year. On 19 July the Teachers Training College at

Black children protesting against enforced teaching in Afrikaans, Alexandra township, June 1976

Lovedale in the Cape, once one of the most famous of the old mission schools, was badly damaged by fire. The administrative buildings at the University of the Western Cape, for Coloureds, went up in flames on 5 August. There was rioting and attempted arson at Fort Hare during the same period with the university closed for a month; strikes and violence disrupted both the University of the North and the University for Indians at Durban-Westville. It was an outpouring of years of discontent.

The government can hardly claim to have had no warning. When Dr Werner Eiselen, Verwoerd's right-hand man, headed the Commission in 1951 that provided the basis for the Bantu Education Act, he reported that 'the Bantu child comes to school with a basic physical and psychological endowment which differs, so far as your Commissioners have been able to determine from the evidence, so slightly, if at all from that of the European child that no special provision has to be made in educational theory or basic aims.' He also stated that Africans who had given evidence showed 'an extreme aversion to any education specially adapted for the Bantu.' But then Verwoerd and his fellows, like Lord Somerset and Lord Milner before them, did not always trouble themselves with other peoples' views.

16

'With propaganda you never let up'

An SABC political commentator

For all the Apartheid energy that went into reorganising black education, yet more was devoted to resolving once and for all the way young
whites should be taught. Above all, the gurus of the Broederbond
who dominated Nationalist thinking on the issue, insisted that impressionable Afrikaners of school age must be removed from the
influence of English language and thought. The policy of the Smuts
government had been to work towards a broad South African nationhood by sending Afrikaans and English speakers to the same schools,
albeit to different classrooms. The Nationalists had long been committed to putting that system into reverse.

As with blacks, so with whites. Separation was the keynote. 'We
want no mixing of languages, no mixing of cultures, no mixing of
religions,' said the Broederbond blueprint on education in 1948.
Bilingualism was an evil to be avoided at all costs.

All researchers in this field are agreed that bilingual children show backward-
ness in development compared with unilingual children'[wrote Piet Meyer in
1945]. It is definitely certain that godlessness is more prevalent among
bilingual people than among those who are unilingual.[1]

During a language debate in the Assembly in 1952, Harm Oost, a
member for Pretoria said that the bilingual child was a bad Afrikaner
because he was 'neither fish nor flesh and had no national backbone'.

For Meyer and Oost and all those who thought like them the
Afrikaner had to be nurtured with his own and by his own. In their
eyes what made the Afrikaner different from his fellow South Africans
was more important that what made him the same. Afrikaner academics like Malherbe who, from a lifetime of research and experience,
argued precisely the opposite, were ignored.

[1] *Moedertaal en Tweetaligheid (Mother-tongue and Bilingualism)* Verkenners-Necks
No 8; 1945.

198

The emphasis on difference had helped restore the Afrikaner to the position of power in which he now found himself in 1948. Now the whole philosophy of difference would be used to keep him there. The means would be what the Broederbond called 'Christian National Education' through which 'our children will be saturated with the Christian and National spiritual stuff of our nation'. Alan Paton never had any doubts about the real meaning of such a concept:

This is a system of education that has two supreme goals, to make a child a Christian and to make him a Nationalist, but it comes very close to identifying the two goals so that being a Christian and being a Nationalist become almost the same thing.[1]

By 1967 the machinery was in place. The National Education Policy Bill of that year decreed that Afrikaner and English children, at both primary and secondary level would go to separate schools, or where numbers made that impractical, at least to separate classes. The medium of instruction would be the home language only. The parents had little say in the matter. If the home language was English, the child would go to an English school and vice versa. If the child was equally proficient in both languages the parents could choose the school but in cases of doubt the principal or school inspector had the last word. As Verwoerd had explained in 1953: 'The fundamental thing about education is not the wish of the parents, often a selfish wish, but the interests of the child.'

Not that all parents objected to the notion of separate education. Smuts's dual medium schools had not been the success that bilingual South Africans like Malherbe had hoped; and that was by no means the fault only of Afrikaners. Conservative English speakers, particularly in Natal, had thought it was an excellent idea for Afrikaners to be taught through the medium of English but not at all so desirable that their own children should be given some of their lessons in Afrikaans. The superiority complex of English speakers had not been destroyed by a couple of adverse election results.

So the dual medium schools were gradually disestablished. Many new schools had to be built. It was a huge and costly venture of duplication but it was vital, Nationalists believed, if young Afrikaners were to be saved. Indeed, many more of the Volk were now exposed to the dangers of anglicisation as the Afrikaner trek from the land to the towns and cities had continued in the post-war years. Once the chil-

[1] 'The Afrikaner as I know him', from *The Afrikaners*. Edited by Edwin S. Munger; Tafelberg, Capetown, 1979.

dren were safely corralled again in their own language schools Malherbe believed the temptation to indoctrinate them was irresistible. As one teacher put it to him: 'If you have the children of only one section in the class, then you can really go to town with the teaching of history.'

For the Broederbond, the formal separation of Afrikaner and English schooling was one of their most important achievements. At their secret fiftieth anniversary congress in 1968, Piet Meyer, now the Chairman, expressed everyone's satisfaction:

It is our Brotherhood, that with unstinting labour at Bond Councils, in study committees and in consultation with education heads at provincial and national levels, who were and are Broeders, has been able to formulate the ideal of a national educational policy for our nation and country. We have carried it through to its present stage, and will continue to do so in the years that lie ahead.

At that time the full extent of Broederbond control of education was still not known but in 1973 Hennie Serfontein, an Afrikaner journalist, writing in the Johannesburg *Sunday Times*, published a series of secret Broederbond minutes and documents passed to him by a dissident member. They confirmed all the fears that Malherbe had expressed to General Smuts at the end of the war about the spreading Broederbond influence.

Out of close on ten thousand members of the Broederbond in 1972, 1,691 were in the teaching profession: 121 school inspectors, 468 head masters and 647 ordinary teachers were Broeders. In higher education the Bond could claim 24 rectors of universities and teacher training colleges, 171 professors and 176 lecturers. Even more important were the Broeders who filled top administrative positions in the Department of Education. The Directors of Education in the four provinces were all members and so was the Chairman of the National Education Advisory Council.

The Broederbond has thus placed its stamp on every aspect of education. They influenced policy, the curriculum of state schools, examinations and teacher training.

Education [said Hennie Serfontein in our BBC television series] is not open education. It is education with a specific task. The aim is the preservation of the white man in general and of the Afrikaner in particular. That means that if you come from twelve years in school, where you have been under Broederbond control, then four years in a teacher training college, being indoctrinated with Broederbond thinking, with separation and the whole of that

200

philosophy, by the time you are a teacher it is not important whether you are a Broeder or not. The fact is, you will teach Broederbond philosophy because you do not know any other. You have not been exposed to any other thinking.

We filmed a striking example of the effect of Afrikaner education at a Voortrekker Easter Competition Camp outside Pretoria. Voortrekker units from all over the Transvaal had gathered for a week of Afrikaner togetherness. There was rifle shooting, tracking, sentry duty, assault courses and competitions for knowledge of Afrikaner history as well as for the more traditional scouting skills. But also there were political sessions under a senior Voortrekker organiser, Jan Oelofse, a Pretoria attorney, who also happened to be a member of the Broederbond.

The subject for discussion that day, as Oelofse put it to the group, was:

the insistence of the Western world that South Africa should allow a vote to everyone, so that the majority (i.e. the blacks) will rule here. There will be no more talk of separate states but one parliament in which everybody will sit together and where affairs in this country will be decided by the majority. Just as it works in other Western countries.

What were the views of his group of Voortrekkers?

From one innocent young Afrikaner after another came the same answers. Our system is different. It is wrong that the outside world should see us as one country because here there are different volk with different identities. We give the vote to each nation in its own homeland. In their own states the blacks can work out their own destiny. We already have one man one vote, said one pretty girl not more than thirteen, it is simply that each man votes for the parliament in his own country. Although one volk is in the minority, said another, the one with the highest intellectual development should run the country because in the long run this works out best for everyone. It would be suicide if everyone voted together, was another view. We would lose our identity. It would make a faceless mass of the volk with a few leadership figures, as it happens in communist countries. If we give each volk its own government, said a boy treading delicate ground, it does not necessarily mean we will take them out of our cities. There would not be enough jobs for them. And finally, you cannot expect different blacks to live together – look at Soweto – that is why we give each volk its own territory.

No one, that day, questioned government policy, although Oelofse assured us that young people often did. All we heard was a constant juvenile repetition of the same views which pour forth from Pretoria.

It was a chilling experience.

The Voortrekkers, of course, are all part of the Afrikaner training ground. A boy or girl who shows leadership qualities is carefully nurtured through the three levels of the Voortrekker movement, the *Penkoppies*, the *Verkenners* and the *Staatmakers* (cubs, scouts and 'stalwarts'), until at the senior level the leaders, often university students by then, take their turn in training the juniors. For all of them it is the most natural thing in the world to espouse Afrikaner Nationalism.

At every stage, as Oelofse explained, young Afrikaners are being tested, screened and selected. Some go to special leadership courses run by the South African Bureau for Racial Affairs, SABRA, one of the Broederbond affiliates. Others prove themselves in the junior Rapportryers.[1] For the chosen few, although that Oelofse did not say, there will be membership of the junior Broederbond. Only Afrikaner men between the ages of eighteen and twenty-eight are eligible. At a secret ceremony they dedicate themselves to much the same aims as the parent Broederbond itself.

When Afrikaners go on to one of their own universities they are, except at Stellenbosch, automatically made members of the ASB, the *Afrikaanse Studentebond*, the Afrikaner student union founded by Piet Meyer in 1933. The ASB, like all the other Afrikaner 'cultural' organisations is affiliated to the FAK. Its offices are in the Broederbond headquarters at Auckland Park, Johannesburg. Thus the Broederbond oversees the activities of Afrikaner youth, doing its best to keep them from dangerous contact with the outside world.

In 1965 when a new university was proposed in Johannesburg to provide a base for Afrikaner scholarship in that largely English-speaking commercial centre, the Minister for Education, Senator de Klerk outlined the major task that awaited it. The role of the Rand Afrikaans University, he said, was to uproot 'the destructive forces' of liberalism, communism and humanism which, he implied, flourished at the existing English-language University of the Witwatersrand. It would be the duty of the new university, of students and lecturers alike, to foster those things which were truly South African. On this the future of white civilisation depended.

The dangers of English so-called liberal thought had long been pointed out to Afrikaners. Albert Hertzog, from his position as Minister of Posts, Telegraphs and Health to which he had been appointed

---

[1] Literally 'Dispatch riders'; an organisation not unlike the English Rotary movement but usually more active.

by Dr Verwoerd, warned parents in 1964 not to send their children to English medium universities because of their 'disregard for national pride and the pride of being of white descent.' Hertzog went on:

They foster among our future leaders, a disrespect for our community's customs and even its laws and policies . . . They permit the erosion and destruction of souls of our young people because of the liberalistic or leftist, perhaps even semi-communistic, influences at work in the English-speaking universities.

But the leaders of Nationalist thought did more than rail against this 'erosion of souls'. They proposed to begin a counter-process of their own. The secret minutes of a Broederbond Executive Committee meeting on 1 December 1965 record a remarkable discussion about relations with English speakers. The chairman was Piet Meyer; among the members of the Executive who were present were Piet Koornhof, in due course to become Minister of Education and later Minister of Black Affairs; Dr Andries Treurnicht, Meyer's successor as chairman of the Broederbond and later leader of the National Party in the Transvaal; and S. P. Botha, known as 'Fanie', Minister of Labour under both John Vorster and P. W. Botha.

Under item twenty-one the executive resolved 'that a committee be set up to investigate the possibility of Afrikanerising English speakers and to see what role the teaching of history in school can play.' In the words of the Chairman, returning to this theme in his address to the general council of the Broederbond ten months later, the English were to become 'English-speaking Afrikaners'.

The Afrikanerisation of the English speakers in our country thus means in essence that the English speaker has to make the Afrikans world-view his own; that he will integrate his ideals and life-style with those of the Afrikaner; that he will adopt Afrikans history as his own; that he will accept Afrikaans as his national language, alongside English as the international community language.

It was an extraordinary enterprise, to attempt to achieve in reverse precisely what Milner had failed to do to the Afrikaners themselves; but the Broederbond was better placed to succeed. The educational hierarchy was dominated by Broeders. When headmasterships came up in the English-speaking schools, many went to trusted members of the Volk. In the staff rooms too, Afrikaner headmasters recruited Afrikaner teachers. The process had been going on for years. Within a few years of the 1967 Education Act sixty per cent of the staff at some of the English schools in the cities were Afrikaners. In the country

203

areas the imbalance was even more marked.

The government also insisted that in every school a certain quota of teachers should be men. Particularly at primary school level there were not enough English speakers to fill the vacant posts; so they went instead to yet more Afrikaners. Nationalists said that the English had only themselves to blame if their young men preferred the more lucrative world of commerce to teaching. But as the promotion prospects for English speakers worsened so their numbers decreased still further.

Subtly, and not so subtly, Afrikaner teachers have placed their imprint on impressionable English minds. Not a few parents have had reason to complain of the lessons carried home by their offspring. One favourite amounted to a child's guide to racial classification with always the emphasis on difference. The white man had: 'fair skin' and 'straight hair'. The Indians, 'brown skin', and 'black hair', while the 'Natives' had 'thick lips', and 'crinkly hair'. Similarly the children were taught that whites lived in 'houses', the 'Bantu' in 'huts'. As for their jobs – white men were lawyers and doctors; Indians shop-owners and waiters; 'Natives' were garden boys and miners.

Such a view of the social hierarchy in South Africa was further reinforced by school text books. Dr Franz Auerbach, who became President of the English-speaking Transvaal Teachers Association, wrote a thesis on *The Power of Prejudice in South African Education*. One of the most striking examples of Nationalist propaganda he found was in the following extract from a school book:

It is, however, not only the skin of the White South African that differs from that of the non-White. The White stands on a much higher plane of civilisation and is more developed. Whites must so live, learn and work that we shall not sink to the cultural level of the non-White. Only thus can the government of our country remain in the hands of the Whites.

The Afrikaner view of history that began to permeate the classroom soon went well beyond an undue concentration on the Great Trek or a convenient lapse of memory concerning who really fought at Blood River.[1]

An English-speaking girl recalled that when she was at school and

[1] One of the researchers for our BBC television series recalled, only half-jokingly, her memories of history lessons in her English-speaking school. 'In the first year we learned about the Great Trek, how many had gone, how they lived and what happened to them. In the second year we were taught the names of all the families on the Trek and learned by heart all the parts of a trekker wagon.' And in the third year? 'We revised the first two years.'

wrote an essay about the Voortrekker battle of Vegkop, 'where the Bantu fought the Boers', her Afrikaner teacher made it clear that if she wanted a better mark she must 'always put the Boers first'. Auerbach today says that many of his English-speaking contemporaries are now completely cynical about teaching history. 'Often we simply tell a class, "Look, this is really what happened but if you put that in your examination paper you will fail".'

Elsewhere in his thesis Auerbach traced other Nationalist obsessions. One of them was the threat to the state from outside forces. He found it vividly portrayed in a textbook exercise:

The *Special Branch* of the South African Police is responsible for the *Internal Security* of the country. Although these men receive no publicity, they have the most difficult task of all the police. It is *Common Knowledge* that *Spies* from other countries are even at this moment trying to obtain *Vital Information* about South Africa. Every hour of the day *Secret Transmitters* transmit *Messages in Code* to various parts of the world.

In an era of *Phone Tapping* and *Hidden Microphones*, of *Riots* and *Sabotage*, the security forces have to *Combat Espionage* tactfully and efficiently without causing *International Incidents*. This extremely difficult task is further complicated by the fact that *Unscrupulous agents use Embassies* of their country and *Abuse the Immunity accorded to Diplomats in Foreign Countries*.

It is fortunate that the *Average Citizen* is unaware of the *Plots and Counterplots* that are hatched daily . . .

Oral composition: C (i) You are head of the Security Branch of the S.A. Police. In a secret interview with the Minister of Justice, tell him why you are so alarmed.

The propaganda onslaught is continued at what is known as the *Veldskool*, or bush school, which has become part of the educational programme of all young whites in the State system, English and Afrikaans speakers alike. The week-long courses, separate for boys and girls, are run by the provincial authorities. Most children attend at least once in their school career, usually at the age of fifteen or sixteen. On occasion, some of the teachers go with them. The letter to one headmaster explained that the aim of the course was 'to lead the child towards self-realisation, to emphasise his place within the Creation, and to cultivate a love for his Fatherland'.

The emphasis at first is on physical preparedness; on long marches, assault courses, tracking and map-reading. At night there is guard duty round a fire which must be kept burning; there may be a mock alarm in the small hours. Reveille is soon after five a.m., followed by inspection, flag raising and morning prayers. 'If you don't sing the anthem well enough,' said one boy who had been through it all, 'the Uncles [the Afrikaner camp leaders] make you "go through the tunnel", crawl through the legs of other boys as they wallop you on the backside.' In the afternoon or evening there are lectures, films and discussions.

Communism is a regular subject. 'We had one lecture on it', said the same boy, 'that lasted for three hours.' To their captive audience the Uncles explain the way that communists are trying to undermine the South African way of life. Arms boycotts, oil boycotts, sports boycotts, one course was told, were communist-inspired as was the unrest in Iran. 'The communists are everywhere. They are even in the government of the United States. I am not giving names but you will see in the 1980 elections.'

Above all, and this is confirmed by virtually anyone who has been to a Veldskool, children are warned of the way the communists are concentrating on them, the future leaders of South Africa. They must beware of pop music, of drugs, of jeans, of T-shirts, the insidious weapons that are being used to break down their moral fibre. Butterfly signs on trousers mean a girl of easy virtue, so does a badge of an apple with a worm in it.

Everyone must be on his guard against the terrorists. There are hundreds of them in Soweto. Speak to your servant about them, was one instruction, and if you notice something strange about her behaviour do not be afraid to tell the police. On one course the pupils were given a police telephone number and told to ask for Jasper, who like his Northern Irish equivalent would gratefully receive all information given confidentially. On another, in the Orange Free State, twelve-year-olds were taught to sing with appropriate actions, a song that included the lines 'We hate Mugabe, we hate terrorists. Kill them all'.

And at the end of the week at the Veldskool, what sort of impression is left? 'Look,' said my young friend, 'the *Ous* (the fellows) really enjoyed it. All that marching and PT. They come back saying when can we go again?'

In its bid to impose a so-called Afrikaner 'world-view' on the whole of South Africa, the Nationalist government had not neglected to give itself a monopoly in perhaps the most persuasive medium of all: broadcasting. When Albert Hertzog was appointed Minister of Posts, Telegraphs and Health in 1958 one of his first acts was to invite his

friend Piet Meyer to take over the Chairmanship of the South African
Broadcasting Corporation, a post he held from 1 August 1959 until he
retired in 1980. In November 1960 Meyer also became Chairman of
the Broederbond.

Before Meyer the SABC was modelled very much on the BBC. In
1936 the Prime Minister, General Hertzog, had even invited Lord
Reith to suggest how South Africa's infant broadcasting service, at
that time commercially run, could be developed. In fact the SABC
virtually adopted the BBC charter. It also regularly relayed BBC news
broadcasts: when they were ended after the war there was strong
reaction, and not only from English listeners. But since then the
SABC has gone its own way. As Meyer told his General Council of the
Broederbond in 1972: 'We must harness all our communications
media in a positive way in order to gather up the Afrikaners' national-
political energy in the struggle for survival in the future . . . Our
members must play a leading role.'

The first casualty under Meyer's reorganisation was the Director-
General, Gideon Roos. An Afrikaner, a former Rhodes scholar and
Oxford rugby blue, Roos was one of the pioneers of broadcasting in
South Africa; his daily reports on the 1938 Trek had virtually established the new service in Afrikaans. A fervent nationalist, he saw
nevertheless the broadcaster's role as a reporter, and not a propagan-
dist. Gradually his responsibilities as Director-General were whittled
away and the break finally came in 1961 after Meyer had announced
that the SABC would have its own editorial policy. Roos resigned. 'I
told Piet Meyer that he would destroy all I had built up, I did not want
to be a member of the demolition squad. The SABC should serve all
the people. It should have no editorial policy of its own.'

Steadily Meyer filled key managerial and editorial posts with his
fellow-thinkers. By 1977 Serfontein's contact could name forty-nine
Broeders in the SABC. By 1978 at least four of the nine members of
the Board of Management were members of the Broederbond.

The man who was later appointed as Director General was
Douglas Fuchs, a leading Broeder, himself and a former broadcaster.
Now retired, he speaks with a missionary fervour of 'the cultural
heritage of the different Bantu nations', of the SABC's role as 'the
custodian of that tradition in song and language' and of his pride in the
eight separate language services the SABC broadcasts twenty-four
hours a day. He believes with passion that 'there is a sanctity in
divergence'; and as for Apartheid: 'People tell us that it is impossible,
that it is utterly illogical. We say we don't mind. We say it must work.'

As the government strives to put its ideals into practice, he is con
vinced the SABC must play its part. 'We are at war', says Fuchs. 'W
are involved in the politics of survival. The SABC cannot stand aside.
The role of the South African broadcaster, he maintains, is to repor
on 'positive achievement', to prevent dissension among South Africa'
different nations and to counteract the negative criticism of the Eng
lish language Press and of the outside world. 'We cannot cast doubt o
the rulers of the country. No useful purpose can be served by causin
the public distrust of our leaders' policies.'[1]

Within the terms they have assigned themselves, the broadcastin
Broeders have made an undeniable impact. The government view
point permeates every news bulletin. No minister can officiate at th
opening of a dam or a power station without the attentive presence o
an SABC camera. There are few worrying discussions about th
problems of implementing Apartheid. The Minister for Co-operatio
and Development or the Prime Minister himself pays a state visit t
one of the 'black states' and is received by grinning acolytes an
singing children.

No critics of the regime appear in live discussion; a tightly edite
snippet is all that Helen Suzman, Gatsha Buthelezi or Nthatho Mot
lana can expect, but enough for the government to be able to say i
parliament that the opposition is not unrepresented. At election time
the SABC purports to remove itself from the actual politicking an
does not broadcast party political programmes. The statements o
Ministers, nevertheless, continue to fill the air waves; as members o
the government they are said to be above the party political fray. Wha
they say, goes the SABC argument, is not so much politics as news.

The visitors to South Africa who are interviewed are always reliable
the retired General from NATO who reaffirms the importance of th
Cape sea route; the governor of New Hampshire who insists they hav
ghettos back home worse than Soweto; the British Conservative MI
who supports sporting contacts – 'I've had letters from all over Bri
tain', he says, offering sweet music to the ears of every red-bloode
white South African. No one speaks for the other side.

From 'overseas' the news suggests a world continually obsesse
with matters South African. For years figures like President Amin o

[1] During our research for the filming of *The White Tribe of Africa*, David Dimbleby
researcher Mike Dutfield and I spent a stimulating evening as Fuchs' guests on hi
farm near Warmbad, north of Pretoria. Some months later Eschel Rhoodie, th
Secretary for Information, told us that Fuchs had been deeply offended by ou
questions and had let it be known on the Broederbond network that we were to b
treated with suspicion.

Jganda provided reams of ridicule and revulsion. Amin, it could be rgued, did more for the cause of Separate Development than Eschel Rhoodie himself. Setbacks like the sabotage at the prestige oil-from- oal plant at SASOL, blown up by black nationalists in 1980, provide he opportunity to stiffen the resolve of the white population. 'The .ttack', said the SABC news on 4 June 1980, 'was a Communist plot . . the work of the Russian-led ANC'. Meanwhile SABC hit tunes xtol the bravery of 'The Boys on the Border' and in 'Forces Favour- tes', their favourite, Pat encourages troopies and loved ones alike to *Vasbyt!'* (Be strong!) and 'Keep the beers on ice'.

For the programme makers who work inside the SABC, life is often lemoralising. Nothing goes out unchecked; the Uncles are every- vhere. Films are constantly re-cut and re-scripted; some are simply ut on the shelf. A producer who initiated too daring a political nterview was moved to sport; another was rapped over the knuckles or allowing an uncomplimentary remark about politicians by com- dian Max Bygraves. An imported television series for children was ensored because it included a sequence of children making fun of a carecrow, and hence authority. The studio director of one of the first nixed variety shows to be televised in South Africa in front of an udience of mixed race was instructed not to cut from a shot of a black erformer to a white person applauding or vice versa. The cuts were to e from black to black or white to white.

As a constant background, after the radio news, morning and even- ng, come the editorials: 'News Comment' and 'Current Affairs' in nglish, Afrikaans and in each of the African languages, praising the overnment here, attacking its opponents there. They tell of pro- ress, of constitutional evolution, of consolidation and co-operation. They speak of 'self-determination' and of 'separate freedoms'. They ing of 'coexistence in this multi-racial, multi-ethnic and multi- ultural population'. The African reserves have become homelands; he homelands have become national states bound together in a con- tellation of contentment. On SABC radio, all is for the best in the best f all separate worlds. 'It is through this medium', wrote black author Vltutuzela Matshoba, 'that the minds of my people are stolen.'[1]

Alexander Steward, one of the senior political commentators, was nce asked by journalist Marshall Lee why 'Current Affairs' never leviated from the government line; would not the message carry more onviction if there was occasional criticism of Pretoria's mistakes? 'By

Call me not a Man, Ravan Press, Johannesburg 1979.

asking that,' said Steward, 'it shows you do not understand the ways of propaganda. With propaganda you never let up'.

The Broederbond seems well content with the machine it has created. At the fiftieth anniversary congress in 1968 Henning Klopper was loud in praise of his chairman: 'When you stand at the helm there, at the SABC, you must know that we are with you in spirit. We support you in your service and we thank God that we have such a man as Piet Meyer who can serve Afrikanerdom.'

For all its good work in the cause of Nationalism the small box in the corner may yet prove too much for even the Broederbond to control. South Africa introduced television only in 1976 after a long and painful debate. Albert Hertzog, as Minister of Posts and Telegraphs responsible for broadcasting, had always opposed it. 'Friends of mine recently returned from Britain,' he confided to the Assembly in 1967 'tell me one cannot see a programme which does not show black and white living together, where they are not continually propagating a mixture of the two races.' It was not until Vorster dropped Hertzog from the cabinet in 1968 that the plans for television went through.

The SABC cannot make enough programmes to fill the air time so, like television stations throughout the world, they import to fill the gaps. Thus South Africans have become the best informed nation in the world on wild life. But even at the SABC there is a limit to the amount of bland fare that can be recycled. South Africans, like viewers everywhere, enjoy their ration of transatlantic cops and robbers. And there's the rub. In American series like *Starsky and Hutch* which now fill Saturday nights, few can fail to notice that the heroes' boss is a black man.

Evenings of viewing divided between programmes in South Africa's two official languages may well have improved English speakers' knowledge of Afrikaans, certainly a first step towards understanding that Broederbond 'world view'. But the obverse is equally true for Afrikaners. Increasingly the youngsters of one group watch the programmes of the other, regardless of the language. But bilingual children, warned the Broederbond, are backward and godless. 'The moral values which give expression to the individual's attachment to the Volk Group,' wrote Meyer himself in 1945, 'are disturbed by an early bilingualism.' If he was right, and doubtless Broeders debate it still, the Nationalists may have more to fear from the 'little bioscope' than even Albert Hertzog feared.

17

'You can carry on interrogating my dead body'

Extract from a 'suicide' note from Mapetla Mohapi,
found dead in his police cell

Where their powers of indoctrination have failed, the Nationalists have always been ready to impose their will by force. From the start the government gave itself the widest powers to silence dissidents. Everything was done in the name of law and order but under a concept of these matters found nowhere else in the western world.

The principal enemy, Nationalists maintained, was Communism. In 1943, Eric Louw, later to be Malan's Minister of External Affairs, had written a pamphlet outlining the main charge:

Communism recognises no distinction of colour or race . . . At meetings of the Communist Party, White, Black and Brown persons sit together. At socials they drink tea together and at dances the Black native whirls with his arms round the waist of the White girl and what follows . . . ?

Decorum forbade Louw from going further but he was clearly not alone in believing that such Communist activities as mixed dancing resulted in 'the impertinent and even challenging attitudes of natives towards Europeans'. For here was the essence of the Nationalist charge, Communism undermined traditional South African attitudes towards race. Communists advocated equal civil and political rights for all and it required no great leap of Nationalist imagination to believe that those who advocated equal civil and political rights for all South Africans must therefore be Communists.

Within a year of the Nationalists' coming to power a government commission on Communism was warning of, 'the danger to our national life, our democratic institutions and our Western philosophy.' Twelve months later in 1950 the Minister of Justice, C. R. Swart, put before Parliament the Suppression of Communism Act that gave him the fullest powers to deal with Communism and a good deal else besides. It was not just 'Marxian socialism as expounded by Lenin or Trotsky' or 'any related form of that doctrine' that was

211

proscribed, but any doctrine that was adjudged to encourage 'hostility between the European and non-European races'.

The Act made the Communist party unlawful and empowered the Minister to declare any kindred organisation unlawful too. By simply using the process of what was known as 'naming' anyone who held office or was active in such a body, the Minister could prevent him from taking any further part in its activities. The Bill also gave the Minister power to ban publications or people if he 'deemed' they were trying to further 'any of the objects of Communism'. From the Minister's decision there was no appeal to the courts.

Among the first to feel the weight of the new law were the trade unions which, in the early fifties, were still allowed multi-racial membership. By the end of 1955 over fifty union officials had been 'named' and forced to give up their positions. The case of Solly Sachs, General Secretary of the Garment Workers' Union, gave a good illustration of how the process worked and of the intense feelings that were aroused at the time.

Sachs' union had long withstood all assaults from the Nationalists, confident in its General Secretary whom it continued to re-elect, confirmed in its multi-racialism in 1951 by a unanimous vote of three hundred shop stewards, English-speakers, Afrikaans-speakers and Coloureds alike. It is true that Sachs had been a member of the Communist Party but he had been thrown out in 1931. The Party journal of the time had defined his deviation as 'a steady drift away from all Party activities and a growing sabotage of all revolutionary work in the trade unions'. Since 1946 he had been a member of the South African Labour Party and by 1952 he was its national treasurer. But none of those considerations was enough to save him.

On 19 May 1952 he returned to his office to find two detectives waiting. They handed him two notices signed by C. R. Swart, the Minister of Justice. The first ordered him to resign as an officer of the union within thirty days; the second restricted him to the area of the Transvaal for two years and prohibited him from attending any gatherings except those of a *'bona fide* religious, recreational or social nature'.

The following Saturday the Garment Workers held a gathering of their own to protest at Sachs' banning outside the City Hall in Johannesburg. Some ten thousand workers attended, black, white and Coloured. Sachs showed his defiance of the ban by addressing the crowd. After he had been speaking for ten minutes a posse of policemen appeared and bundled him into the City Hall. The crowd tried to

rotesters against the banning of trade union leader, Solly Sachs, under the
uppression of Communism Act, Johannesburg, May 1952

torm the building and the police responded with batons. At least fifty
eople were injured of whom thirty-five required treatment in hospi-
al.

When Sachs came up for trial a month later eighteen thousand
arment workers went on strike in the Johannesburg area as well as
everal thousand in other centres. Sachs was released on bail and
romptly tried to address another crowd at the City Hall; just as
romptly he was re-arrested. In July 1952 he was found guilty on two
ounts of attending gatherings in contravention of orders of the Minis-
r of Justice and sentenced to six months hard labour on each count.
he Appeal Court confirmed the sentence but suspended it for three
ears. The case had made headlines for months but at the end of it,
lthough Sachs never went to prison, his career was finished. He had
ot been tried for his beliefs nor for his activities as the leader of one of
e biggest unions in the country, still less as the champion of working
lass rights for black, Coloured and white alike, but because he had
hallenged a ministerial decree. In January 1953 Sachs went into
oluntary exile and left South Africa for ever. Although he wrote from
far of his own bitter experience, his protest went unheard in his
omeland. For under the ban imposed upon him, his books could not
e published in South Africa.

Sachs died in 1976, but long before then the Nationalists had introduced a battery of laws which put an end to all that he and his colleagues had worked to achieve. Mixed unions of Coloured and whites could no longer be registered; those that continued to exist were required to have separate branches and separate meetings. Blacks were excluded from registered trades unions altogether. They were offered only what were called 'liaison committees' and were forbidden the right to strike. The Native Labour Act of 1953 even redefined the term 'employee', specifically to exclude all blacks.

'Naming' and banning by the 1950s were the standard means of silencing opponents. The legislation allowed a variety of restrictions. Teachers could no longer teach; journalists could no longer write; attorneys could no longer practise. It became an offence to quote what a banned person had said. Some had to report daily to the police; others were virtually under house arrest. For ten years, Abdul Docrat was allowed out of his Durban flat for only two hours a day. Banned people are not allowed to speak to one another; Yusef Cachalia, under continuous restriction over twenty years, had to obtain special government dispensation to talk to his wife, Amina, when she was banned as well. For most, 'gatherings' of more than two people were forbidden. Winnie Mandela, the wife of the ANC leader, Nelson Mandela, has been banned almost continuously for nineteen years; once she was charged with taking part in a 'gathering' which turned out to be with a nine-month-old baby and a two-year-old child. As well as being banned, Winnie Mandela was also banished from her home at Orlando in Soweto to the black township outside Brandfort in the Free State where she knew no one. On the day the order was served the police arrived at her house, loaded all her possessions on to a truck and drove her and her daughter, Zinzi, to Brandfort. There she was allocated a house with no electricity, no running water, no stove and no bath.

'If you were to ask me what I miss more than anything else,' said one man under a five year banning order, 'and what I feel to be the greatest loss, it is the lack of normal human communication with people on a personal level. A spontaneous communication whether I know them or not.'

'Banning frightens away a lot of friends,' wrote another former victim, 'only a few are prepared to risk meeting you, while others don't want to make things awkward . . . the effect is to increase alienation. You feel disappointed and hostile, even paranoiac, since you are anyway looking over your shoulder whenever you break your ban. . .'

People can be broken.'

Harassment is a regular accompaniment. Repeated searches, day or night are allowed for in the legislation, but other attentions not listed are commonplace: telephone tapping, calls in the night, obscene messages, shots from passing cars, tyres slashed, petrol bombs. Mewa Ramgobin, a Durban attorney, was banned for five years in 1971 and placed under house arrest; two years later he was sent a parcel bomb which exploded injuring two of his children. In 1972 the skinned body of the Rev. Basil Moore's cat was left on his doorstep; a former acting general secretary of the University Christian Movement, he had been banned for five years. Such crimes tend to go unpunished and are often put down to right-wing terrorists; but once, when Winnie Mandela was in court, security policemen did admit that harassment was, as they saw it, part of their duty.

Since 1950 over fourteen hundred individuals have been subject to the banning laws, 'the closest thing any modern state has devised', *The New York Times* once wrote, 'to George Orwell's *1984*'. Part of the tactic was to silence potential leaders but organisations were also banned when they grew too troublesome, like the African National Congress and its off-shoot, the Pan Africanist Congress, both picked-off after Sharpeville. In one spectacular burst of legal gun fire on 19 October 1977 the government silenced eighteen organisations in a single day. Included were student and parent groups, community organisations and black consciousness movements. At the same time they closed two black newspapers, arrested one editor, banned another and put forty-two people behind bars.

The Afrikaners' own tribesmen are not exempt. The seven people banned that day included Dr Beyers Naudé, one of Afrikanerdom's most famous sons. His father, Dominee Joshua Naudé had been a chaplain with the Boer Commandos, a delegate at the Vereeniging Peace conference in 1902 and one of the six who had voted to continue the war (see page 85). In 1918 the Dominee had been a founder member of the Broederbond with Henning Klopper and its first President.

Beyers Naudé himself was a minister of the Dutch Reformed Church and, as Moderator of the Synod of the Southern Transvaal, one of its most senior pastors. He was also a member of the Broederbond for twenty-two years. But his Christian conscience had long been troubled. He went back to the Bible to seek justification for Apartheid but could find none; his break with Nationalist Afrikanerdom became inevitable. In 1963 he caused a sensation by resigning from the

215

Broederbond and making public his letter to Piet Meyer, the chair
man.

In it he denounced the Broederbond's influence in the church, it
support of Apartheid and the legislation enforcing it,

all of which contains stipulations that violate the demands of the Bible fo
neighbourly love, justice and mercy. I also wish to mention the impossibilit
of implementing total Apartheid without seriously endangering the existenc
of the Afrikaner people, and the injustice perpetrated on millions of non
whites. . . . And I want to assert that the road which the Broederbon
prescribes, no matter how sincere and honest its intentions, will eventuall
break the Afrikaner people, not preserve it.

The whole episode took place against the background of a series o
revelations about the Broederbond in the Johannesburg *Sunda*
Times. It transpired that they were based on confidential Broederbon
documents that Beyers Naudé had passed to a friend. Soon afterward
Naudé was offered the position of Director of the Christian Institute, a
non-denominational centre of research and Christian study. He wa
informed by the DRC that if he took it, he would lose his status as a
minister. On 3 November 1963 Beyers Naudé preached a farewell
sermon at Northcliff in the northern suburbs of Johannesburg, picked
up his Bible and his notes and left the pulpit of the Afrikaner church
for the last time. A Dutch girl, who had been taken to the church by
her father, remembered how she and many of the congregation were in
tears.

From then on, Beyers Naudé was a marked man; the telephone
tapping, the abusive calls, the watch on his house, became part of his
daily life. In September 1972 a church hall in Cape Town where he
had been holding a meeting of the Christian Institute was burned
down. On 19 October 1977 the Institute itself was closed through
banning and its Director was silenced. The Broederbond had had its
revenge.

Bannings, of course, were only part of the government's armoury.
The laws which allowed detention without trial were another. For the
first few years after the Nationalists came to power anyone arrested
was required to be charged in court within forty-eight hours. Just
before Sharpeville the period was extended to twelve days. The Minister of Justice said forty-eight hours was 'unrealistic' in time of great
unrest. Before long he was back asking for, and being given, powers to
hold suspects first for ninety days and later still for one hundred and
eighty.

A year after John Vorster became Prime Minister, the Government

eyers Naudé (right) with Rev. Theo Kotze in the burned-out Church
all where they had just held a meeting of the Christian Institute; Cape
own, September 1972

itroduced a Bill that was even more draconian. It was the infamous
'errorism Act of 1967 which allowed for indefinite detention without
rial. If a definite period of detention were stipulated, said the Minis-
er, 'terrorists' would be indoctrinated and prepared in advance to
vithstand questioning for that period. Terrorism was defined as
ommitting 'any act whatsoever with intention to endanger the
naintenance of law and order'. Conviction carried a minimum sen-
ence of five years' imprisonment; the maximum sentence was death.

The fine print gave the Act extraordinarily wide application; it also
hifted the onus of proving innocence on to the accused, overriding
ompletely the long cherished principle of South African law that left
he burden of proving guilt to the State. For example, an act likely to
ripple or 'prejudice' any industry or undertaking could, unless it was
roved that such was not its intention, be interpreted as terrorism. So
ould an act 'likely to cause financial loss to any person', such as a
trike or a boycott; and so too could anything 'likely to embarrass the
dministration of the affairs of state' or 'cause feelings of hostility
etween the white and other inhabitants of the Republic.'

Sidney Kentridge, one of the barristers who represented the Biko

217

family at the inquest after the death of their son, recalled the case of young black man who wrote a violent anti-white poem. By sending i to a seventeen-year-old girl he was deemed to have published it. 'It wa held, no doubt correctly,' said Kentridge, 'that this poem was likely t encourage feelings of hostility between blacks and whites in the hear of this seventeen-year-old girl. He could not discharge the onus on hin to prove that was not his intention; he was sentenced to the minimun of five years' imprisonment.' Under the Terrorism Act, as with al political offences, there is no remission and no parole.

When the Act was promulgated in the Assembly, the Minister o Justice, Piet Pelser, admitted that it was very far-reaching but said h was offering no excuse. The police had warded off the first onslaugh by terrorists entering South West Africa through Zambia and Angol but 'had been in contact only with the vanguard.' He also made the Ac retrospective to June 1962 because 'this was the date when terrorist first commenced their training.' It meant that people could be, an were, prosecuted under the Act for things which they had done befor it came into force. *1984* was another step nearer.

The early sixties had been a period of considerable violence Although the ANC and PAC were banned they were active under ground. *Umkonto we Sizwe* (The Spear of the Nation), the ANC': military wing had launched a campaign of sabotage; governmen offices were bombed, electric pylons blown up, telephone lines cut. I was like a repeat of the days of the Ossewabrandwag although th sabotage was more extensive if not always more efficient. Hundreds o arrests were made. In raids again reminiscent of the wartime years th police discovered secret radio transmitters in Johannesburg and Cap Town and seized quantities of dynamite, detonators, time-bomb kit: and photographs of both civil and military establishments.

A new movement called *Poqo* favoured much more violence. Poq means 'only' or 'pure' in Xhosa, implying that unlike the ANC, it wa exclusively a black movement working for black people. Its member: were mainly militants from the PAC who found their own leaders to moderate. The group was believed to have been responsible for th brutal murders of several Africans suspected of giving information t the authorities in the township of Langa near Cape Town. When sever men were arrested in connection with the murders a mob went on th rampage in the white part of town, killing two whites and injuring three others.

The main activities of Poqo were in the Transkei where thei attempts to bring down Chief Kaiser Matanzima, involved them ir several bloody clashes with the police. Elsewhere they were believed to have organised armed assaults on police stations and, according to judges at a series of trials, to have planned a concerted attack on Pretoria itself that included blowing up power stations and murdering whites. Domestic servants were to have been instructed to poison the food of their employers. By the middle of 1964 two hundred and two members of Poqo had been found guilty of murder and three hundred and ninety-five of sabotage.

One of the most spectacular trials had begun in October 1963 when eleven men, six blacks, an Indian and four whites appeared in court in Pretoria on charges of sabotage. The case became known as the Rivonia Trial', after the suburb of Johannesburg where the group had been arrested. Seven of the men in the dock, including Nelson Mandela and Walter Sisulu, made up, so it was alleged, the high command of The Spear of the Nation. They were charged with committing or instigating almost two hundred acts of sabotage as a prelude to revolution within the country and invasion from without. The trial provoked perhaps the most famous statement from the dock in South Africa's recent history. It came from Nelson Mandela, the leader of the group; he admitted that he had planned sabotage, although 'not in a spirit of recklessness' but 'as a result of a calm and sober assessment of the situation, after many years of oppression and tyranny of my people by the whites'. He added that as all other means of opposing the principle of white supremacy were 'closed by legislation, we had either to accept inferiority or fight against it by violence. We chose the latter.'

Mandela said that they had decided on sabotage rather than terrorism because they did not want to kill anyone. Their aim was to scare away foreign capital and draw world attention to South Africa. On 12 June 1964 the seven-month trial ended; Mandela and seven others, including one white, were sentenced to life imprisonment. The verdict was followed by a fresh outbreak of sabotage, again mainly buildings and pylons but on 24 July a time-bomb, left in a suitcase, exploded in the concourse of the main railway station in Johannesburg. A number of people were seriously injured by burning petrol and flying glass. Fifteen were admitted to hospital and one white woman died. John Harris, a teacher and former chairman of the South African Non-Racial Olympic Committee, was arrested and charged with murder. A statement was produced in court in which Harris admitted he had planted the bomb; he had meant it as a spectacular demonstration. He had telephoned a warning and had expected the concourse to be cleared. Harris was found guilty, sentenced to death and hanged.

Against this background of violence the Terrorism Act wa accepted by many non-Nationalists as a necessary response by th state. René de Villiers was Assistant Editor of the Johannesburg *Sta* when the Bill was introduced in 1967; both he and the newspape opposed the legislation from the beginning but de Villiers was in n doubt what many of the readers felt: 'The station bomb affair probabl did more than any one single act to frighten and anger people. Th whole Rivonia Trial, of course, had shaken them. For the first tim people realised that a widespread organisation was forming in th wings. It was seen as a tremendous coup for the security people to hav pulled in the brains of the whole outfit. So the whole sequence o events dragged a lot of English-speakers along with the government.'

In the same way that Macmillan's wind of change speech ha propelled many English-speakers into the Nationalist camp over th Republic, so many more now accepted that white South Africans ha to stand together to face what they saw as the terrorist onslaught. As i did in later years, danger, real or imagined, helped to bring Englisl and Afrikaans-speakers together and provided the politicians with th perfect rallying cry. The fear of the avenging black masses, whethe Communist or not, provided the justification for all measures t safeguard the security of the state. Most white people, therefore, wer not going to quibble that some of the provisions of the Terrorism Ac were more suited to a police state. When the Bill went through parliament only the vote of Helen Suzman, the lone Progressive Party member was cast against.

The most ominous provision in the Act gave the authorities almos limitless power to lock up whom they liked without going near a cour of law. Under the notorious Section Six any police officer, 'if he ha reason to believe a person is a terrorist or is withholding from th police any information relating to terrorists or to offences under this act', may detain him until he has answered questions to his satisfac- tion, or, in a chilling phrase, 'otherwise until the Commissioner o Police is satisfied that no useful purpose will be served by his furthe detention.' In other words, he may be detained indefinitely. No one, other than an officer of the state is entitled to access to such a detainee or to any official information about him.

Once a person has been detained the police are under no lega obligation to tell his family or his lawyer or his doctor. So he may simply vanish without anyone knowing. He can be held indefinitely in solitary confinement. Nor need he ever be brought before a court. 'You can understand how you feel when you are locked into a tiny cell only ten feet by twelve. Understand how one feels when they slam that iron door shut . . . you feel like beating on the door with your fists. So, if you do not take yourself in hand immediately, I can readily understand how you can go insane.' Thus wrote John Vorster about his own experience of solitary confinement during the war. Unlike Vorster in 1942 many black detainees are not simply left to their own devices; they are interrogated.

Shun Chetty is an attorney who has defended many black clients; he was also involved in the Biko affair, called in by the family the day the Black Consciousness leader died. In 1978 he fled the country. In exile he described what he came to regard as a regular pattern of events under the detention laws:

You simply hold a detainee in solitary confinement until he breaks. The kind of people who may be involved with some sort of political organisation are usually outgoing, extrovert types who need other human beings. With no human contact, nothing to read, few clothes, they break sooner or later.

There may be some assault but probably not torture. Keep them awake. Use the imaginary chair. Make a detainee sit against the wall on an imaginary chair. It puts tremendous pressure on the thigh muscles. Then put a knee into your thigh as you start to slip down the wall. Or hold a sharp point under your chin so that if you sink towards the floor it sticks in your throat. The black policemen often do this. They are given the menial jobs and are much harder.

Every detainee I have ever represented has always been broken by this sort of treatment. No one can hold out. In the end you tell them everything. You even make it up. It all comes out. Fifty, sixty pages of confession. I have known as many as a hundred and twenty pages. You tell them everything about yourself and your friends.

What concerned Chetty was that once the confession was on paper, the detainee could suddenly be brought to trial. 'You would have no notice for the defence. Before you know it, sentence is passed and your man is on Robben Island.' Chetty was not the only one to make such accusations. In May 1978 the Johannesburg *Sunday Express* reported four cases in detail: a nineteen-year-old youth, detained incommunicado under the Terrorism Act for several months, was tried at Ermelo in the Eastern Transvaal in March 1978 and sentenced to twelve years' gaol for terrorism. His parents, who had heard the evening before of the pending trial, were refused admission to the court. The attorney, whom the parents had instructed on their son's behalf, was not notified. The young man, Sipho Madondo, was defended by *Pro Deo* (for God) counsel appointed and paid for by the state. The trial lasted three hours.

Petrus Molefe, aged twenty-three, was detained in February 1978 and brought to trial in April without the knowledge of his family or a legal representative. He was sent to prison for fifteen years. His lawyer believed he was not represented at all. The lawyer had informed the Security Police nine days after Molefe's detention that he was representing him. In another example, a charge of sabotage was brought against a detainee and the Security Police wrote to inform his attorney the day before the case came to court. The letter was received by the attorney two weeks later, after his client had been both convicted and sentenced.

Some detainees have not survived to reach court. Looksmart Solwandle Ngudle was detained on 19 August 1963 in connection with the Rivonia investigation. On 5 September he was found hanged in his cell. At the inquest counsel for the state said Mr Ngudle had been interrogated on a number of occasions, and it had been made clear to him that he was to be brought to trial and what the consequences might be. On the day before his death he gave information to the police that led to other arrests. He apparently then realised, said counsel, that he faced death either by the proper processes of law or at the hands of his previous associates. A Pretoria magistrate said he had visited Ngudle three times with an interpreter but out of earshot of the police. On the first two occasions Ngudle had nothing to say. On the third he complained that he had been assaulted to force him to make a statement, and said he had coughed up blood as a result. The magistrate reported this to the police. Next day he heard of Ngudle's death. A medical expert who carried out the autopsy reported no evidence of ill treatment. The police denied that assault had taken place. The presiding magistrate found the suicide of Looksmart Solwandle Ngudle had not been the result of any act or omission amounting to an offence on the part of any person.

In the course of the next sixteen years, forty-one detainees are known to have died in the hands of the Security Police. The official cause of death was not always given but those that were included five deaths by natural causes, eighteen by hanging, two 'other' suicides; 'falls down stairs', two; 'falls from windows', four; 'injured in scuffles', two; and 'slipped in shower', two.

Mapetla Mohapi was one of those forty-one cases; he was reported to have been found hanging by a pair of jeans from bars in a police cell at Kei Road, near King William's Town in August 1976. He had been detained for three weeks under the Terrorism Act. Mohapi's widow said the police told her that no note was found in her husband's cell but

Alleged suicide note found in the cell of Mapetla Mohapi, who died in police detention, August 1976

at the inquest one was produced, written on lavatory paper. It began: 'Death Cell, Kei Road, 5/8/76' and was addressed to a security police officer, Captain P. A. Schoeman. The note read: 'This is just to say goodbye to you. You can carry on interrogating my dead body. Perhaps you will get what you want from it. Your friend, Mapetla'.

Mrs Mohapi later sued the Minister of Police claiming that the Security Police had caused her husband's death. In court, a handwriting expert demonstrated the differences between the handwriting of the note and that of Mapetla Mohapi and called it 'a clumsy imitation'.

By far the most notorious case concerned the death of thirty-year-old Stephen Biko, the charismatic spokesman for the Black Consciousness Movement in South Africa, believed by many to have been a potential national leader. Already under a banning order that confined him to the King William's Town district in the Eastern Cape, Biko was picked up at a police roadblock outside Grahamstown seventy miles away, on the night of 18 August 1977. The Security Police said they had received information that 'inflammatory pamphlets' were being distributed; they understood that Biko was involved and was on the way to Cape Town. According to police evidence at the inquest, Biko was held in a police cell at Walmer Street, Port Elizabeth for the next eighteen days. It was stated that he was kept naked in order to prevent him hanging himself with his clothes.

On 6 September he was transferred to the Security Police office, still naked and now in leg irons and handcuffs. Major H. Snyman led a five man interrogation team which began the questioning that day. According to Snyman's evidence, Mr Biko became violent. On the morning of 7 September, said Snyman, after being presented with certain facts regarding his involvement in compiling and distributing pamphlets, Biko had to be subdued by the entire interrogation team. In the scuffle that ensued, said Major Snyman, Mr Biko hit the back of his head against a wall. As Sidney Kentridge, representing the family, pointed out, the incident had not been mentioned in any of the twenty-eight affidavits sworn by doctors and policemen involved in the case.

After the 'scuffle' the Divisional Commander of the Security Police, Colonel Goosen, called in a district surgeon, Dr Ivor Lang, to examine Biko. Dr Lang signed a certificate stating that he found 'no evidence of abnormal pathology'. Under cross-examination he admitted this was incorrect because Biko had refused water and food, was weak in all four limbs, had lacerations on his hip, a bruise near his second rib, swollen feet, ankles and hands, slurred speech and could not walk properly. Dr Lang said that Colonel Goosen had suggested to him that Mr Biko could be shamming.

On the following day, 8 September, Biko was examined again by Dr Lang and the chief district surgeon, Dr Benjamin Tucker. At their suggestion he was moved to a prison hospital for observation. A Port Elizabeth specialist, Dr Colin Hersch, carried out his own examination and wrote a report, but not until 16 September, four days after Biko had died. Dr Hersch admitted at the inquest that he had sus-

Major Harold Snyman, of the Security Police, Port Elizabeth, who led the interrogation of Steve Biko

pected damage to the brain but did not mention it specifically in the report. 'It was not a good report', he said.

On 11 September, Biko was sent back to his prison cell; the next day he was transferred to Pretoria for treatment in a prison hospital. He made the seven hundred mile journey naked on the floor of a police Land Rover with a blanket thrown over him. No medical report about his condition was sent with him. In Pretoria he was given an intravenous drip and a vitamin injection but not treated for brain damage. 'We end,' said Kentridge at the inquest, 'with Biko dying a miserable and lonely death on a mat on a stone floor in a prison in Pretoria'.

The magistrate found that death was due to brain damage but 'the available evidence did not prove that death had been brought about by an act or omission involving an offence by any person.'

The death of Steve Biko provoked much hostile comment abroad and outrage at home from the liberal establishment and its English language Press. Twenty thousand mourners attended the funeral. But few government supporters added their voices to the protest. Perhaps some of the other reactions showed just how far many white South Africans, English and Afrikaners alike, had now gone in accepting Nationalist norms.

The first public response from the Minister of Police, Jimmy Kruger, to the news of Biko's death was, '*Dit laat my koud*', ('it leaves me cold'). At the Transvaal Congress of the National Party, Kruger said Biko had died 'following a hunger strike'. (He later denied saying that Biko died *of* a hunger strike). A delegate from Springs commended the Minister for allowing detainees 'the democratic right to starve themselves to death'. An English-speaker, with whom I discussed the whole affair in Johannesburg two weeks later put another view: 'Well, who was Steve Biko anyway?'

18

'It's known as the Persian Solution'

Eschel Rhoodie on a lesson learned in Iran

Many South Africans may not have known who Steve Biko was but within days his name had gone round the world. His death and the manner of it caused an outcry. The calls for boycotts and sanctions echoed once more from Washington to Westminster and round the United Nations Plaza. A South African Foreign Minister had once reported that his country was generally regarded as 'the polecat' of the world. It was never more so than in September 1977.

In their early years of government, the Nationalists had not paid particular attention to what people thought 'overseas'. The conviction that they were right and the rest of the world did not understand them merely fortified them in their isolated laager at the tip of Southern Africa. It suited politicians to see only hypocrisy and double standards in the criticism of Apartheid and to blame foreigners for some of their own misfortunes. 'If we hadn't been handicapped by these incessant attacks over the years,' said Verwoerd to an American journalist in 1966 shortly before his death, 'we would be much further along than we are now.'[1]

But the flight of capital after Sharpeville had taught South Africans that they could not exist in isolation. The country needed arms, machines, computers and aeroplanes. Sports boycotts hurt the pride of a sports-mad nation anxious to test itself against the best of the world.

A young information officer named Eschel Rhoodie, charged with upholding South Africa's good name abroad, was appalled at the view of his country presented wherever he went. By the end of the sixties he believed something drastic had to be done to change the image.

The major achievements in South Africa, [he said] the background to the social and political problems, the objectives, the *bona fides* of the people and

---

A Very Strange Society Allen Drury, Michael Joseph, London 1967.

the positive aspects were being obscured by Petty Apartheid and reporting which concentrated only on brutal highlights and isolated incidents.

We were facing a situation where, if this had continued, if there were another two or three major disturbances in South Africa, similar to, say, Sharpeville or to the riots of the Indians in 1949 [where one hundred and forty-two died in fighting between Zulus and Indians in Durban], the country would have found itself in a state of isolation, where there would have been a one-way traffic of bad news going out into the world and nothing else being published.

Rhoodie's forthright views soon brought him to the notice of the Minister of Information, Dr Connie Mulder who was also the powerful leader of the National Party in the Transvaal. In 1972 Rhoodie found himself promoted to the senior post in the department, charged with leading an assault on world opinion that might restore South Africa to a place at the top table. So began a story that was to span four continents, cost the South African taxpayer millions, involve elements more suited to a James Bond movie and finally bring about the downfall of the two most powerful men in South African politics and the humiliation of the man who had begun it all.

Much later, in 1979, Rhoodie gave many of the details himself. By then, the whole scheme had gone awry. Rhoodie was on the run from the South African government; after long negotiations during which we had come to know him well, we met in a hotel room in Zurich where he had agreed to a filmed interview with David Dimbleby. From that and other discussions we were able to piece together much of the story.

Eschel Mostert Rhoodie was all that traditional Nationalists were not. Service in South African Information bureaux in Australia, the United States and Holland had given him a social agility and sophistication plus a knowledge of the outside world that none of his masters could equal and not a few might have envied. In Sydney he had chafed under a conservative ambassador who insisted on traditional methods of dispensing information; in New York he had found his way into the world of the CIA, eagerly espousing their unconventional attitude to making friends and influencing people. In the Hague he had helped a Dutch publisher start a news magazine called *To The Point*, backed by secret South African money. In 1971 he had himself become deputy editor of a South African edition of the magazine, with the role of keeping an eye on both the government's funds and the editorial policy.

When Mulder engineered Rhoodie's promotion to Secretary of

Dr Eschel Rhoodie, former Secretary of Information

Information he ignored the recommendations of the Civil Service Commission. Rhoodie was not a Broeder and was virtually unknown to the establishment. At thirty-eight he was the youngest man to have been appointed to such high office. But he soon had friends in even higher places; Prime Minister John Vorster immediately took to his unconventional methods; General van den Bergh, head of the Bureau of State Security, South Africa's CIA, later described Rhoodie as, 'one of the most intelligent men I have ever met', and they became close working partners.

By the end of 1973 Rhoodie had drawn up his plan of action. South Africa would go onto the attack, aiming at the 'opinion-formers and decision-takers' in four main target countries, the United States, Britain, France and West Germany. Mulder arranged a meeting with Prime Minister John Vorster and the Minister of Finance, Dr Nico Diederichs, and Rhoodie set out his case:

I spoke for about an hour, presenting the state of affairs, South Africa's increasing isolation and the fact that we were not getting through. There were perhaps twenty or thirty reasons which I presented to the Prime Minister why we should undertake a fairly dramatic and drastic programme in the field of what is commonly called psychological and propaganda warfare.

I said to him that if it was necessary for me for example to influence a particular journalist to stop writing anti-South African articles, anti-investment articles, if it was necessary for me to send him to Hawaii with his girlfriend for a month's holiday at our expense, then I should be able to do so. If it was necessary to purchase a fur coat for a politician or an editor, I should be able to do so ... I said to him 'You should understand what I mean by propaganda war. This should be a war, an effort, a programme in which no rules or regulations would inhibit us', and I twice asked him whether he understood what I meant, and on both occasions he replied: 'Yes, I understand perfectly well, and it is in order for you to go ahead.'

Diederichs too, said Rhoodie, was enthusiastic and emphasised the need for absolute secrecy. There would be no auditing of the books and Diederichs would not even inform the two most important people in his department, the Secretary of Finance and the Secretary of the Treasury.

Rhoodie drew up a detailed five-year plan and submitted it to the three Cabinet Ministers. Two weeks later, he said, it came back signed by Mulder. 'The entire programme is approved.' Some R64 million (£40 million) were to be assigned to the project, most of it transferred from the huge budget of P. W. Botha's Department of Defence.

If, in retrospect, the whole venture seemed somewhat quixotic, especially in the light of some of the absurdities that later emerged, it was not so surprising that in 1973 Vorster and his inner cabinet should have given it their wholehearted approval. In twenty-five years of government the Nationalists had established control over the means of fashioning much of South African thought. Now similar methods would be applied to selected areas of the outside world. There was one major problem still at home but as Rhoodie and his agents set to work abroad that was also receiving attention.

The Nationalist government had long been aware that much of the adverse publicity they received overseas could be traced back to South Africa's own English language Press. For years the English newspapers had chronicled the errors and abuses of Apartheid; for years they had backed the parliamentary opposition, giving them a hearing far beyond their numbers. Since most visitors, tourists, businessmen, politicians and journalists were unable to read Afrikaans, many of the impressions they carried away with them were those they found in the English press.

In 1963, when Piet Koornhof was Secretary of the Broederbond, he had put forward a recommendation for what was called a 'Press task group' to establish English language newspapers of their own 'to reach the top level of English-speakers and by that means exercise influence'. Koornhof himself led an attempt to take over *The Natal Mercury* in Durban but it came to nothing. By the early 1970s the government itself was ready to launch a more sustained attack on the printed enemy. Rhoodie was to be the staff officer to plan the assault while the blunt instrument to batter at the actual portals was a self-made millionaire named Louis Luyt, said to have risen from railway clerk to fertiliser tycoon in seven years. Luyt testified later that the first approach to him was made at a rugby test match to which he had gone with his friend Piet Koornhof plus General van den Bergh and Rhoodie. Their first project was to buy up no less than South African Associated Newspapers, the group that published *The Rand Daily Mail*, *The Sunday Times* and *The Sunday Express*.

When the take-over failed they resolved to start their own newspaper and on 7 September 1976, *The Citizen* was born. The government had coolly handed over £7 million of tax payers' money to set the presses rolling, having laundered the cash through a Swiss bank account. Luyt had arranged that the actual printing was done by the Afrikaans newspaper group, Perskor, publishers of *Die Transvaler* and *Vaderland*, thus keeping some of the benefits nicely in the Afrikaner family. The editorial guidelines agreed by Luyt and Rhoodie laid down that *The Citizen* would support the broad objectives of the government in respect of separate development and the fight against communism. Luyt was chairman of the board but Rhoodie, as the link man with the government, retained a considerable influence.

The newspaper had an unhappy start. The first editor lasted only three weeks. In order to impress the opposition and potential advertisers, *The Citizen* let it be known that they were selling ninety-thousand copies daily; in fact, as diligent reporters from *The Rand Daily Mail* discovered, thirty thousand copies were being driven each night to one of Luyt's properties and destroyed. So the costs soared. Luyt said later that with their lack of experience the board had been one hundred per cent out in their estimates. He had invested most of the original £7 million in his own fertilising company, Triomf, hoping to finance the newspaper from the interest, but far more cash than that was needed. Luyt insisted that the capital could not be touched so Rhoodie had no option but to look elsewhere. He raised some money in Switzerland but much more came directly, although secretly, from the government. Over the next two years some £20 million were

231

poured in to keep *The Citizen* going. But the Nationalists now had what they wanted, a securely pro-Apartheid English language newspaper for visitors to read with enough of an independent image to attract a steady following of its own. For the moment Rhoodie had covered his tracks, no one could prove that *The Citizen* had a government godfather.

Meanwhile from abroad, Rhoodie's men had other progress to report. In Britain they had bought their way into the publishing firm of Morgan Grampian. It was to be the launching pad into British hearts and minds producing books, magazines and newspapers. They tried to take over *The Daily Express* and had designs on *The Observer* and *The Guardian*. A bid for the *Investors Chronicle* failed, according to Rhoodie, only because Vorster held up the money. They set up front organisations like the 'Committee of Fairness in Sport' and 'The Club of Ten' to make the case for South Africa's readmittance on to the world's playing fields.

In Britain also there was a scheme known as 'Operation Bowler Hat'.

We had a Conservative Member of Parliament who ran it for us, [said Rhoodie] and the project was secretly to finance through him visits to South Africa by British MPs. We believed that it was an important way in which to expose them to South Africa and its complex problems. If they had known where the money originated they would have refused to come. So our Tory contact would find likely members, men who were showing an interest in our problems and he would invite them to South Africa.[1]

On the other side of the House of Commons, Rhoodie claimed there were two Labour MPs who had each received £2,000 per annum over a period of three or four years. They lobbied for South Africa and provided information on the activities of anti-Apartheid organisations thus enabling Rhoodie's men to mount 'disinformation and disruptive' operations. This included sending out fake petitions and notices cancelling meetings.

France and Germany were important targets with the emphasis on the secret buying of magazines and the setting up of extensive public relations networks. In Norway a right-wing magazine, funded directly from Pretoria, was so successful that in the 1976 elections the editor formed his own political party and had four MPs elected. 'When I reported this to Mr Vorster,' said Rhoodie, 'it was one of the few

---

[1] When we contacted the MP who Rhoodie alleged fronted 'Operation Bowler Hat', he refused to talk about the project and threatened legal proceedings if his name were revealed.

occasions in my life that I saw him really laugh, and he said "Well, it just shows what can be done by people with initiative and enterprise".'
In Japan, two MPs were bribed to use their influence with trades unions when South Africa's extensive iron ore trade with that country looked to be at risk. In all these ventures, Rhoodie had the enthusiastic support of General van den Bergh, who could see opportunities to infiltrate his own agents, sometimes under journalistic cover, into foreign countries.

In the United States there were more bribes for trades union leaders to dissuade them from joining an international week of protest. Two Senators, John Tunney of California and Dick Clarke of Iowa, known for their opposition to South Africa, were singled out for special attention, and both were defeated in subsequent elections. Nothing was ever proved, and Rhoodie claimed his front men never told him how they did it, but it was assumed that yet more public money had gone to support the special interest groups who backed the Senators' successful opponents.

One of Rhoodie's concerns in the United States was to blunt the influence of *The Washington Post* with its consistent anti-Apartheid line. He found an ally in John McGoff, an American newspaper owner who also had a printing business in South Africa. In 1974, with the help of a loan from Pretoria, McGoff made a bid for the rival *Washington Star*. When that failed, McGoff used some of the money to buy *The Sacramento Union* in California. Rhoodie was none too pleased, but later McGoff made a much more satisfactory deal, from Pretoria's point of view, by acquiring a fifty per cent share of UPITN, the international television news agency. It had been set up jointly in 1967 by the American news agency, United Press International, and ITN, Britain's Independent Television News, and soon became one of the world's two biggest television news suppliers, servicing nearly one hundred countries. Its weekly news round-up, 'Roving Report', was seen from Salisbury to Santiago to Sydney.

Rhoodie claimed that they were able to influence the news agency into making a number of film stories on the strategic importance of South Africa and on the value of its Defence Force. Once, he arranged a film interview for them with the South African Prime Minister, and remembered telling Vorster he did not have to worry about any tricky questions as the agency was partly owned by the South African government. ITN in London recalled that they had not thought much of the interview at the time, but for some months insisted that there was 'no possibility whatsoever' that their news film agency was partly financed by South African money. Eventually, in June 1979, after a government commission in South Africa admitted that it was in fact so, ITN bought out McGoff's share.

Throughout those salad days money was splashed over four continents. Some went into the 1976 presidential election funds of Governor Jimmy Carter. Some went to President James Mancham of the Seychelles to help secure landing rights for South African Airways and a friendly voice at the Organisation of African Unity; some went to golfer Gary Player to organise yet more visitors to South Africa; some went to James Chikerema, a Rhodesian nationalist leader identified as a possible rival to Bishop Muzorewa, head of the provisional government, set up as part of Ian Smith's attempted internal settlement. There was some embarrassment in Pretoria when it was discovered that from a separate source of funds Vorster was offering backing to Muzorewa at the same time. Another scheme to finance films for black South Africans went awry when the generous budget supplied through the Department of Information found its way into financing a mighty flop for the cinema called *Golden Rendezvous*. Rhoodie's men had some success with another venture aimed at blacks when after failing to take over the established magazine *Drum*, they started their own rival called *Pace*.

As a haven for friends and associates, Rhoodie enterprises bought property in Miami, Cannes, London, Soweto and Cape Town, plus a half share in a Transvaal cattle station. In Pretoria they leased a private box at the new Loftus Versfeld stadium where selected clients could watch rugby at its Afrikaner best. At a luxurious office nearby, owned by a front organisation called Thor Communicators, it was reported that other manly pleasures were also available, regularly sampled, so it was whispered, by the home team as well.

But there was nothing frivolous about the major part of the Rhoodie operation. Regularly and tirelessly he flew to African capitals establishing unofficial contacts that he believed were beyond the capabilities of the more staid Department of Foreign Affairs. It was Rhoodie who claimed to have paved the way for Vorster's unannounced visit to the Ivory Coast in May 1974, although he and van den Bergh always claimed, 'we had to drag John Vorster kicking into Africa'. They had their own name for the Prime Minister. 'We called him the "cork in the bottle". He was always stopping the flow of development.' Rhoodie was reported to have been in Zaire and also in Saudi Arabia. He took Mulder to Iran in the days before the Shah was toppled, in search of friends and, of course, oil.

Rhoodie recalled a lesson they learned in Iran that stood them all in good stead. The Prime Minister, Amir Abbas Hovayda, had been telling his South African visitors about the friendly relations Iran enjoyed with Israel. They were so good, said the Prime Minister, that the Israeli Airline, El Al, had established an office in downtown Tehran. One day a delegation of Arab ambassadors had come to him complaining that, as a good Moslem, he could surely not allow such a thing.

So the Prime Minister said: 'Very well gentlemen, I will investigate the matter personally.' Two days later he called in the ambassadors and after they had exchanged greetings he said: 'My chauffeur has taken me up and down the main street of Tehran four or five times. I spent literally three or four hours in the car and I passed the place where you said the *El Al* office was. Gentlemen, I can guarantee that there is no *El Al* office.' And the Arab ambassadors bowed and shook hands and went off completely satisfied. And to this day that is known as 'the Persian Solution' to a problem.

Rhoodie also made a dozen trips to Israel to prepare the way for Vorster's visit in 1976. He was always reluctant to talk about the details but it was an open secret that the establishment of close relations between two similarly beleaguered countries had led to an exchange of nuclear know-how. When Rhoodie was on the run from the South Africans in 1979 and we met him in the South of France, he was at least as concerned about Israeli hit men, should he say too much, as he was about any Afrikaner vengeance.

His troubles really began in April 1977 when the South African government's Auditor-General began an audit of the Information Department's books. Rhoodie did his best to hide behind the Official Secrets Act but F. G. Barrie, the Auditor-General, was not to be put off, his zeal for proper accounting doubtless sharpened by the memory that he was the man whom Rhoodie replaced as Secretary of Information. A steady drip of leaks told of expensive government printing contracts and lavish editorships with some benefits finding their way into private bank accounts, including that of one of Rhoodie's brothers, a Professor at Pretoria University. By mid-year one of the top three men at the Department of Information had resigned his post in New York for no convincing reason.

The South African election campaign in November 1977 diverted much attention until, one week before polling day, a bizarre murder released a further flood of rumour. A Nationalist Party candidate, Dr Robert Smit, and his wife, were shot and repeatedly stabbed one night at their home at Springs, a gold mining town twenty miles east of

Johannesburg. Smit had once been a South African representative on the International Monetary Fund and was believed to have been investigating the illegal movement of currency out of South Africa at the time of his death. Had he discovered too much for his own good? Another version suggested he was demanding high government office as a price for silence. Much later a former judge told of a one-time pilot with South African Airways who had come to him with a story of a contract killing involving a flight in a private plane carrying two former mercenaries from Luton to South Africa and back. But nothing was proved.

In February 1978 the Auditor-General tabled his expected report in Parliament, criticising unnamed officials of the Department of Information for undertaking unnecessary and extravagant trips abroad. He also stated that for three years the Department had been using funds without Treasury approval. Within a few weeks the Johannesburg *Sunday Express* was revealing details of an expensive jaunt to the Seychelles led by Rhoodie in Louis Luyt's private jet. In the first week in May the same newspaper trumpeted its intention, the following Sunday, to reveal 'startling new facts'.

Mulder, the Minister of Information, immediately began to distance himself from the scandal. Full of outrage, he announced that two senior officials of the department would be retiring immediately. One was J. F. Waldeck, the head of administration. It transpired later that his only crime was to have tipped off the Auditor-General about some of the goings-on. The other was Eschel Rhoodie's brother, Deneys, number two in the Department. His position had been put at risk when a few weeks before, returning from an Information mission abroad, he had been stopped at customs on Jan Smuts airport in Johannesburg after failing to declare some £350 worth of dutiable goods, including some doubtful literature.

Rhoodie himself launched an immediate counterattack in the form of a lengthy statement to the Press. He defended the lack of formal accounting in the department on the basis of the need for secrecy and virtually accused the Auditor-General of leaking a secret document to the newspapers. He spoke, almost casually, of the secret projects that were designed to counter 'the propaganda war being waged against South Africa'. They were, and this was the crucial point, 'overseen by a secret, though unofficial three-man Cabinet committee'.

Far from calming the situation, Rhoodie's pre-emptive strike, containing the first public reference to secret funds and an even more secret Cabinet troika, provided invaluable ammunition for opposition press and politicians. It was quickly pointed out that only three government departments were empowered by law to maintain secret funds: the Foreign Ministry, the Bureau of State Security and the Ministry of Defence. So what was Dr Rhoodie doing with secret funds, where did they come from and which cabinet ministers had apparently consented to supervise the way they were being used?

In the wake of such questions, the Prime Minister John Vorster, finally spoke up in Parliament. It was 8 May 1978. He accepted full responsibility for allocating funds to combat 'the psychological and propaganda onslaughts against the Republic' but deplored the irregularities in the way some of the money was being spent. As a result of the Auditor-General's findings, Vorster now proposed a total 'restructuring' of the Department of Information. Dr Eschel Rhoodie would be taking an early retirement. A further investigation had been placed in the hands of 'another capable person' (who eventually turned out to be the auditor for the Bureau of State Security, one of General van den Bergh's employees).

Underlining the government's contention that its hands were clean, Mulder announced in Parliament the next day that as far as the funding of *The Citizen* was concerned 'The Department of Information owns no newspaper in South Africa and runs no newspaper in South Africa. The Department of Information and the Government do not give funds to *The Citizen*.' It was a perfect example of what Rhoodie had called 'the Persian Solution'. Unfortunately for the government, the investigative reporters on the story did not, like the Arab ambassadors in Tehran, bow and go away satisfied. Numerous contacts inside the civil service were busy leaking to them yet more details of the secret projects – perhaps in a bid to save their own skins. Opposition members on a Parliamentary Committee on Public Accounts continued to ask awkward questions. More important, by trying to make Rhoodie into the scapegoat, Vorster had made an enemy of the one man who knew enough to implicate them all. The government's public contention that the only problem was the misuse of some of the secret money by Rhoodie and his cronies was simply not credible.[1]

Assailed from all sides, Vorster began to show the strain. Cabinet colleagues told of his inability to make decisions and of his leaving one particularly difficult meeting complaining of feeling unwell. The

---

[1] Mulder maintained later before a judicial enquiry that he had lied to Parliament only after receiving a handwritten instruction from Vorster. He was never able to produce the note and Vorster always disputed Mulder's claim.

John Vorster, whose resignation first as Prime Minister, then as State President, was brought about by the Information Affair

strong man who had ruled South Africa for twelve years looked increasingly vulnerable. On 20 September 1978 he announced to a news conference in Pretoria that, for reasons of health he was resigning as Prime Minister. He let it be known that he was making himself available for the ceremonial office of State President, and was duly elected, thus easing himself out of active politics altogether.

Dr Connie Mulder had always been regarded as Vorster's natural successor as Prime Minister. As leader of the National Party in the Transvaal, he commanded almost half the votes in the parliamentary caucus; and Transvaal had supplied each of the country's three previous Prime Ministers.[1] The previous January Mulder had been entrusted with the ministry that dealt with black affairs, one of the most sensitive of the government's portfolios. Many believed the promotion was a mark of Vorster's confidence. But as the man who had been in charge of the now defunct Department of Information, Mulder was deeply enmeshed in the scandal. If it became known that he had lied to Parliament the party that prided itself on its probity was unlikely to elect him as their leader.

The other candidates were P. W. Botha, Minister of Defence and leader of the Cape Nationalists, and R. F. (Pik) Botha, the Minister of Foreign Affairs who was popular with the electorate for his forthright sallies against the hypocrisy of the outside world which he made regularly on television and at the United Nations. There would need to be not a few defections from the Mulder supporters to give either of them a chance, and a week before the elections there was no such prospect in view.

On Saturday 27 September, to the astonishment of the English language Press, the Afrikaans language paper *Die Transvaler* published a report saying that Vorster's special investigator into the Department of Information, the BOSS auditor named Loot Reynders, had completed his enquiries and had cleared Mulder and his Department. 'According to the registers and documentary evidence submitted and the explanations given to me,' wrote Reynders in a three-sentence account of his findings, 'it is my opinion that proper account was kept of all receipts and expenditures . . . and comprehensive tests which I carried out brought no misexpenditures to light.'

It was a cynical piece of manoeuvering by the Mulder camp and

---

[1] The National party caucus which elects the Parliamentary leader comprises Members of Parliament and Senators. In 1978 there were 172 members – eighty from the Transvaal, fifty-five from Cape Province, twenty-four from the Orange Free State and thirteen from Natal.

P. W. Botha making his acceptance speech outside the Senate Building after his election as Prime Minister; Cape Town, 27 September 1978

General van den Bergh, to ensure the election of the faltering favourite. But the plan went astray. A Pretoria attorney named Retief van Rooyen knew Reynders and had discussed with him their joint misgivings about Information spending. Van Rooyen himself was heavily involved as the front man for Rhoodie's Thor Communicators. He could not believe that the bland assurances of the statement carried by *Die Transvaler* represented Reynder's real views. So he went secretly to Pik Botha and told him about Thor Communicators and all he knew of the secret funding of *The Citizen*, of the way the money had been channelled through a Swiss bank and back again to Louis Luyt.

Pik Botha, apparently astonished, took van Rooyen with him to Cape Town by government jet to repeat the story in front of P. W. Botha and the party leader of the Orange Free State, Alwyn Schlebusch. Vorster, confronted with the details, agreed that they were true and that he had known all along. Next day, for the first time, the facts of the whole *Citizen* project were outlined to the cabinet. Mulder was asked to withdraw from the premiership race but refused.

On Thursday 27 September the National Party caucus assembled in

Cape Town for the crucial vote. After three hours the 172 members emerged on to the Senate steps where the Chief Whip hesitantly read the results to background chants from the crowd of 'We want Pik'. P. W. Botha had beaten Mulder by ninety-eight votes to seventy-four and was the new leader of the National Party. In the first round the voting was: P. W. Botha seventy-eight; Mulder seventy-two; Pik Botha twenty-two. The transfer of virtually all of Pik Botha's votes to P. W. Botha in the second round had been crucial. The last minute disclosures by van Rooyen had almost certainly led to Mulder's defeat, although it was Mulder's own determination to become Prime Minister that had led to the disclosures in the first place.

However the story was far from over. The responsibility for clearing up the mess now lay with the new Prime Minister, P. W. Botha. On the steps of the Senate building, in his acceptance speech, he had pledged himself 'at all times to uphold honest public administration'. His intentions were quickly put to the test by an Afrikaner judge named Anton Mostert, who had been carrying out yet another enquiry into exchange control regulations. Mostert had been quietly taking evidence throughout the election period on Information spending. Early in November he let it be known that, 'in the national interest' he was considering publishing some of his findings. There was a fierce row in the Prime Minister's office. Mostert walked out and at a news conference the same day produced his evidence, page after page on the funding of *The Citizen*, on Thor and on various other secret projects. Botha's immediate reaction was to try to prevent newspapers from publishing the details. He issued a confidential note through the South African Press Association warning editors of possible legal consequences. Mostert replied that the regulations Botha had cited were not applicable and the newspapers went ahead. Only the compliant SABC made no mention of the judge and his evidence. Three days later the Prime Minister suspended the Mostert Commission because of 'an evident and untenable difference between the Government's point of view and the action taken by Judge Mostert'.

Seizing the moment, Botha soon rid the government of the embarrassing presence of Connie Mulder. First Mulder had to resign from the Cabinet, then four days later from his chairmanship of the National Party in the Transvaal. The first report of the judicial commission Botha had appointed under Mr Justice Erasmus had provided justification and more. Parliament was specially summoned in December 1978 to hear the once second most powerful politician in the country described as 'incompetent, lax and negligent'. Erasmus

241

raised too the possibility of criminal actions against former members of Mulder's senior staff.

Two months later, at Botha's insistence, Mulder resigned as a Member of Parliament. In April 1979, for good measure, the Party expelled him. Back in the heyday of their secret operations Rhoodie and van den Bergh had often scornfully referred to P. W. Botha, the Minister of Defence, as 'the Pangaman'. As Prime Minister he had certainly lived up to his reputation.[1]

Erasmus found that throughout the Information Affair P. W. Botha had acted honourably. He had been unaware of any irregularity relating to the use of secret funds. Although he had known that money from the Department of Defence was channelled into Information's secret fund, he did not know how the money was spent. 'His hands are clean in every respect,' said the Judge, 'and his integrity remains unblemished for his great task as Prime Minister.' Vorster did not receive quite such a glowing end of term report, but nonetheless his integrity remained 'unblemished'. To come to this conclusion Erasmus had to set aside the combined testimony of Mulder, van den Bergh and Rhoodie, who had all stated and repeated that the former Prime Minister had been involved with the secret projects from the start, and had received regular reports on their progress. Six months later Erasmus reversed his view about Vorster and found that after all the former Prime Minister must have lied. He may have been helped to that view by the chorus of contumely heaped upon his head after his first report. Van den Bergh was photographed signing a petition demanding that he himself be put on trial in order to test in court the truth of his insistence about Vorster's involvement. Mulder had continued to cry foul to anyone who would listen and Rhoodie had added his twopennyworth in our BBC film interview from a hotel room in Zurich.[2]

At all events, on 4 June 1979, Erasmus announced in his next report that Vorster had in fact known everything about the funding of *The Citizen* and the other projects launched by the Department of Information. He had thus been 'participating in action which in itself was a

---

[1] 'The Pangaman' was originally the nickname given to a black murderer who dispatched his victims with a *panga* (a large knife).
[2] After giving his evidence to the Erasmus Commission, Rhoodie had taken himself into hiding in Europe and South America where he was eventually tracked down by two journalists from *The Rand Daily Mail*, Mervyn Rees and Chris Day. It was thanks to them and their long-standing friendship with Mike Dutfield, a former colleague at the RDM, now at the BBC, that we were able to arrange David Dimbleby's television interview, shown on BBC-1 on 21 March 1979.

serious irregularity, the covering up of gross irregularities.' Vorster resigned as State President the same day. Having finally chosen to believe what Mulder, van den Bergh and Rhoodie had told him about Vorster, Erasmus still could not bring himself to accept their testimony about the involvement of the Minister of Finance, Senator Horwood. Rhoodie had always contended that when Diederichs had become State President in February 1975 and Horwood had taken over as Minister of Finance, he had also assumed the financial responsibility for the secret projects. Indeed, before our camera Rhoodie had produced a letter, dated 12 May 1978 from Mulder to Horwood requesting authorisation from the Minister of Finance for almost R8 million to pay for a list of thirteen secret projects including 'Front organisations' and 'Collaborators'. The letter appeared to have been signed by Horwood himself over a Treasury Stamp and returned to Mulder as due authorisation.

Horwood had always insisted that although he signed vouchers for the dispersal of secret money, he made a point of not looking at the details. The Minister of Finance, said Judge Erasmus, was in a 'pardonable position'. He was like a 'cyclist whom a bigger vehicle has pushed over a white line at an intersection where he is not allowed to be. Who, except perhaps a politician who wanted to make capital out of it would blame him if he were to pick up his cycle and continue on his way?' It was just as well that Erasmus found himself able to come to such a conclusion. After all, P. W. Botha had said all along that if it were proved that any member of his cabinet had had prior knowledge of the irregularities or of the funding of *The Citizen* he would resign.

All that remained was to punish the man at the centre of the scandal. Eschel Rhoodie, after six months on the run, was arrested by the French police at Juan-les-Pins on the Riviera. He was extradited to Pretoria where he was charged with seven counts of fraud, or alternatively theft, involving R83,000 (about £47,000) of the government's secret funds. The court heard of considerable sums that passed through Rhoodie's personal bank account, to buy property and to pay anonymous collaborators. Rhoodie had always insisted that he had not been hired to be a super clerk to keep the books in order but as someone to run a series of costly and unorthodox projects.

'I am not a man for red tape', he liked to explain. 'If the Marxists take over one day will we then be content to say, "Yes, but the books balance"?' The court was unimpressed with such arguments, found him guilty on five counts and sentenced him to six years' imprisonment. On appeal eleven months later the judgement was overturned.

The three judges found that Rhoodie's explanation for the charges brought against him was acceptable when assessed in the context of the 'extraordinary milieu' in which he operated. He had been invested with exceptionally wide discretionary powers and had had to act unconventionally and take exceptional risks. Rhoodie's financial transactions in regard to the payment of anonymous collaborators pointed to a disregard for superfluous detail rather than deliberate concealment. The sentence was set aside and Rhoodie was a free man. 'I feel like a dog who for two years has been kicked by the postman', he said. 'Now I am going to bite back.'

The likelihood, however, of Rhoodie's turning again on the hand that fed him became increasingly remote. While he was on bail awaiting his appeal Rhoodie had been put on the payroll of the Nationalist newspaper group, Perskor, enabling him to complete his own manuscript on the whole Information affair. Perskor, who by this time had also taken over the ailing *Citizen*, seemed the least likely promoters of yet more revelations to embarrass the government. Rhoodie's silence looked to have been effectively assured perhaps by yet another secret project.

As for the one hundred and twenty projects that Rhoodie himself had initiated, many were abandoned in the glare of public exposure. But at least sixty were duly vetted by the Department of Foreign Affairs and continued. For all the ridicule that was heaped upon the more van der Merwe-like attempts to buy friends and influence people, the campaign had achieved some success. At the end of the seventies, despite the Soweto riots, despite the Biko affair, despite Pretoria's continued frustration of United Nations' attempts to reach a settlement in Namibia, South Africa still managed to buy the oil and arms it needed. Calls for sanctions were ignored by the major powers; talk of disinvestment fell on ears tuned more to reports of profits to be made in a booming economy. South Africa somehow went on selling itself as a stable society in a troubled world. How much Rhoodie's secret projects had contributed will probably never be measured although van den Bergh once said that rather than pillory the former Secretary of Information, the government should erect a statue in his honour for all that he had done for his country.

At home, after the biggest public scandal in South African history, nobody was held accountable before the law, although the careers of the country's two most powerful politicians had been ruined. But their downfall had been brought about by their own lies, not because they had initiated a campaign to suborn and bribe and start a party newspaper with public money. Few Nationalists had stood up and condemned the secret projects. As Rhoodie had said, 'when it came to the future survival of South Africa, then of course rules and regulations did not apply and morality flew out of the window.'

There is no doubt that the disgrace of Vorster and Mulder came as a shock to many rank-and-file Nationalists. Since the days of Paul Kruger and before, Afrikaners had always regarded their leaders, with some justification, as righteous, God-fearing men. Vorster, particularly, had been held in much respect, never more so than when he took the Volk into his confidence in his fatherly chats up and down the country, telling jokes at the expense of the opposition and the world outside. On one such occasion at Graaff-Reinet a farmer had been waiting outside the hall for hours before the hall opened. He had driven many miles across the Eastern Cape to be there. Why had he arrived so early? 'I've come to listen to my hero,' was his simple reply. But now that hero had defiled the trust of thousands.

For Rhoodie, the fall of Connie Mulder meant disillusion on a different plane. Once, during a break in our negotiations for a television interview, at lunch in the unlikely setting of the hill-top village of Eze, high above Villefranche in the south of France, Rhoodie recounted how he and van den Bergh and Mulder had planned for the day when Mulder would become Prime Minister. Alongside the Cabinet would have been a special 'Think-Tank' of all the best brains in the country with Rhoodie himself as co-ordinating director. They would have provided the ideas to transform South Africa; not, said Rhoodie, the piecemeal change that was all Vorster could envisage. They would have consolidated the homelands. The showpiece port of Richards Bay in Natal would have become part of Kwazulu along with substantial areas of additional farmland. Even Buthelezi (the Chief Minister of Kwazulu who had always rejected Pretoria's offers of 'independence') would not have been able to refuse that. East London would have gone into the Ciskei. The homelands would have become viable. It might well have meant that the Nats would lose a few farming seats but they had persuaded Connie that it was worth the price.

In Soweto they would have spent a lot of money making life better for everyone, giving them electricity, roads and other facilities. They would have made Soweto into a city state like Berlin. The surveys Rhoodie had done showed that the blacks were more interested in improving their standard of living than in the vote. All these measures would have bought ten years for South Africa and released the pressure. The outside world would have seen a more settled country and a place in which it was worth investing. Connie would have given the vote to the Coloureds and Indians in some sort of Federation. Whether all this was any more than Nationalist policy taken to its logical conclusion was perhaps open to doubt but Rhoodie was convinced that Mulder was the only leader who could have implemented it. Instead, now P. W. was Prime Minister; a man, said Rhoodie, who would only react, who was incapable of initiating, just like Vorster.

Indeed, P.W. was now very much Prime Minister. The Information scandal had given him his chance and he had taken it, quickly dispatching his immediate rivals into obscurity and ensuring that his own reputation remained unsullied. But not everything had gone as planned. When Mulder was forced to stand down as leader of the National Party in the Transvaal, he had been replaced, despite Botha's best endeavours, by Andries Treurnicht, a potential claimant for Botha's new throne. An ideological purist and leader of the Nationalist right wing, Treurnicht stood in the way of any initiatives Botha might wish to attempt in steering Apartheid in a new direction.

The tragedy of Muldergate, wrote Percy Qoboza, the editor of the black newpaper, *The Post*, was that for two years the scandal had diverted attention from the country's real problems. For black South Africans it mattered little that Vorster and Mulder had been pushed aside because of a few untruths; black demands were the same whoever presided over the white Parliament.

Botha had now been presented with an opportunity to sweep away much more than the peccadilloes of the Information Affair. Until then as Minister of Defence he had rarely been called upon to deal with inter-racial affairs, but even his critics agreed that in his new job he made a promising start. In Mulder's place in charge of black affairs he appointed Piet Koornhof, who as Minister for Sport had made a reputation by removing some of the barriers to normal games playing. Would Botha and Koornhof together have the desire or the courage to free Afrikanerdom from the shackles of the old Nationalist dogma? Or would Rhoodie's bitter forecast prove correct?

19

'The Dompas must be ousted'

Dr Piet Koornhof, Minister of Co-operation and Development,
Washington, June 1979

Dr Koornhof said it but could it really be true: 'Apartheid as you came
to know it is dead'? Not only his audience at the National Press Club in
Washington were incredulous on that day in June 1979. Conservative
Afrikaners back home were heard to be calling for the transcript of the
speech. The man they call 'Piet Promises' would have some explaining
to do when he returned to the laager.

For over a year the signs had been remarkably propitious. Koornhof
himself had been appointed to the job of managing black affairs within
a month of P. W. Botha's election as Prime Minister. His reputation as
the man who had changed the public face of sport in South Africa in
his previous ministry was indisputable. Dr Piet Koornhof, the born-
again-Christian; the former secretary of the Broederbond, member
number 6844; the former Rhodes scholar whose Oxford thesis was on
the evils of migrant labour; the Nationalist, reported to have had tears
in his eyes when he visited a resettlement village in the Ciskei; the
Afrikaner who had once driven himself and two American visitors to
dinner with a black household in Soweto.

'We can be, and are well on the way to achieving in my country,
equality for all people before the law as well as equal chances and
opportunities', said Koornhof as he toured America. He had 'declared
war' on the dompas. It must be 'ousted completely out of my country
and I have told my officials to work on it'. Such statements, of course,
were not unknown from South African visitors. Had not Pik Botha
told the United Nations he would not die for separate lifts? Had not
John Vorster invited the world to give him six months? Had not
Hendrik Verwoerd in 1966 said: 'What we need is sympathy from
those who should be wise enough to see what a real problem we have,
and that we are trying honestly to solve in a decent and generous way.'?

Koornhof was not alone in tilting at Apartheid. His Prime Minister
had told Nationalists that whites did not need the Immorality Act to

247

Dr Piet Koornhof, Minister of Co-operation and Development

survive; that there were more important things in life than to stare the whole day at the colour of another man's skin; that he would not tolerate laws that insulted people. Taking their cue, the Nationalist Press had dropped even more hints.

'The stream of Afrikaner thinking,' wrote Dawie, the authoritative political columnist of *Die Burger* late in 1979, 'has become like a river that has burst its banks and even threatens, here and there, to take a new course.' Willem de Klerk, editor of the National Party newspaper *Die Transvaler* and a member of the Broederbond Executive, went further:

Hard, cold, equal negotiation is now on the agenda . . . The whites in this country are increasingly sincerely prepared to establish a new dispensation. A dispensation of human dignity for all. Removal of discrimination. Equal opportunities. Even a new look at the old bastions of separate development. The whites want consultation and discussion, constellation or confederation or however one wants to give joint responsibility to all national groups. The whites want to give their share of meaningful compromise for a political settlement that will link us as partners.

Koornhof changed the name of his ministry to Co-operation and Development; reversed the decision to demolish the black township of

Alexandra on the edge of Johannesburg, having already reprieved Crossroads, the shanty home of twenty thousand blacks outside Cape Town. Within two years he had quadrupled the amount spent on black housing and invited known opponents of the system to join him in committees to advise the Cabinet on issues from coal-smoke pollution to the constitution itself. Even Chief Gatsha Buthelezi, a Zulu leader not given to undue Afrikaner praise-singing, found himself describing the new Minister as 'quite unlike certain people who have occupied this portfolio, and a man who recognises that black people have a God-given dignity'.

During the same period, Apartheid signs continued to disappear in parks and public places; more hotels, under special permit, displayed the signs that made them 'international' and able to serve all races; restaurants learned that they had only to dial Pretoria for exemption from the Group Areas Act should a party of well-heeled blacks like the look of their menu.

In November 1979 the Prime Minister shook hands and sat down to lunch with Harry Oppenheimer at the Carlton Hotel in Johannesburg, something his predecessor John Vorster could never bring himself to do. The entire Cabinet and one hundred and eighty businessmen were there too. At the end of the day's think-scrum, co-operation was promised all round. 'The Anglo-Boer War is finally over', purred a euphoric Press.

Equally far-reaching it seemed were the results of two long-awaited government commissions. Professor Nic Wiehahn had been studying racial barriers in employment and the possible extension of trades union rights for all. Dr Piet Riekert, a former economic adviser to the Prime Minister, had been tackling influx control and the pass laws. Early summaries let it be known that good news was on the way. The world, or most of it, held its breath and forbore to comment. Had the Afrikaner Brothers really seen the light? Mrs Thatcher, in New York, acclaimed 'welcome initiatives' which offered a 'chance to defuse a regional crisis . . . and to make progress towards an ending of the isolation of South Africa in world affairs'. The British rugby unions, going one better, announced that in view of the advances towards non-racialism in South African sport, the Lions would be touring in 1980.

Only slowly did it emerge that not all the walls of Pretoria were about to fall to the trumpets of change. Two Cabinet Ministers, reporting to Afrikaner constituents, let it be known that sex across the colour line was likely to remain forbidden. Section 16 of the Immoral-

ity Act and the Mixed Marriages Act were only being 'reviewed
Population Registration, Group Areas, Separate Schools were no
being altered. The cornerstones of Apartheid were still intact.

Nonetheless, Wiehahn did propose important advances on the sho
floor. Trade union rights were to be extended to all and the statutor
reservation of certain jobs for whites should be abandoned. In labou
relations the lessons of the Zulu strikes in Durban in 1973 had bee
well learned. White managers then had found they had to deal with
football field full of strikers having no apparent leaders. The so-calle
'liaison committees' set up by employers to handle workers' grievance
had achieved very little; more muscle clearly lay with the unoffici
black unions with whom management were not supposed to negotiat
Wiehahn's advice was blunt: accept the black trades unionist as a fac
of life and control him. The African worker, he said, was a 'permanen
part of the economy' who must not be left outside the 'protective an
stabilising elements of the system'. If allowed to continue unsuper
vised, black unions could come under foreign influence with all th
ensuing risks.

Black unions should therefore be registered and operate alongsid
the white unions. They would have access to the industrial court an
to the existing conciliation procedures available to whites, includin
the right to strike after the official thirty-day notification period. Bu
registration would depend on government approval. All existin
unions would have to prove their 'acceptability' to black worker
within their firm and they would have to be responsible, apolitical
free of foreign influence and pursue policies conducive to 'peace an
harmony'. Their accounts would be audited, unregistered union
would not be allowed. It all sounded uncommonly like the measure
used to bring black mission schools under government contro
twenty-five years before (see page 190).

The mixed unions of black and white that Albie Sachs had fough
for were not ruled out but they required permission from the Minister
'Parallel' black unions were more to his and Wiehahn's liking, to sa
nothing of white workers themselves. White officials, under th
umbrella of the white dominated Trade Union Council of South
Africa, began to set up, and supervise, 'parallels' who found them
selves offered facilities by white employers that were not available t
'independents'. So the established black unions faced a crucial deci
sion: register and lose credibility with their members or stay outsid
the system and lose their status. To prod them into the fold th
Establishment did not hesitate to use its own muscle. The leader of ar

nofficial strike at the Ford plant in Port Elizabeth was banned for five ears even though the firm had reached an agreement with its workers. 'he parent organisation for the 'independents' FOSATU, the Federa- tion of South African Trades Unions, had its overseas funds cut off y government decree. And, as if to underline where the power still ay, the Johannesburg City Council, after a ten-day stoppage by ten housand municipal workers in July 1980, simply loaded a thousand of hem onto buses, batoning a few in the process, and dumped them ack in the homelands.

But where black workers came from there were thousands just vaiting to take their place; how to control the flood from the reserves o the cities, that was the ageless South African problem that Riekert's Commission had been called upon to review. The problem had exer- ised the white man ever since he had imposed a Hut Tax to make the lack man work for him. Whether Riekert's approach would amount o a war on the hated pass system, as Koornhoffian hyperbole had inted, was another matter.

None of those in power were likely to have forgotten the warning of Professor Gerrit Viljoen, then Chairman of the Broederbond, to SABRA in 1972. There were 'three Bantu persons for every two vhites in white urban areas,' he pointed out. 'May I remind you once again of the fate of the drowning person in ten feet or thirty feet of water?'

What was certain, at the end of the seventies, was that the bright ights of the cities looked even brighter from the twilight of the homelands. With the astonishing rise in the price of gold the South African economy had thrown off the gloom which had followed the Soweto riots in 1976. Investors were back, trade was up and firms were expanding. Wages for all, for black as well as white, were on the increase (though the gap between black and white earnings was still widening).[1]

Theoretically the only blacks supposed to be enjoying the bonanza were those who lived legally in the white areas, those who had been born there, or who had qualified through long residence or employ- ment or who came on short-term contracts as migrant labourers from the homelands. They were the fortunates known in the bureaucratic

Figures issued by the Bureau of Economic Research at the University of Stellen- bosch in May 1980 showed that in 1970 the average annual income of whites was R3,244, of blacks (in the non-agricultural sectors) R475; a difference of R2,769 or 14% of white earnings. By 1979 the figures were: whites R7,848; blacks R1,872; the difference R5,976 or 23.9%. Had the figures included the wages of black farm workers the difference would presumably have been even larger.

jargon as the 'Section Tens' (i.e. those who qualified under Section 1 of the Bantu (Urban Areas) Consolidation Act). In practice it was no like that and never had been. Despite all the controls, thousands of men and women from the homelands continued to pour into the so-called white areas in search of work. They had no choice; if they stayed at home, they had no work. But without the correct stamp in the pass book they became 'illegal', liable to arrest, imprisonment, fine and deportation.

The courts are daily jammed with offenders. In 1978, 273,000 arrests were made for pass law offences (50,000 more than in 1977), an average of 750 a day. The magistrates work a production line of punishment: a fine here, imprisonment there; 'endorsement out' 'remanded for identification'; two minutes, rarely more, for a case Few of those charged have the money for bail; fewer have any legal representation. The regulars know that an admission of guilt can save time and money and an early bribe on the way to the lock-up may keep them out of court altogether.

No one knows how many 'illegals' are in the cities; in Soweto alone they may be half a million. What is known is that they are the worker who will take any job that is offered for pay well below the recognised rate, just to keep body and soul together, to send a postal order to the family in the homelands, to buy school books and clothes and a better chance for the children. They are the builder's labourers, the factory hands, the shop assistants, the garden 'boys', the domestic servants Employers like them because they make no demands and do what they are told for fear of dismissal. Section 10 workers on the other hand complained Riekert witnesses, were far too choosy and were 'lazy and unproductive'.

Riekert expressed surprise that 'illegals' had 'a contemptuous attitude towards legal processes' and were 'not deterred by the possibility of clashing with the law or being sentenced to a fine or imprisonment'. Some figures prepared by Dr Jan de Lange of the University of South Africa in October 1979 went some way to explaining the reasons. A worker from rural BophuthaTswana who travelled to neighbouring Pretoria, worked for nine months illegally and then spent three months in gaol for a pass offence, could still raise his annual homeland living standard by eighty-five per cent. A Lebowa worker who made the two-hundred mile journey south to Johannesburg, who might work six months and then serve six months in gaol was 170 per cent better off in money terms. And a man from the Ciskei, who worked three months in Pietermaritzburg and spent nine months in gaol earned 234 per cent more than if he had stayed at home.

Riekert knew all about such excesses but what he proposed was not so much to abolish the laws which gave rise to them but to prevent them by making the laws more efficient. Influx control could not be abandoned; the risk to the white population of 'drowning' in a flood of black workers was too great:

control over the rate of urbanisation is, in the light of the circumstances in South Africa, an absolutely essential social security measure. Even though . . . the abolition of such control would lead to faster economic growth, the price to be paid for it in terms of direct and indirect social costs would be too high.

At the same time, for those blacks on the inside, the fortunate Section Tens with residential qualifications, Riekert had good things to offer. They would be given priority for available jobs; they would have more freedom to look for work in other areas; some of the restrictions which prevented families from joining them would be lifted. Whether there would ever be the homes to house them was another matter. But the intention was clear; Riekert was aiming to produce a more stable and efficient work force. The 'insiders' were to be given a degree of permanence hitherto unknown in South Africa; but the 'outsiders' would have to pay the price.

Riekert proposed to step up the war against those he called 'unregisterable migrant labourers' by shifting the onus of obeying the law from the worker to the employer. Fines for workers would be abandoned since they had little effect but fines for those who gave work to 'disqualified' people would be increased; up to R500 (£275) for a first offence; a minimum of R500 from then on. Koornhof responded immediately and introduced the new fines for employers forthwith but kept the fines on 'disqualified' workers as well, threatening later to increase them. New legislation also proposed to fine anyone housing such workers and to impound the cars of those found guilty a second time of the crime of transporting them.

In the meantime the prospect of a R500 fine caused panic in the white suburbs; Koornhof offered a three-month moratorium provided employers now registered their 'illegals'. Eighty-four thousand were flushed out but given only one year's papers. Hundreds of others, presenting themselves in good faith at their local pass office, found themselves unable to meet unexpected requirements and were endorsed out to the homelands. 'Piet Promises', they said in the townships, had conned them.

A white builder on the East Rand explained the small employer's problems. He had sixty blacks on the pay-roll half of them 'illegals'. He preferred them because they worked harder. During the moratorium his brother went each day to the pass office to see what could be done for them; by six a.m. the queue already stretched right round the block. When the moratorium ended on 31 October 1979, fifteen of the 'illegals' were registered. The other fifteen he sacked. The new law had done its work but fifteen black breadwinners were out of work.

At the Black Sash Advice offices in the city centres, hundreds of blacks thrown up by Riekert's R500 fine now add to the queues. But the white ladies of the Black Sash face much more than those caught in the Riekert trap. Here, every day, they are confronted with thirty years of Nationalist government. Here, every day, they witness the toll on family life the system takes, the misery of the contract worker who seeks to have near him the children who are growing up without him, the incomprehension of the wife who asks only to live with the man she legally married; the tears of the young man, a boy really, who does not understand why, since he cannot find work, he is classified as 'idle' and must now leave his parents and be sent to a homeland he has never seen.

Here the language is of '10 (1)(a) and (b) and (c)', of affidavits to prove employment, of letters to prove residence, of witnesses to prove birth, of certificates to prove existence. The labelled files in the Johannesburg office tell the story of the rows of patient black South Africans who wait: 'Workman's Compensation', 'Name Change', 'Employer's Abuse', 'Pensions', 'Administration Board', 'Farm Labour', 'Bribery and Corruption', 'Work Permit', 'Endorsed Out', 'Successfully closed'. This last one is no thicker than any of the others. For fifty per cent of the fifty thousand Africans who have come to seek help since the Johannesburg office opened in 1963, the Black Sash has been able to do nothing – and those who find the bus fare into town are but a tiny percentage of those in trouble with the Nationalist bureaucracy.

The ladies of the Black Sash may be the first whites who have ever listened sympathetically to their problem. They are middle class and mainly middle-aged housewives from the northern suburbs, moved by common humanity for their fellow South Africans. Elizabeth Rowe, one of the founder members, probably knows the ins and endorsed outs of the Nationalist system as well as anyone in Pretoria. All her family have now left South Africa, but she stays on: 'I'm sixty and people keep saying I must ease up but if I want to work myself to the grave that's my affair.' Work starts at eight. No one stops for lunch.

Adeline Phologi and Mabel Makgabutlane, the two black interpreters, bring round tea between translations; there is do-it-yourself bread and cheese in another room.

Elizabeth is constantly interrupted; Nana Wynberg wants to know why the township superintendent will not hand over this man's house permit; should they ring him up? Beulah Rollnick wants advice with the case of a delivery driver, waiting in another room. He had been working in Johannesburg for six years. His boss never bothered to register him and paid him R25 a week (about £14). Now he has lost his job and has been endorsed out. 'It's pure harassment'. Ginna Portman asks a fine point about 10 (1)(c)s. She is an American over on an exchange grant who used to teach poor whites in the Appalachians. 'Questions keep cropping up and I hate to keep asking but if you make a mistake you can easily ruin someone's life'. Her view of South Africa is 'negative and getting more so every day'.

'Where is your home place?' Elizabeth asks through Mabel. 'Can you remember where you were born? Did you go to school?'

A case can take half an hour [she says]. We have terrible trouble getting the story straight. Then we have to decide if it is worth trying for proper registration. Here's a young man who might make it under the moratorium. He's brought three letters to prove he's been employed for all but six months of the last three years. For the rest of the time he was selling fruit, so that's a problem. He stays with a policeman's family in Soweto. If he can bring an affidavit saying that the family will take their 'cousin' as a lodger and that they know he was self-employed during that six months blank period it might come right. I am not very hopeful but we will try.

'Links' Harris comes in with a typed-out affidavit. She and her husband moved to Sasolburg three months ago. Yet she drives in to the office several times a week, one hundred kilometres each way. Barbara Waite arrives for an afternoon stint after a full shift as a nursing sister in a children's hospital. Sheena Duncan is there too. Joyce Harris, the President, comes in after addressing a lunchtime meeting. They all do their turn, hearing cases, drafting letters and affidavits.

How many Afrikaners are in the Black Sash? 'Well,' says Barbara, 'there's Lynette Naudé, Beyers' daughter-in-law. But she is a special case.' So is Beyers Naudé himself, of course, a senior member of the Broederbond who publicly denounced the secret society and all its works. 'Apart from her and Anna Marais, one of the early members, I can't think of any others. But it must be difficult for Afrikaners to join us. It takes a special kind of courage.'

Afrikaner housewives have founded their own organisation, 'Kon-tak', to work for better relations between black and white. But they have not yet made it their business to confront the government in the market place on matters of principle. To put themselves out of step with the mass of white thinking, as the Black Sash have done, is to invite abuse and ridicule, telephone tapping, mail opening and vicious hoaxes. Joyce Harris, the President, was telephoned one day: 'This is the police', said the voice. 'Your husband has just been killed in a road accident.'

'When we ring up employers,' said Elizabeth, 'I always tell the girls to say "This is the Advice Office", not "The Black Sash". That way you can usually get further.'

Black Sash was founded in 1955 to protest against the removal of Coloured people from the common roll, and thousands then joined their 'Women's Defence of the Constitution League'. They could draw thirty thousand to a meeting on the steps of Johannesburg's City Hall. Although they failed to save the Coloured vote they have gone on protesting, even though now they are only eleven hundred strong. The government loathes them. Where once they had marched and carried posters and chanted slogans, they were allowed only to stand in silence. Then they were permitted to demonstrate only in certain places. Then the size of the placards were regulated; next the wording that went on them had to be submitted to the police. Finally, under the Riotous Assemblies Act, they could no longer protest in groups. Not even two women were allowed to stand together. So now members of the Black Sash protest singly, holding a placard in silence, demonstrating their opposition.

Throughout these years, the seven Advice Offices have handled all the cases they can manage and more. In the four months after the Riekert report in July 1979, their workload doubled. Most of the additional cases were men and women from the homelands who had found possible jobs but who had been told by employers, fearing the R500 fine, that they would not take them on until they were registered. When they went to the pass office, they were endorsed out. In November, the Black Sash issued an emergency report:

Never in the sixteen years since this office was opened, [wrote Sheena Duncan, the Director of the Advice Office] have we experienced such anger expressed by black people or such a sense of impending catastrophe. Never have we felt more urgently the need to try to communicate to white South Africans the reality of what is happening.

The pass laws have always been one of the main causes of black alienation but if historians who in the future write of our times are able to isolate the final straw which precipitated disaster, it may well prove to be this year's legislation introducing the fine of R500 which can now be imposed on the employer of an unregistered person . . .

Over and over again during the last few weeks men and women have said to us: 'But my children have no food.' 'My children are hungry.' 'What will my children eat?' Poverty, hunger and the diseases of malnutrition have been a way of life for thousands of South African families for many years. Work seekers in the homelands are not allowed to move to the cities to seek for work, and if they do so, are not allowed to register in jobs they have found. The only way in which they can obtain legal employment is if they are recruited or requisitioned from the labour bureau in their home area. Such recruitment is now being strictly controlled and cut back.

Until this year people have been able to find illegal work and so have survived. Now for the first time in our experience, we have no hope and no comfort to offer to the unregistered and the endorsed out. Always before, we and they have known that they would be able to go on somehow, even if it meant arrest and imprisonment from time to time. All hope has now been removed and when you take away all hope, all that is left is rage and anger, bitterness and hatred.

Yet the other side of the Riekert coin does exist. In the black townships, those who are protected by the new rules enjoy a life more settled than they ever knew before. In 1978 we met and filmed the family of Solly Madlala living in the heart of Soweto, at number 1477 in Zondi, a district like any other. The house was rented with four rooms, no bathroom, just one cold tap outside next to the lavatory. There was no electricity and the only heating was provided by the coal stove which was also used for cooking.

Madlala worked for a jeweller in Braamfontein, on the northern edge of Johannesburg's city centre. He was what was called a 'delivery boy', bicycling around the city carrying diamonds and pearls, necklaces and rings, mostly to the Post Office. He was paid R30 a week (£16.50) with which he did his best to maintain a household of twelve, eight of his own children, two grandchildren plus his wife Maria and himself. His eldest son had been killed by *tsotsis* (thugs) and Solly Madlala himself had lost an eye when he had been attacked on the way home with his pay packet.

The money was just enough to keep the family going, after rent and coal and school and candles. There was bread and tea for breakfast, ten cents (about six pence) for each of the four schoolgoers, Charles, Anna, Ruth and Denis, to last them until evening when the family had their supper of *sadsa* (mealie porridge) and vegetables. Meat was a treat at weekends when Solly would sometimes also splash out and enjoy a can of 'Castle' or 'Lion' beer.

He had lived in Soweto all his life, so he had '10 (1)(a)' in his dompas. 'Without that', said Solly, 'you are nobody in Soweto'. The children were all qualified as residents too but none of the three oldest had regular work. Twenty-one year old Maria spent most of her time around the house with her four-year-old son, Peter. The twins, Judas and Andries, did any odd job they could find, running errands or working as weekend 'garden boys', but they brought in no regular money.

Life in Soweto is bad, even terrible [said Madlala as we filmed his candle-lit supper in 1978]. There is actually no life worth living in Soweto. At any moment you can be killed or murdered. You are just not sure of what you are doing, or where you are when you are not white. But the white people of this country are not playing ball with us blacks, in more ways than one, especially when it comes to living conditions and these pay conditions of theirs. We are being unhappy in such a way that we are starving. But they live splendidly; they have got everything. They've got flashy cars, they've got mansions, not to compare with these matchboxes we've got here. This is not a house, it's just a hovel. So life for them is quite all right, but not for us blacks.

Two years later Solly Madlala was a changed man. Judas and Andries had full-time jobs, perhaps because of the uplift in the economy, perhaps because, as part of the Riekert proposals, 'insiders' with permanent residence were being given precedence for available work. Whatever the reason, the money coming into the Madlala household had more than doubled. Madlala's own wages had gone up by ten rand a week (£5.50).

'If you have a full stomach,' he said, as we all sat in the back yard next to the cabbages, sipping 'Castle,' 'life is quite different.'

He had been busy plastering the bare breeze blocks of the inside walls of the house. Painted white they had already brightened up the kitchen; they would keep it warmer too. There was even the promise of electricity soon. Since the plugs and points had already been installed for eight years, Madlala was not counting on anything. 'But if the white man tells me the electricity is coming soon, who am I to disbelieve him?'

In one other respect Solly Madlala's life had changed. The abolition of separate queues for blacks and whites at the Post Office had transformed his working day:

Coming to the Post Office now, and having to wait and do all that jazz because

258

there were three whites; we had to wait hours on end, we being a hundred or so. But today all that has been eliminated and it satisfies me in such a way that what I used to do in two hours, today I'm doing it in about forty-five minutes. So now everything is easier for everybody. Other than having my boss shouting at me and asking what hours I've been wasting, doing my own things when I was on his job. All such things have come to end now. Without any commotion everybody is being served, like a person. Even we black people are being seen as people living, human beings. Not like before.

In front of the house in Zondi, where before had been only waste ground, there was now a football pitch. Not Wembley turf but a pitch nonetheless. The community had clubbed together and had rented the ground from the West Rand Administration Board. Volunteers had cleared the rubbish and flattened the mounds. The pitch was in use for as long as there was light; in addition to kick-abouts, regular matches were organised with teams of different age groups playing in local leagues. Solly Madlala was convinced that the drop in hooliganism in Zondi was a direct result. One of his twin sons, Judas, now aged twenty-three, was a regular player, so was seventeen-year-old Charles, a promising centre forward. He played for the junior team, the 'Winter Roses'. Madlala had great hopes that Charles might soon be accepted at a trade school and might one day become an electrician. The family, and the community, were putting down roots.

Under Verwoerd's theories the flow of blacks to the cities should have been halted by the end of the seventies. The development of the homelands was by then to have become a magnet in the other direction. No such miracle had occurred because of the Nationalists' own refusal to develop or extend the meagre black reserves. So now Apartheid has changed. The Solly Madlalas of the townships are being allowed to stay because the white economy cannot do without them. The government hopes that they will be content with their improving lot, that they will provide a buffer against the great unwashed of the homelands now penned behind the even taller fences of the new pass laws.

The 'illegals' are steadily being expelled as they are thrown up by the system. The numbers of the 'insiders' are now ever more rigidly controlled. Black Sash sees them as the top twelve per cent. The Nationalists are ready to hold back the economy rather than allow the numbers of urban blacks to become unmanageable. Perhaps all that is what Koornhof meant when he spoke of the death of Apartheid:

The last thing I would do would be to want to mislead anybody [he said in 1980]. I am a straightforward and honest man and what I say I literally mean.

259

Apartheid as the world came to know it, and the caricature of Apartheid as they knew it, I think, was dying and I hope is dead . . . But you must remember that you are dealing with a highly complicated human problem; and you are dealing with a deep-going reform and it seems to me that it is bound to lead to some misunderstandings, if one doesn't understand . . . But because of the fact that you are dealing with a tremendous, mammoth task, it can't be done before breakfast.

20
'Moses had a mixed marriage'
Prime Minister P. W. Botha, September 1980

Just what would be achieved *after* breakfast and beyond would depend very much on Pieter Willem Botha. He had been thrust into the Prime Ministership by the events of Muldergate. Until then as Minister of Defence he had hardly seemed a likely candidate to take over the mantle of Malan, Strydom, Verwoerd and Vorster.

His life spanned the events of the Nationalists' rise to power; his career touched many of them. His only employer had been the National Party. He was the official turned politician, the longest-serving Member of Parliament, the longest-serving minister; known as an administrator but not as a visionary. At Defence they called him *Piet Wapen* (Piet Weapon), partly because of his temper. 'No one will ever accuse me of too much self-control', he once told Piet Cillie. Helen Suzman, in a famous epithet, said 'If he was female, he would arrive in Parliament on a broomstick.'

On the day that he was elected Prime Minister, an hour or so after the official declaration on the steps of the Senate in Cape Town, a small group of people was waiting outside the Members' entrance at the House of Assembly. As Botha came down the steps a coloured man moved forward, spoke briefly and shook him by the hand. Some months later I asked the Prime Minister what the man had said. 'Just that he would pray for me', was the answer.

P. W. Botha had always enjoyed a particular relationship with the South Africans known as Coloureds. During the Anglo-Boer War his mother, Hendrina de Wet, a distant relation of the Boer general, was married to a farmer in the Free State named Prinsloo. He was captured by the British and sent to a prisoner-of-war camp in Ceylon. His wife stayed on at the farm near Senekal until the British advance began. Then Hendrina Prinsloo, like Henning Klopper's mother ninety miles away at Heilbron, hitched the family's oxen to the wagon and fled with her three children; the youngest was three months old. With

261

them too went Hendrina Prinsloo's fourteen-year-old sister and the family's Coloured gardener who hid them in a cave. For three months he and his wife looked after them but then they were captured by the British and the family were sent to a concentration camp at Winburg.

Two of Hendrina Prinsloo's children died in the camp at Winburg but after the war she went back to the farm where she had hidden £600 in gold under the floor of the house. The homestead had been destroyed but the money was safe. With it the family were able to start again and the Coloured gardener stayed with them until he died. Prinsloo himself was repatriated from Ceylon but did not long survive. In 1915 his widow married Botha's father who had fought right through the war. 'He called himself a wild Boer, and was very proud because they hadn't been able to catch him.'

Pieter Willem, their only child, the future Prime Minister, was born in 1916. He grew up in a political family, committed to the Afrikaner cause; but while his father supported the more moderate views of General Hertzog, his mother was for Malan and his 'Purified' Nationalists. 'We argued politics very much', he said. But there was no disagreement on the Afrikaners' ultimate objective. By the time Botha went to high school in Bethlehem, he said 'we were so motivated that we thought of only one thing and that was our freedom'. From there, in 1934, he went to the University College of the Orange Free State in Bloemfontein to study economics and law; but he never obtained a degree. It was not so much that he was 'not quite a brilliant student', as one of his contemporaries, Professor Hennie Coetzee of Potchefstroom University put it, but that he left before taking his final examinations.

In his third year at Bloemfontein while Botha was not yet twenty, Dr D. F. Malan the leader of the Cape Nationalists came to address the students. Malan had just broken with Hertzog over Fusion and gone his own way with his group of 'Purified' Nationalists. Botha made the address of welcome on behalf of the students and afterwards Malan told him 'he was looking for young men in the Party's service in the Cape'. So in 1936, Botha gave up his studies, falling out with his father in the process, and went to work for Malan in Cape Town as one of the six Party organisers. When he became Prime Minister some of his opponents were not slow to point out that South Africa was now governed by 'a matric boy'.

Travelling through the Cape collecting funds, selling Nationalist literature, setting up branches of the Party, Botha gained a reputation as an organiser; he was also well known as a famous disrupter of opposition meetings. It was a bitter period with Afrikaners deeply divided over the issue of Fusion. The technique of the Nationalists was to infiltrate United Party meetings and then challenge the impartiality of the chairman when he refused to take their questions. If that did not work they regularly broke up the meetings. 'When Afrikaners fight', said Piet Cillie then a reporter and later editor of *Die Burger*, 'it's like the family. It gets rough.' Rival groups regularly came to blows although Botha always said he did not enjoy that part so much. He never lost the ability, learned during those years, to produce a wounding phrase.

Botha worked for the National party in the Cape for ten years and at the outbreak of World War Two helped found the Ossewabrandwag in the province. But as the split between van Rensburg's paramilitaries and the National Party developed (see pp. 133–139) Botha stayed firmly on his employer's side. In August 1941, at the height of the row, he took the initiative of writing to *Die Burger* complaining that van Rensburg was leading the Ossewabrandwag in a 'disastrous direction'. It was heading, said Botha, towards National Socialism while the party stood for Christian Nationalism. Two days later the newspaper published a reply from the Ossewabrandwag saying that Botha had been 'suspended'.

In 1946 Botha's loyalty to the Party was rewarded when he was promoted to become national publicity secretary in the run-up to the 1948 elections. The party paid him the further compliment of nominating him, an employee, as a candidate. It gave him the chance to win the seat at George on the Cape coast which he has held ever since. In election year, Botha was also appointed secretary of the National Party in the Cape, an office he filled for a decade, smoothly orchestrating party activities throughout the province. In 1966, Botha became provincial leader and immediately increased the number of professional party organisers. He also arranged for more of them to be put forward as parliamentary candidates. In 1948, when Botha entered parliament he was one of three such nominees; by 1978 eleven Cape parliamentarians out of the total of fifty-five had come up by the Botha route, all of them owing personal allegiance to their leader.

In the Transvaal, the nomination process for the province was quite different. There Dr Connie Mulder encouraged the recruitment of professional men as candidates. The different approach had an important effect on the elections for the party leadership when Vorster resigned. While several of Mulder's professional men defected to Pik Botha and ultimately to P. W. Botha, it was believed that no more than three or four Cape members failed to vote for their provincial patron.

Botha's experience in government began as Deputy Minister of the Interior in 1958. Three years later he was a member of Verwoerd's cabinet as the first Minister for Coloured Affairs, with additional responsibilities for Community Development. If he had grown up with feelings of gratitude towards individual Coloured South Africans, those feelings never impinged upon his Nationalist beliefs. He had already been part of the campaign to remove the Coloureds from the common voters' roll. As the Minister for Coloured Affairs he prepared the way for the end of any representation at all for the Coloureds in the white parliament, although by the time their four seats were abolished in 1968 Botha himself had moved on to become Minister of Defence.

As Minister of Defence, Botha the organiser made a lasting impact, building up the most powerful armed forces in Africa. The Institute for Strategic Studies in London calculated in 1979 that the combined strength of South Africa's seven northern neighbouring states, Mozambique, Angola, Tanzania, Botswana, Zambia, Malawi and Zimbabwe were appreciably less than South Africa's 'total mobilisation force'. Put more succinctly by R. W. Johnson, the Oxford author of *How Long Will South Africa Survive?*: 'There is no army in Africa which could last more than an afternoon against the South Africans if they put their backs into it'.

To improve efficiency Botha broke with tribal loyalties and promoted English speakers and Afrikaners alike purely on merit. He also started to recruit Coloureds, Indians and Africans who by the end of his fourteen years as Minister made up a quarter of the regular armed forces. While most blacks went into the army's so-called 'ethnic' battalions, Coloureds and Indians who joined the navy were much more integrated. 'There is no room for Apartheid on ships', said a naval commander in Simonstown. 'We break the race laws of this country every day but we don't make a big noise about it.'

Under Botha South Africa developed a formidable armaments industry through the government agency of Armscor. South Africa became self-sufficient in helicopters, armed vehicles, artillery and missiles and produced its own standard automatic rifle, the R4, plus the ammunition to go with it. In 1968 Botha told the Senate that South Africa had developed napalm bombs, aerial bombs, smoke bombs, two types of cheap, highly effective shrapnel mines and an anti-armour mine. English and Afrikaans firms alike played their role; even companies with British connections were not indifferent to Botha's

Prime Minister P. W. Botha visiting the Bushman Battalion in
South West Africa

blandishments and fat contracts.

For years one firm near Johannesburg produced thousands of
mortar bomb casings a day that were collected every morning by eight
Bedford trucks and driven away to be charged with explosives. That
many were then fired at black Nationalist guerrillas in Rhodesia, as
part of the secret war effort to assist Ian Smith, was not a matter on
which there was any discussion in South Africa where such topics are
highly restricted. Meanwhile Rolls-Royce Viper turbo-jet engines
were being built under licence in South Africa for two versions of the
Impala so-called 'trainer' which, when fitted with two 30mm cannons
was particularly suitable for counter-guerrilla activities. The British
arms company Plessey trained South African soldiers in the use of

radar air surveillance equipment; despite the United Nations arms embargo of 1977, Atlas Aviation, set up with French help, continued to make complete Mirage fighter bombers, every piece manufactured in South Africa, even though the licence from France had been withdrawn.

As for the much debated question of whether or not South Africa possessed nuclear weapons, as Minister of Defence Botha always chose to follow a policy of what was called 'deterrence by uncertainty', thus allowing his Prime Minister John Vorster to delight audiences up and down the country with his nudge-and-wink confidences:

We developed the process to enrich uranium, [said Vorster at Graaff-Reinet in 1978] and we built a pilot plant; and it rather amuses me that when I announced it a couple of years ago there were those who laughed at us and said we are talking big, we haven't got it. Now they are accusing me that we have got it. They then said we couldn't do it, now they say that we want to do it.

There is some evidence that South Africa, with the help of the Israelis, did do it, that is explode a nuclear device in the South Atlantic at three o'clock in the morning on 22 September 1979. An American satellite which had not failed to monitor forty-one previous tests in various parts of the globe left the Pentagon in no doubt that a test firing of a tactical nuclear weapon had taken place. Naturally South Africa and Israel made appropriate denials and the White House, presumably embarrassed that its protégé Israel had broken the Nuclear Test Ban Treaty, made no public issue of the event. But it remained highly probable that with their combined resources, technical know-how and above all motive, South Africa and Israel had given their nuclear scientists rather more than theoretical know-how.

This arming of South Africa took place under the direction of a man with no military training who still earned the respect of his senior military hierarchy. In return, the advisers Botha gathered around him, like General Magnus Malan, the head of the Defence Force, put their own imprint on their Minister's thinking. It was said that Malan even used to suggest Botha's reading matter, on subjects from the French Algerian war to American counter-insurgency in Vietnam. Botha was impressed by the way the military got things done in contrast to the inefficiency and duplication in the civil service which after thirty years of Nationalist rule was clearly suffering from the over-promotion of Afrikaners. Even a leading Broeder at Stellenbosch, Professor E. C. Pienaar, had complained that after the fifties there had been far too many '*baantjies vir boeties*' (jobs for pals).

266

When Botha moved on from the Ministry of Defence to become Prime Minister he kept the Defence portfolio for himself during the first two years and he took with him both military men and methods. He also took a broom to the civil service, reducing some forty government departments to almost half that number under eighteen managers with the new rank of Director General. In those £20,000 a year posts Botha placed men of proved ability, not hesitating to by-pass more senior civil servants or those whose loyalty he doubted.

The civil servants met in fifteen policy planning committees on all of which the military was also represented. Their activities in turn were coordinated by a new 'Office of the Prime Minister'. Similarly Botha reduced the number of Cabinet committees to four: internal affairs, social affairs, financial affairs and foreign affairs, presided over by ministers who were close to his own thinking. At the top of this slimmed-down pyramid sat not only the Cabinet, but also what was called the 'State Security Council'. It had been in existence since 1972 but under Vorster had met barely half-a-dozen times.

Under Botha's chairmanship the State Security Council has met regularly and has become a vital instrument in managing the affairs of the nation. Under General Malan's tutelage it developed the much publicised concept of 'Total Strategy' which, as Malan explained in a speech in 1977, was simply a response to the 'Total War' being waged against South Africa:

What then is total war all about? In effect every means of a state and community or society becomes a weapon; every capability in whatever field of endeavour at the disposal of an enemy becomes a target. It is the kind of battle in which the soldier is relegated to a minor role. The politician, diplomat, economist, industrialist, psychologist and similar professionals now take over the centre stage.

The weapons have become diplomacy, industry and trade, technology, the written and spoken word, the public media, demonstrations, strikes, boycotts, subversion and so forth. The whole of South Africa must be attuned to applying its total effort in an organised way by continuous coordinated action in all the various terrains of action.

Thus, when Prime Minister Botha tries to push recommendations in almost any field through the Cabinet or Parliament he can justify them as being in the interests of national security and the military can justify their own activity in almost any sphere of South African life, because they are part of the machinery of co-ordination.

Senior officers were clearly aware of the difficulty, in a democratic society, of implementing the action that might eventually be required

if the 'Total War' against South Africa were stepped up. In a somewhat chilling speech in 1977 the Chief of Staff Operations, Lt General
J. R. Dutton, anticipated the measures they might have to ask government to take:

The requirements for the application of Total Strategy would appear to
favour a system of unified command. . . . Conventional organisations in
democratic systems do not as a rule lend themselves to those procedures.
Therefore organisational changes or adaptations would appear to be imperative.

If Botha continued to listen to his military advisers there was the
unmistakeable hint that the State Security Council might one day find
itself by-passing the parliamentary institutions altogether. In 1975,
when Botha was Minister of Defence and Vorster Prime Minister,
South Africa had mounted a major military operation in Angola
without consulting Parliament, so there was already a precedent.

In 1980, Botha had given a further hint of these somewhat anti-
democratic tendencies. He announced the government's intention of
increasing the strength of the House of Assembly by twelve nominated
members. Four would be chosen by the State President, eight by MPs
themselves on a basis in proportion to the seats already held. That
meant one additional member for the Progressive Federal Party and
eleven more Nationalists. A government hand-out praised an innova-
tion that allowed for 'the introduction of specialists'. Others saw it as
the beginning of a move to erode powers of an elected parliament.

Simultaneously Botha abolished the partially elected Senate and
established instead a President's Council whose members were nominated. No one suggested that the upper house in recent times had
applied much of a brake to the Nationalist machine but nonetheless
another check on government had gone. As South Africa moved
steadily away from the Westminster system of government P. W.
Botha seemed to be giving himself more powers than any Prime
Minister since Union.

In a cabinet re-shuffle in August 1980 Botha brought in two more
outside specialists. He promoted General Malan to become Minister of
Defence and nominated none other than the Chairman of the
Broederbond, Professor Gerrit Viljoen, to be Minister of Education
and Sport. It was a shrewd appointment that promised several
benefits. The obvious one was that Botha, Broederbond member
number 4487, was publicly seen to be drawing to his side the senior
executive of the somewhat less than secret society that nonetheless still

played a crucial role in holding Afrikanerdom together. Botha had already sent Viljoen to Namibia as Administrator General to bang together the heads of warring Afrikaner elements who were not anxious to accept the changes Pretoria was proposing for the territory. Now Viljoen, a classicist and first Rector of the Rand Afrikaans University, would bring his considerable intellectual powers to the Cabinet. He was known to share his Prime Minister's views on the need to adapt Apartheid to South Africa's changing circumstances. Furthermore, in 1974, when Viljoen had been elected chairman of the Broederbond, he had defeated the more conservative Dr Andries Treurnicht. In due course, with Botha behind him, Viljoen might well beat Treurnicht again for the Transvaal leadership. In that way Botha might rid himself of his main rival.

Viljoen's promotion meant an election for a new Chairman of the Broederbond. In September 1980 Botha took the unusual step of addressing the secret General Council before they made their choice but he cannot have been happy with the outcome. The natural successor to the so-called moderate, Viljoen, would have been Professor W. L. Mouton, the Rector of the University of the Orange Free State, whom Botha had made Chairman of the South African Broadcasting Corporation. The right-wing candidate was Dr D. P. N. Beukes, former Vice-Chairman of the Broederbond, a long serving member of the Executive Council, and one time head of the Dutch Reformed Church in the Transvaal.

In the event the Broederbond flexed its muscles and elected Professor Carel Boshoff, the chairman of one of their own front organisations, the think-tank called the South African Bureau of Racial Affairs. Boshoff was the son-in-law of Dr Hendrik Verwoerd, and the man to whom writer Hennie Serfontein used to send visiting journalists for an articulate expression of full-blooded Afrikaner Nationalism. Boshoff had been known to expound on the possibilities of an Afrikaner retreat to a white homeland if the going became too rough. His election was a clear sign that the arch-conservatives were not to be underestimated.

As Botha tried to decide how the old Verwoerdian concepts should be developed, the right-wingers with their fear of change would never be far from his mind. But there were other forces, no less powerful, pushing him in a different direction; chief among them, perhaps surprisingly, were his close advisers, the military. Malan and his generals had pointed out many times that while the Defence Force had the capacity to resist external aggression it could not deal with continuing internal unrest as well. Malan had spoken of the need to 'gain and keep the trust of our different population groups'. The obvious way to do that was to give blacks, Coloureds and Indians a better deal. Discrimination on the grounds of colour, went the reasoning, could be removed without necessarily undermining the basic principles of the separation of the races.

The Defence Force needed manpower. White employers were continually irritated at losing their bright young men for two years' National Service as well as for regular spells of reservist duty that could last as long as three months. That was one reason why the military had been prepared to put aside their doubts about giving guns to black men and now sought recruits among all population groups. Another was the lesson learned from Rhodesia. Black soldiers had done much of the fighting there against black Nationalist guerrillas giving Ian Smith an opportunity he never missed, to point out that his was no race war but part of the world conflict between democracy and Communism. South Africa would do exactly the same. But to encourage blacks, Coloureds and Indians to help the government face the 'Total Onslaught', went the military reasoning, they must be given more of a stake in the country they were to defend. So there was another reason for reforms at home. The generals, for all their autocratic tendencies, were arguing for more liberal policies.

Overseas pressure was urging South Africa in exactly the same direction. Eschel Rhoodie liked to recall his regular discussions with his political masters about the difficulty of selling South Africa to the outside world. His theme was that if ever they were to break out of their isolation they would have to look very carefully at the practices and the laws which affronted the dignity of the black man. Repeating the Nationalist assertion that such things had 'nothing to do with the overall objectives of separate political freedoms, or the establishment of independent homelands for blacks' Rhoodie nonetheless recognised that, 'they deeply affronted the friends of South Africa abroad'.

Multi-national companies, with branches in South Africa, were particularly well-placed to insist on change. What they wanted was a contented work force. If Botha's government would not move towards them by abolishing some of the discrimination on the shop floor, they would take their capital and their new plant elsewhere. And to maintain the growth rate, said the economists, South Africa could not manage without foreign investment. After the Soweto riots the pressure for real black advance increased. The boom that followed the rise in the price of gold emphasised the urgent need for skilled labour. Answering both demands came the recommendations of both

P. W. Botha in Soweto, the first South African Prime Minister
to go there; with him, Piet Koornhof and David Thebahali, Chairman
of Soweto Council

Wiehahn and Riekert. Limited though they were they did represent
some advance. Thus the government hoped to take the wind out of the
sails of the groups pressurising foreign firms to disinvest.

At the same time Botha himself began to behave as no Nationalist
Prime Minister before him. In 1979, a year after succeeding John
Vorster, he did what no Prime Minister had ever done and visited the
black township of Soweto showing quite clearly that his intention was
to win black city dwellers to his side. But before any of his right
wingers could take fright he also explained exactly why he was doing it.
'The aspirations of urban blacks and the fulfilment of them', he said to
the Soweto Council and the seven Cabinet ministers he had taken with
him, 'must form part of the strategy for the protection of everyone in
South Africa.' General Malan could not have put it better.

Perhaps there was also a less definable motive for change that Botha
sensed and seized. By the end of the seventies the Afrikaner had grown
in self-confidence as his role in the running of South Africa's affairs
had expanded. Most Afrikaners were now city dwellers where they
worked in business and industry and the professions alongside English

271

speakers. The Afrikaner 'identity' nurtured by the Broederbond, was no longer under the threat that it had been before 1948. The Republic had been won and had endured. The country was prosperous and the Afrikaners' place in it secure.

It began to appear as more and more reasonable that black office workers and factory hands should also share in some of the good things of South African life. The Afrikaner could begin to relax. He was discovering that the world did not come to an end when the signs on separate lifts were removed or when he stood in the same queue as a black man to be served by an Indian bank teller. René de Villiers, President of the South African Institute of Race Relations, considered that Afrikaners had long been anxious to come in from the cold of world opprobrium. 'The real Afrikaner', he said, 'is a man who longs to be accepted, a man who longs to be wanted and to be loved.'

In the Afrikaner universities like Potchefstroom and Stellenbosch there was growing disenchantment with the political status quo. Students were questioning not just the practice of Apartheid but the principles as well. In the churches, Afrikaners were heard to voice doubts as to why the divine mission of civilising Southern Africa had to be attended by so much suffering. In Dutch Reformed Church halls, like the one in the Johannesburg suburb of Parktown North, Afrikaner matrons were spending two evenings a week teaching their black servants how to read and how to sew.

Botha gave ear and expression to some of this concern. He berated hardliners who objected to Coloured players taking part in a schools rugby week, 'What sort of mentality is it', he barked to the National Party Congress in the Transvaal, 'when we cannot accept Coloureds playing sport together with white, while on the border they fight with us?' and in Cape Town he complained to his home team Nationalists that 'at a time when the Russian bear is at the door, there are people who are arguing about immorality and sport.'

Dr Ernie Malherbe, in retirement on the Natal coast, believed Botha's major contribution was towards:

the creation of a new tolerance in white Nationalists towards the blacks. His image is more that of a concerned man than that of a racist. He has repeatedly lectured his own followers on how they should improve race relations and his reformist ideas are slowly seeping into the public service. From his speeches it is clear that his approach is quite different from that of Verwoerd.

Where Malherbe saw real hope was in the attitude of young Afrikaners. He perceived the simmerings of unease at Stellenbosch and Potchefstroom as the start of a revolt:

Young people are essentially pragmatic, [he wrote] especially Afrikaners who have become educated enough to realise what the ultimate consequences of Apartheid will be. They know that Apartheid will not work in the long run and while they have no cut-and-dried solution themselves they are now prepared to seek another solution.

Towards the end of 1980 even Botha himself appeared to be approaching that Rubicon when he publicly admitted that the Verwoerdian ideal of independent homelands was no longer attainable. 'It is impossible to consolidate the geographical area of each national group', he told his own national group in Pretoria, 'in such a way that it will become economically viable on its own . . . We cannot give away the whole of South Africa merely to create economically viable states.' Setting aside the fact that no Nationalist government had ever really attempted to make the homelands viable, here was a reversal of policy with colossal implications. Botha had appointed his own commission to study homeland consolidation and he was not even waiting for its report to be made public.

But it was known that the amount of white farming land the van der Walt Commission proposed would have to be transferred to the 'Black States' to give them even a remote chance of independence was completely out of the political question. Van der Walt had spoken too of the need to create two hundred thousand new jobs a year in the homelands, a ludicrously high figure in the light of previous government achievement. What Botha's bright young men were now proposing was regional development that ignored the homeland boundaries. Where it made economic sense to build what was euphemistically called 'a co-prosperity development zone' that is where it would go. Transport facilities, natural resources, markets and labour would be the determining factors rather than the demands of an ideology. Just how much the 'black states' would get out of the 'co-prosperity development' was not clear. Botha had spoken of the need 'to extend the hand of co-operation over the borders of states'. But if a new factory was to be built in, say East London, in white man's land, it was difficult to see how Chief Sebe of the Ciskei next door would be able to insist on a share of the profits that labourers from his 'black state' would help ensure.

Nonetheless Nationalist right-wingers took immediate fright at the prospect of economic integration. 'Any nation that tries to turn its living area into an open market', Andries Treurnicht told his Transvaal faithful, 'cannot retain its identity and control'. The new Chairman of the Broederbond, Professor Carel Boshoff, was equally critical. 'Economic integration in a system of separate political sovereignties', he said, 'is a false doctrine'. It was perfectly evident, he maintained, that blacks would use their economic power base in the 'white country' to promote further integration until they had obtained full citizenship and power. It was exactly the same argument used by those same Nationalists who opposed integrated sport on the grounds that it led to social mixing. For that, in turn brought love across the colour line, plus demands for intermarriage, unsegregated living areas and ultimately, the Nationalist nightmare of shared political power. And it was hard to dispute the conservatives' logic.

P. W. Botha, however, had no intention of going too far. Even though homeland consolidation was no longer a priority and the overcrowded black islands that Nationalists insisted on calling 'states' had no prospect of viability, they were still the only place where black South Africans would exercise political rights. 'There is not one single black man in the country who is not linked to a black homeland', he reassured the Volk; and black political aspirations would be channelled only through these 'black states'. He had 'given the answer to this ten times already but some people are so foolish you have to say it again and again'. On the issue of citizenship he was equally unyielding. As a homeland accepted Pretoria's version of independence each one of its citizens and all those judged by officialdom to be such, automatically lost their status as South Africans and became citizens of states recognised by no government in the world. In his days as Minister of Plural Relations, Connie Mulder had once said that ultimately there would be no black South Africans at all. It is one of the fundamental aspects of the Nationalist Grand Design that black South Africans refuse to accept.

Botha told blacks as he toured Soweto that 'We are all South Africans', and Mulder's successor, Piet Koornhof, in his renamed Ministry, promised both co-operation and development. But all that Koornhof produced was confusing talk of common citizenship and separate nationality; two years into his stewardship no change that would remotely satisfy his black charges had been proposed. The act which potentially made every black South African a foreigner in his own land remained on the statute book.

In truth, although Botha had tried to give Apartheid a new image the edifice remained intact. After the Riekert Report and the legislation that followed, the pass laws had not been abolished. They had simply been refined. While Botha created a stir by reminding Nationalists that 'Moses had a mixed marriage' he did nothing to alter the law that, had the Israelite patriarch and his Ethiopean wife been re-incarnated in South Africa, would have put them in front of a magistrate for contravening the Mixed Marriages Act. For Botha knew as well as anybody else that once such legal cornerstones were removed the whole structure upon which Afrikaner Nationalists believed they depended for survival was in danger.

Botha committed his government to establishing compulsory education for all, but no amount of money poured into black schooling (and the allocation for blacks was increased by thirty-two per cent in the 1980 budget) would convince the black population that their education was anything but inferior to that of whites for the simple reason that it was different. When Botha set about reorganising the civil service and government he chose not to bring the separate systems of black and white education under a central ministry. By a single administrative act he could have done more to convince the blacks of his good faith than on a hundred visits to Soweto. But the ideological arguments prevailed, The white teacher training college in Johannesburg was only half full in 1980 but despite the continuing shortage of qualified African teachers, no black could find a vacancy there. Separate schooling separately administered remained inviolate and one more major black grievance was ignored.

So the former Chairman of the Broederbond, Gerrit Viljoen, took over the Ministry of white education only and naturally, there too, Broederbond Nationalist thinking remained paramount. Not only was white education to remain separate from black, but Afrikaans speakers would be equally separate from English speakers. Nationalists could not accept that white children speaking either language should go to school together to develop a common loyalty to South Africa. For all the expansion of the Afrikaner's self-confidence they still feared they might be swamped by the English. Botha called for an end to the old feud between South Africa's two groups of whites and for the promotion of what Pretoria's hand-outs called 'the Anglo-Afrikaner nation' but as a Nationalist could not take the one step that might bring about real union, and send the children of both white groups to school together.

If the Afrikaner has an almost over-anxious fear of losing his identity, [explained Professor Gerrit Viljoen to me in 1977] that is because he is not the branch of the tree but the tree itself. If the whites of Rhodesia are defeated, they are merely a branch and the tree of English culture still grows . . . If the Afrikaners go, then the whole tree of Afrikaner culture goes with them.

But the Nationalist's motive was more than just self-preservation. After more than thirty years in power the branches of the Afrikaner tree were inextricably entwined around the very tree of South African life. It was little part of P. W. Botha's intention to loosen that hold.

In fact by the time Botha had become Prime Minister Apartheid was far more than a policy which could be repealed, an ugly aspect of an otherwise normal society. It was a total way of life, written into the constitution and enshrined in law. Apartheid had developed an unstoppable momentum of its own. As John Kane-Berman reported to *The Guardian* in 1980, 'Botha and his generals may now see some of the folly but Apartheid is greater than they are'.

In schools the Broederbond machine continued to print its racist pattern on youthful minds. In the civil service the Afrikaner bureaucracy remorselessly enforced the laws of the land. If Botha really had abandoned the chimera of homeland independence and the strict territorial separation of the races, the forced removal of Africans from 'white man's land' into the reserves might have been expected to drop away. Piet Koornhof had spoken of a halt to mass removals of whole communities. But in the absence of legislation that told them to do otherwise, the civil servants in government and local administration went on doing what they had always done. So black South Africans continued to be dumped in the 'closer settlements' where they had no prospect of making a living and where, as the eighties commenced, their children continued to die from diseases contracted through malnutrition.

Prosecutions under the Group Areas Act also continued. Coloureds and Indians caught living illegally in the central Johannesburg area were fined and evicted. Late in 1980 two test appeals to the highest court in the land were dismissed. Bulldozers continued to flatten good solid houses in the traditionally Indian district of western Johannesburg called Pageview. Householders were sent thirty miles away to find what accommodation they could in the already overcrowded Indian township of Lenasia.

Rather than change Apartheid legislation, and face protests from the ultra-conservatives, the government proceeded stealthily to reform by exemption. Thus in 1980 Mrs Susan Green, a woman classified Coloured, was given permission to marry Mr Aubrey Jooste, a man classified white. The ban on mixed marriages remained intact. Thus a ticket to a football match in Soweto became the white visitor's permit to be in a black area. The Group Areas Act was not altered. But such a practice left enormous power in the hands of government officials, to give or to withhold, inviting abuse and inconsistency of every kind.

Thus a white employer, who knew the right official at the pass office, also knew how much he had to pay for one of his 'boys' to be 'fixed up' with the right papers. Thus, also, seven black boxers on their way to the 1980 Transvaal Amateur Championships were arrested for not having passes; they were locked up overnight and missed the tournament.

Piet Koornhof likened the bureaucracy to a tortoise and told of a friend who gave him one as a present to remind him of the fact. 'If you allow it to go at its pace then it goes at a tortoise pace, which is slow. But if you push it, what happens? It pulls its head in and then it sits; and then the pace gets even slower.'[1]

The upper echelons of the civil service 'tortoise', of course, had long been the preserve of the Broederbond, as had the top jobs in education and the Dutch Reformed Church. While it was reasonable to assume that the Broederbond was as riven with doubt as the rest of Afrikanerdom over the future course of Apartheid, its members remained dedicated to one goal, and that was the secret promotion of their own. Botha may have had a broader view of Afrikanerdom than any Nationalist Prime Minister since Hertzog but it did not extend to renouncing the secret politicking of his fellow Broeders. He remained an undiluted Nationalist.

In June 1979 a letter to *Die Burger* calling for an end to the secrecy of the organisation brought forth a rare public response from an anonymous member. The Broederbond required its secrecy, went the letter, to be an agent for change. The call for an end to secrecy underestimated the threat to the country and 'especially to the leadership and initiative which Afrikaners were called upon to take in these circumstances'. This leadership

sometimes demands drastic reconsideration of existing positions and practices and sometimes radical changes. This can only happen after penetrating and frank discussion and persuasion within the Afrikaner ranks. To conduct all this delicate reflection and discussion in public would lead to confusion and would in any event be mercilessly exploited by the hostile Press and politicians. This we cannot allow because the debate also concerns the survival of the Afrikaners.

So the Broederbond philosophy remained clear. The changes to be

[1] Interview in June 1980 for part five of the BBC television series, *The White Tribe of Africa.*

made were only those that twelve thousand Nationalist Afrikaners accepted in their secret cells and the Broederbond view of the future was still enclosed by Nationalist blinkers. Gerrit Viljoen liked to maintain that Apartheid was an open-ended policy capable of adaptation to meet South Africa's changing circumstances. But when in 1978 he held a much-publicised meeting with Dr Nthato Motlana, the Soweto leader, Motlana recalled being left with a feeling of real depression:

Here was a man who was courteous and ready to listen, [said Motlana] but here also was a man steeped in the outrageous policies of the National Party, unwilling to budge from this idea of Separate Development. And one came away with a feeling that there is no movement, that there is going to be no movement in the foreseeable future that will lead the National Party to abandon this rejective policy.

21

'A wheelbarrow full of tins'

A Zulu politician on the quality of change under P. W. Botha

A further pointer to Nationalist thinking about change was evident in the constitutional proposals that P. W. Botha announced during 1980. At the centre of them was the President's Council which was to replace the Senate. Its sixty members were to be drawn from across the nation. The Council, said Botha, 'transcended political and racial barriers', its task was to formulate a new deal for South Africa, to find a constitutional framework that could satisfy everyone. It should be seen, the Prime Minister insisted, as a 'sincere attempt to ensure constitutional peace'. Its chairman, who also became the republic's first Vice-President, was one of Botha's close allies, the former Minister of Justice and the Interior, Alwyn Schlebusch. Three other former Cabinet ministers were drafted in to head various sub-committees.

But while the Council had provision for ten Coloureds, five Indians and even one Chinese, no blacks were included. They were offered only a separate and subordinate council of their own. It transpired that Piet Koornhof, for one, had wanted blacks as part of the main council but when right-wingers led by Andries Treurnicht had threatened to walk out of the party caucus if the 'moderates' had their way, the Prime Minister gave in to avoid an open split in the party.

Predictably black South Africans were scornful in their rejection of a separate Council. Chief Buthelezi of Kwazulu called the proposals 'half-baked' and refused even to sit down and discuss them with the government. Within months Botha withdrew the offer of a black council but proposed nothing in its place. Most Coloured and Indian politicians said they would not serve on the Council unless blacks were included and the official white opposition in the Assembly, the Progressive Federal Party, refused to have anything to do with it for the same reason. Undeterred, the government went ahead with their proposals. All sixty members of the Council were to be nominated, thus avoiding the ignominy of an electoral raspberry from the

279

Coloureds and Indians had representatives been subjected to the ballot box. The students of the Coloured University of the Western Cape let it be known they would burn down the university if their Rector accepted a nomination. The Chinese Association expelled the man appointed by Pretoria to represent them. One Indian among that community's five nominees promised to resign in a year if by then, blacks had not been invited to join as well.

So with a motley collection of Coloured politicians, white businessmen and academics and a Nationalist hardcore of aged Senators and MPs on free transfer from the Assembly, the President's Council took shape. It was also seen to include one or two hardliners whom Botha was thought to have been anxious to put on the sidelines. Some non-politicians whose names would have added prestige to the gathering were known to have refused invitations.

On 3 February 1981 the Council held its first session in an assembly hall, spruced up at great expense close to the Cape Town shopping centre, for it transpired that this prestigious President's Council was not prestigious enough to sit in the old Senate chamber in the same building as the House of Assembly. Perhaps, whispered the cynics, it was to avoid the risk of right-wing members of the lower house having to share the Members' dining room, or worse still, the lavatory, with men of colour.

Schlebusch, with a touch of Koornhoffian hyperbole, called the Council the most important negotiating body in the country's history 'able to consult at a high level and serve the government with advice'. And it was true that for the first time Nationalists were sitting down to discuss the country's constitutional future with men who were not white. Some observers, accustomed to the tortoise pace of change in South Africa, hailed that moment as a watershed in the history of the republic. Botha had provided a forum where the most sensitive issues facing the government could be discussed outside the National Party caucus. He could use the Council as a platform from which the Vice-President, a leader of undoubted status, with no electoral responsibility, could call for changes that Botha himself, as leader of the Nationalists could never be seen openly to demand.

The Council, went the argument of the optimists, could justify itself through the results it delivered, even though its members were not representative. They could recommend some sort of vote for the Coloureds and Indians (although hardly on the same roll as the whites); they could discuss Apartheid legislation like Mixed Marriages or Group Areas; they could even put forward the arguments for the eventual inclusion of blacks in their deliberations. But at the end of the day such proposals still had to be passed by Parliament because the President's Council had no power to legislate. It was merely an advisory body. If the Council made the kind of recommendations that would win credibility outside the ranks of the National Party, in other words among blacks, there seemed to be no chance at all that such notions would be acceptable to a parliament dominated by those very same Nationalists.

Botha was clearly aware of the potential impasse and late in 1980 hinted at a way round it. He announced that, if necessary, he would call a referendum in order to push through what he called 'drastic constitutional reforms'. There was a perfectly good precedent. The Nationalists had used a referendum to win endorsement for their Republic in 1960. Nationalists were also adept at bypassing constitutional hurdles. They had been equal to the task twenty-five years before when it came to taking the Coloureds' vote away from them. It was a great South African irony that a Nationalist Prime Minister might now have to consider similar stratagems in order to give it back to them.

A much more likely scenario was that the President's Council would come forth with no recommendations that would split the National Party, or if they did, the government would ignore them. Botha knew as well as anyone that what Afrikaners called *Broedertwis* (fraternal feud) could prove fatal to the Nationalist cause. He had lived through the split over Fusion, the wartime rift between the Ossewabrandwag and the Party, and the break away by Albert Hertzog in 1969. His early record as Prime Minister suggested he had no intention of precipitating another such crisis.

At the end of the parliamentary session in 1980 the leader of the opposition, Dr F. van Zyl Slabbert, reflected sadly that Botha had two choices: either to make the National Party an instrument of reform or to maintain party solidarity. He could not do both. 'At the moment,' said Slabbert, 'I get the impression that he prefers to maintain party solidarity rather than bring about reforms which he knows have to come.'

Botha himself continued to put forward his new Council as the panacea for political ills, backed by the threat of nasty medicine in reserve. 'If the President's Council fails,' he told a nationwide television audience in June 1980, 'and there are forces who want it to fail, then there will be confrontation.' Pretoria was quite prepared to create consultative bodies for Coloured, Indian and African leaders, he insisted, but not on the condition that it accepted majority rule in South Africa as the ultimate end. One man one vote in a unitary state was not an option. Botha had always been quite clear about it. 'If confrontation must come over that, then it must come . . . But if people choose this above reasonableness, above sensible discussion and above consultation, then the state has no choice and will have to use all its might.'

'Piet Wapen' had already shown what the state could do. His television broadcast came some days after the fourth anniversary on 16 June of the nationwide unrest of 1976. The government had banned all gatherings and even church services to commemorate the start of the protest in which five hundred blacks had died. If Lord Milner, years before, had forbidden Afrikaners to celebrate their own heroes' day on 16 December the result might well have been the same. Young bloods turned out to prove their virility and taunt authority. Stone-throwing provoked baton charges, tear gas and then shooting, rioting and arson followed.

The arrogance of some Nationalists at such moments can invite only profound pessimism for South Africa's future. On the eve of that Soweto anniversary I spoke to Jimmy Kruger, former Minister for the Police and then President of the Senate, about the possibility of a weekend of unrest. He was supremely confident that the police could handle any problems disaffected blacks might offer. 'They have only got their second team out', he boasted. 'We have picked up all the first team.'

On the tactics the police might use he was equally forthright:

It's not like Europe where the police with shields can push demonstrators into a limited area, baton them a bit and arrest who they want. Soweto is not like that. It's wide open so they have to use guns.

Our police don't like riot shields. The police are the sort of people who wear shorts, who went into action in the Western desert with no shirts on, despite what the rule book said. You are never going to get them to use shields.

And rubber bullets? 'They wouldn't work on black crowds. You've got to know these Africans. They're not like your European crowds.' Within a few days over forty South Africans were dead; two hundred were injured and, by early July, twice that number of so-called activists were in detention.

Since Sharpeville in 1960 close on seventeen thousand South Africans have been detained under the state's emergency powers. 1,400 have been banned, 160 banished to outlying areas. Twenty-two organisations have been declared unlawful although usually without recourse to the law itself. These are the figures that touch black South Africa, not the soaring sums that Pretoria is now spending on much publicised reform.

It may be that Botha's government does not understand the depth of hatred that is building up in the townships and in the poverty-stricken homelands. Cut off by their own laws from regular contact with blacks perhaps they are duped by their own propaganda and believe that their reforms are enough. After all, a month before the Soweto riots in 1976, the Chairman of the West Rand Administration Board, Manie Mulder, had reported that 'the people of Soweto are perfectly content, perfectly happy. There is no danger of a blow-up at all.'

On the other hand, some whites, convinced of their own superiority might welcome confrontation with an enemy they despise. Thirty years in power has bred in many Nationalists a dangerous complacency. When one of Botha's ministers dropped the reformist mask in the Assembly long enough to speak of the 'slower thought processes' of blacks he was saying only what thousands of South African whites believe. Jimmy Kruger showed the same arrogance when he brushed aside suggestions that the homelands might yet become centres of unrest fuelled by guerrillas infiltrating from across the borders. 'We can pick them up as they come in,' he told me. 'It's not like Rhodesia.'

To bolster whites' morale as they await the advancing enemy, South Africans believe they now have the most powerful ally in the world. The election of Ronald Reagan has installed in the White House a leader who needs no persuading that the biggest danger to Southern Africa comes from creeping Communism and that the Cape sea route and South Africa's minerals are much more important to the West than his predecessor believed. High-ranking South African military men were soon spotted in Washington; the intelligence links between the United States and South Africa, cut off by Carter, appeared to have been restored. When a South African commando unit raided African National Congress quarters in the Mozambique capital, Maputo, early in 1981 Samora Machel insisted, despite Washington denials, that American satellite photographs had helped pinpoint the target.

The Republican landslide that brought in Reagan also swept away two Democrats who led the anti-Apartheid lobby in Congress. Frank Church of Idaho was Chairman of the Senate Foreign Relations Committee, George McGovern, Chairman of the Africa subcommittee. Pretoria could simply not believe its luck. It seemed unlikely that pressure for change in South Africa's internal policies would be the same under Republican replacements.

At home, too, there were also reasons why change might be less urgently pursued. In April 1981 Botha called an election to put his two and a half years of leadership before white voters. They had seen his cautious attempts at reform; they had been lectured on the important consultations taking place in the President's new Council. Now they were being asked to offer an opinion at the ballot box.

As expected, the results gave the National Party a huge majority, (one hundred and thirty-one seats out of one hundred and sixty-five) but that was no great comfort to P. W. Botha. The fact that the Progressive Federal Party carried six of his seats off to the left was nothing to cause alarm. He could even stomach the first defeat of a Nationalist Minister since 1948. Only five per cent of Afrikaner votes were cast for the Progressives, despite the personal appeal of van Zyl Slabbert, their Afrikaner leader. But one Afrikaner voter in three had voted to the right for the ultra-conservatives whose only platform was to slow down reform and return to the ideology of Verwoerd. The Herstigte Nasionale Party, founded by Albert Hertzog, won no seats but increased its vote five-fold. 'It is more than worrying', said Piet Cillie, 'It is ominous . . . It shows a gut reaction'.

Botha maintained that the National Party had received enough votes to continue with 'the direction we have taken and not be pushed from our course.' But thirty-three per cent of the voting Volk had now expressed the view that Botha's course was going too far and too fast towards reform. 'Afrikaner unity in the political sense of the word', said the Afrikaans Sunday newspaper, *Rapport*, 'no longer exists.' It was unthinkable that an Afrikaner leader should ignore the message from his unhappy people. But if he would now bend his efforts to restoring unity it could only be at the price of change.

Blacks were already cynical about Botha's promises. The election result did nothing to alter their views. 'The Prime Minister's noises about change are like a wheelbarrow full of tins,' said a member of the Kwazulu Legislative Assembly some months before. 'We have heard the noise of the tins, but the wheelbarrow has been put down. What now?'

The answer perhaps lies in the muscle of the black man himself. After all, in South Africa, *he* pushes the wheelbarrow. However hard Botha may try to apply the brake, the processes he has set in motion cannot be halted. It is no longer a question of limited rights on the shop floor or better wages or more schooling. Botha's black subjects now have hope for real change and, what is more important, the confidence to go on demanding it. Before them they see the example of Angola, of Mozambique and, more lately, of Zimbabwe and Iran. They see Polish trade unionists exacting concessions from a reluctant central government. The benefactions that Botha is steadily being persuaded to make convince many blacks that the Boers are already on the run.

Experience teaches [wrote Alexis de Tocqueville in 1850] that generally speaking the most perilous moment for a bad government is when it seeks to mend its ways. Only consummate statecraft can enable a king to save his throne when, after a long spell of oppressive rule, he sets out to improve the lot of his subjects. Patiently endured so long as it seemed beyond redress, a grievance comes to appear intolerable once the possibility of removing it crosses men's minds.

But what is equally intolerable for Afrikaner Nationalists is to share government with black men who outnumber them. In this regard Nationalist policy has not changed. Theirs is a holding operation, to retain power and privilege for as long as possible. To do so they will not hesitate to use every weapon at their disposal. Limited reform is part of the strategy but so too is repression. Opponents of Pretoria's system are tolerated for only as long as the 'security of the state' allows. Black union officials, student leaders, teachers, politicians are singled out and, as they rise to any sort of prominence outside the framework of Apartheid, are systematically cropped off. The army is increasingly employed as well as the police, to man road blocks around the black townships. Over one hundred people were detained without trial in the first six months of 1981. After all, no one knows better than the Afrikaners how small beginnings, centred around dedicated individuals, can produce ends that change the course of history.

So what now? Will the Boers negotiate as they did at Vereeniging or must there first be bloody conflict? Milner once faced just such a moment. 'There is only one way out of the troubles in South Africa,' he said, 'reform or war. And of the two war is more likely.' In fact both sides will tell you the war has already begun.

BIBLIOGRAPHY

Adam, Heribert & Hermann Giliomee *The Rise and Crisis of Afrikaner Power* David Philip, Cape Town 1979

Arnold, Guy *The Last Bunker* Quartet Books, London 1975

Barnard, Lady Anne *South Africa a Century Ago* Smith, Elder & Co. 1901

Benson, Mary *South Africa: The Struggle for a Birthright* Penguin, London 1966

Biko, Steve *The Testimony of Steve Biko 1978* Granada Publishing Ltd (Panther Books), London 1979

Böeseken, A. J. *Slaves and Free Blacks at the Cape 1658–1700* Tafelberg 1977

Bunting, Brian *The Rise of the South African Reich* Penguin, London 1964

Burger, Jan *The Gulf Between* (Racial Problems in S.A.) Howard Timmins, Cape Town 1960

Burgess, J., *et al. The Great White Hoax* Africa Bureau, London 1977

Butler, Jeffrey, Rotberg, R. I. & Adams, John *The Black Homelands of South Africa* California Press 1977

Carter, Gwendolen M. & O'Meara, Patrick *South Africa, The Continuing Crisis* Indiana University Press 1979

Cassar, George H. *Kitchener, Architect of Victory* William Kimber, London 1977

Chivers, Hedley A. *The Seven Wonders of Southern Africa* South African Railways & Harbours 1929

Cubitt, Gerald & Helfet, Arnold *South Africa* C. Struik, Cape Town 1975

Davenport, T. R. H. *South Africa – A Modern History* Macmillan, South Africa 1977

Davenport T. R. H. *The Afrikaner Bond 1880–1911* Oxford University Press, Oxford 1966

286

Bibliography

Davidson, Basil *Report on Southern Africa* Jonathan Cape Ltd, London 1952

Davidson, Basil, Slovo, Joe, & Wilkinson, Anthony *South Africa: The New Politics of Revolution* Penguin, London 1976

Desmond, Cosmas *The Discarded People* (African Resettlement in South Africa) Penguin, London 1971

D'Oliveira, John *Vorster the Man* Ernest Stanton, Johannesburg 1977

Doyle, A. Conan *The Great Boer War* Smith, Elder & Company, London 1902

Drury, Allen *A Very Strange Society* Michael Joseph, London 1968

Education Commission Report *Education Beyond Apartheid 1971* Published by Christian Institute of South Africa in 1971

Farwell, Byron *The Great Boer War* Allen Lane, London 1976

First, Ruth, Steele, Jonathan, & Gurney, Christabel *The South African Connection* Temple Smith, London 1972

Fisher, John *Paul Kruger* Secker & Warburg, London 1974

Fisher, John *The Afrikaners* Cassell, London 1969

Gann L. H. & Duignan, Peter *Why South Africa will Survive* Croom Helm, London 1981

Gordon, Ruth & Talbot, Clive *From Dias to Vorster* (Source material of South African History) 1488–1975, Nasou Ltd 1977

Griffith, Kenneth *Thank God we kept the Flag Flying* Hutchinson, London 1974

Hellmann, Ellen & Lever, Henry *Conflict and Progress* (Fifty Years of Race Relations in South Africa) Macmillan, South Africa 1979

Hepple, Alexander *Verwoerd: Political Leaders of the 20th Century* Pelican, London 1967

Herd, Norman *1922, The Revolt on the Rand* Blue Crane Books, Johannesburg 1966

Hobhouse, Emily *The Brunt of War and Where it Fell* (1902)

Horrell, Muriel *Bantu Education to 1968* South African Institute of Race Relations, Johannesburg 1968

Jaarsveld, F. A. van *From Van Riebeeck to Vorster 1652–1974* Perskor Publishers 1975

Jaarsveld, F. A. van *The Afrikaner's Interpretation of South African History* Simondium Publishers, Cape Town 1964

Johnson, R. W. *How Long Will South Africa Survive* Macmillan Press, London 1977

Judd, Denis *The Boer War* Granada, London 1977

Kane-Berman, John *Soweto, Black Revolt, White Reaction* Ravan Press, Johannesburg 1978

Keatley, Patrick *The Politics of Partnership* Penguin African Library, London 1963

Kenney, Henry *Architect of Apartheid* Jonathan Ball, Johannesburg 1979

de Kiewiet, C. W. *A History of South Africa: Social and Economic* Oxford University Press, Oxford 1941

de Klerk, W. *The Puritans in Africa* (The Story of Afrikanerdom) Rex Collings, London 1975

Knightly, Phillip *The First Casualty* André Deutsch, London 1975

Lacour-Gayet, Robert *A History of South Africa* Cassell, London 1970

Laurence, John C. *Race Propaganda in South Africa* Victor Gollancz, London 1979

Laurence, Patrick *South Africa's Politics of Partition, The Transkei* Ravan Press, Johannesburg 1976

Lee, Marshall & Magubane, Peter *Soweto* Don Nelson 1978

Le May, G. H. L. *Black and White in South Africa* Purnell & Sons, Paulton, Someset 1971

Malherbe, Ernst G. *Education and the Poor White* Juta & Co 1932

Malherbe, Ernst G. *Education in South Africa* Juta & Co, Cape Town Vol 1–1925 Vol 2–1977

Malherbe Ernst G. *The Bilingual School* Longmans, Green & Co, London 1943

Malherbe, Janie A. *Predikante – Prestasies en-Petaljes* Maskew Miller Beperk, Cape Town 1949

Marquard, Leo *A Federation of Southern Africa* Oxford University Press, Cape Town 1971

Martin, A. C. *The Concentration Camps 1900–1902* Howard Timmins, Cape Town 1957

Matshoba, Mtutuzeli *Call Me Not a Man* Ravan Press, Johannesburg 1979

Meiring, Piet *Smuts the Patriot* Tafelberg 1975

Millin, Sarah G. *The South Africans* Constable, London 1926

Moodie, T. Dunbar *The Rise of Afrikanerdom: Power, Apartheid & the Afrikaner Civil Religion* University of California Press 1975

Munger, Edwin S. *The Afrikaners* Tafelberg, Cape Town 1979

Naudé, Louis, 'Dr. A. Hertzog, die Nasionale Party en die Mynwerkers.' Potchefstroom Herald (Pty) Ltd, 1969

Pakenham Thomas *The Boer War* Weidenfeld & Nicolson, London 1979

Paton, Alan *The Life and Times of Jan Hofmeyr* Oxford University Press, Cape Town and London 1965

Bibliography

Pelzer, A. N. *Die Afrikaner-Broederbond: eerste 50 Jaar.* Tafelberg, Cape Town 1979

Ransford, Oliver *The Battle of Majuba Hill (The First Boer War)* John Murray, London 1967

Report of the Carnegie Commission, 5 volumes, Stellenbosch 1932

Rhoodie, Nicolas *South African Dialogue* McGraw-Hill Book Co., Johannesburg 1972

Ritner, Susan R. *Salvation through Separation* University Microfilms, High Wycombe 1971

Rosenthal, Eric *Encyclopaedia of South Africa* Vol 1 A–L, Vol 2 M–Z Frederick Warne, London 1961, 6th Ed 1973

Roux, Edward *Time Longer than Rope: The Black Man's Struggle for Freedom in South Africa* University of Wisconsin Press 1978

Sachs, E. S. *Rebel's Daughters* MacGibbon & Kee, London 1957

Sachs, E. S. *The Anatomy of Apartheid* Collet's, London 1965

Sachs, E. S. *The Choice Before South Africa* Turnstile Press, London 1957

Serfontein, J. H. P. *Brotherhood of Power* Rex Collings, London 1979

Spies, S. B. *Methods of Barbarism* Human & Rousseau, Cape Town 1977

South African Institute of Race Relations, *Laws Affecting Race Relations in South Africa.* Annual Surveys 1970–1978

Strangwayes-Booth, Joanna *A Cricket in the Thorn Tree* Hutchinson, London 1976

Stultz, Newell M. *Afrikaner Politics in South Africa 1934–1948.* University of California Press 1974

Temkin, Ben *Gatsha Buthelezi – Zulu Statesman* Purnell & Sons, Cape Town 1976

Thompson, Leonard & Butler, Jeffrey *Change in Contemporary South Africa* University of California Press 1975

Vatcher, Wm Henry Jr *White Laager – The Rise of Afrikaner Nationalism* Pall Mall Press 1965

de Villiers, David *The Case for South Africa* Tom Stacey Ltd, London 1970

Visser, George Cloete *O.B. Traitors or Patriots* Macmillan, South Africa 1976

van Warmelo, Dietlof *On Commando* A. D. Donker, Johannesburg 1977

Wilkins, Ivor & Strydom, Hans *The Super-Afrikaners* Jonathan Ball, Johannesburg 1978

Wilson, Monica & Thompson, Leonard *The Oxford History of South Africa* Vols I & II Clarendon Press, Oxford 1969
Woods, Donald *Biko* Paddington Press, London 1978

GLOSSARY

Afrikaanse Handelsinstituut— Afrikaans Institute of Commerce

Afrikaanse Taal en Kultuurvereniging (AKTV)—Afrikaans Language and Cultural Organisation

Afrikaans Studentebond—Afrikaans Students Union

Afrikanerbond van Mynwerkers— Afrikaner Union of Mineworkers

Agterryer—outrider, attendant on horseback

Amandla—power

Apartheid—lit. apartness; separation

Baas—lit. master; boss

Bantu—lit. The People, but used as singular noun to denote a Black man

Besembos—lit. broom-bush; student journal of the University of Potchefstroom

Bittereinders—bitter-enders; Boers who fought on to the end of the Anglo-Boer War

Boeresport—Boer sport i.e. jukskei

Boerewors—Boer sausage

Boere Universiteit—Boer University

Bondsraad—General Council

Braaivleis—lit. grilled meat; barbecue

Broeder—brother

Broederbond—Band of Brothers; Afrikaner secret society

Broedertwis—fraternal feud

Burger—citizen

Burger, Die—Cape Town newspaper

Bywoner—squatter

Dominee—Vicar; Minister

Donga—gully

Duiwelstad—devil's town; Kruger's description of Johannesburg

Dompas—pass

Eike, die—lit. the Oaks; head offices of the Afrikaner Broederbond in Auckland Park, Johannesburg

Eerste Vryheidsoorlog—First War of Independence i.e. First Anglo-Boer War, 1880–81

English War—usually refers to Second Anglo-Boer War, 1899–1902

Federasie van Afrikaanse Kultuurvereniging (FAK)—Federation of Afrikaans Cultural Societies

Genootskap van regte Afrikaners, die—the Society of true Afrikaners

Great Trek—mass emigration of settlers, mainly of Dutch origin, from the Cape of Good Hope in the 1830s

Helpmekaar—lit. help each other; Afrikaner mutual assistance society

Hensoppers—lit. hands-uppers; Boers who surrendered during Anglo-Boer War

Herstigte Nasionale Party (HNP)— reconstituted National Party

Hervormingsorganisasie—lit. Reform Organisation; Afrikaner reform movement within the Mineworker's Union

Impi—Zulu regiment
Induna—headman
Inspan—yoke, harness

Jong Suid-Afrika—lit. Young South Africa; original name taken by organisation which became the Afrikaner Broederbond
Jukskei—game played with wooden pin of ox-yoke
Jukskeibond—Jukskei Association

Kaffir—lit (from Arabic) non-believer; pejorative name for African
Kakis—Khakis; Afrikaner name for British soldiers in Anglo-Boer War
Khoikhoi—lit. 'a man' in Hottentot language; nomadic Hottentots
Klerewekersnuus—lit. Garment Workers' News
Kommando—Boer Military Unit
Kraal—lit. pen, fold; term for African village, grouphof huts or cattle enclosure

Laager—defensive fortification formed by circle of wagons

Melktert—milk tart
Monumentkoppie—monument hill; site of Voortrekker Monument, Pretoria

Nasionale Raad van Trustees—National Council of Trustees
Noodhulpliga—lit. Emergency League; Afrikaner organisation similar to Red Cross

Ous—fellows
Oom—uncle; often used by Afrikaner children to refer to male adults

Ossewabrandwag — ox-wagon fire-guard
Ossewatrek—lit. ox-wagon trek, especially 1938 Centenary Trek

Padkos—provisions
Pad van Suid-Afrika, die—lit. Path of South Africa; the symbolic way ahead for South Africa
Pamperlanging—buttering-up
Penkoppies—cubs i.e. junior scouts
Platteland—lit. flat land; country districts.
Poqo—only or pure in Xhosa; exclusive Black Nationalist organisation
Pro deo—lit. for God; e.g. Pro Deo Counsel, appointed and paid for by the state.

Rapportryers—lit. dispatch riders; Afrikaner organisation similar to Rotary
Reddingsdaad—act of rescue
Reddingsdaadbond—Association for Act of Rescue; formed to rehabilitate Poor Whites
Rooi Luisies—lit. red lice; derogatory term to denote South African soldiers in 1939–45 War wearing red tabs signifying readiness to serve overseas
Rooinek—red neck i.e. an Englishman

Sadza—mealie-meal
San people—Bushmen, often cave-dwellers
Skollies—lit. teddy boys, hooligans
Staatmaker—stalwart i.e. Senior Scout
Stem van Suid-Afrika, die—lit. the Voice of South Africa; the National Anthem
Stormjaers—stormtroopers

Suid-Afrikaanse Buro vir Rasse-Aangeleenthede—lit. South African Bureau for Race Relations

Transvaler, die—Johannesburg newspaper

Trek—lit. pull; journey

Tsotsis—lit. young Black children; now used mainly for Black hooligans

Tweede Vryheidsoorlog—Second War of Independence i.e. Anglo-Boer War, 1899–1902, known also as the English War and the South African War

Uitlander—foreigner

Uitspan—unharness, unyoke

Umkonto we Sizwe—Spear of the Nation; Black Nationalist organisation

Uitvoerende Raad (UR)—Executive Council

Vaderland, die—Fatherland; Johannesburg evening newspaper

Veghekke—fighting gates

Veld—lit. field; open country

Veldskool—country school

Verkenner—scout

Verkrampte—reactionary, hard-line

Verligte—enlightened, moderate

Vierkleur—four-coloured flag of the Transvaal Republic

Volk—people

Volkfeeste—People's Festivals

Volksorganisasie—People's Organisation

Volkspele—folk-games

Volksraad—People's Council; National Assembly

Voortrekker—participant in the Great Trek

Vrouefederasie—Womens' Federation

Vrouemonument—Womens' Monument (in Bloemfontein)

Vryheid – freedom

Wildebeeste—large antelope

Wees Sterk—'Be Strong'; the Broederbond motto

PICTURE CREDITS

The publishers would like to thank the following for the use of their photographs, the pages on which they appear is given after the credit. Africamera, Johannesburg 105, 107, 116, 127, 271; The Africana Museum, Johannesburg 34, 77, 86; Argus Group, South Africa 63 (right), 121, 162, 217, 225, 240; BBC Hulton Picture Library 26, 51 (right), 146, 152; BBC-TV 175; Butch Calderwood 11, 12, 90, 171, 248; Camera Press 155; Fox Photos 60; Kenneth Griffiths 39; David Harrison 187, 229; International Defence & Aid Fund 185, 197, 213; Keystone Press Agency 159, 238; Mike McCann 130; Dr E. G. Malherbe 67, 73, 74, 75; The Mansell Collection 51 (left); Marshall Lee 135; National Film Archive, Pretoria 55; Ossewabrandwag Archive, University of Potchefstroom 128; Rand Afrikaans University 98; South African Defence Force 265; S.A. Morning Newspapers 184.

Endpaper maps by Line and Line.

INDEX

Africa Oath 125, 126

African National Congress (ANC) 164, 215, 218, 283

Afrikaans evolution of 48; newspapers 50, 51; in schools 53–5, 59, 141–3, 196–9; discrimination against 56, 58, 101; Broederbond policy 91, 92, 203, 210, 275; spoken by troops in North Africa 142; rejected by Coloureds 159, 194; *see also* bilingualism; education; language discrimination; schools

Afrikaanse Patriot, Die 50

Afrikaanse Studentebond (ASB) 95, 202

Afrikaanse Taal en Kultuurvereniging (ATKV) 96, 103

Afrikanerbond van Mynwerkers 118

Afrikaner Party 148, 151

Afrikaner Reform Movement 115

Afrikaners character 2, 3, 88; attitude to British 84, 85, 87; exclusivity 96, 102, 198, 199; in trade unions 114–19; *see also* Broederbond

Afrikaner Students' Organisation 133

Amin, General Idi 208, 209

Anglo-Boer War 25–47; memories of Henning Klopper 25–8, 30–2, 35; memories of Ernst Malherbe 28, 29, 33, 34; concentration camps 30, 31, 35–9, 45, 46; treatment of prisoners 33; ceasefire 44; Treaty of Vereeniging 45–7

Apartheid philosophy of 150, 215; British attitude 161, 164; Commonwealth attitude 166; Nationalists' policy 169–77, 276, 277, 285; in education 190–206; in broadcasting 208–10; opposition to 176, 227, 230, 247, 249, 250, 273, 274, 283; in navy 264; *see also* Broederbond; education; sport; trade unions

Appeal Court 157, 158, 213

army 264; *see also* defence

Asquith, Henry 45

Atomic Research Centre (Pelindaba) 13

Auerbach, Dr Franz 204, 205

'Autonomy of our Universities and Apartheid, The' (Malherbe) 196

Balfour, A. J. 57

banning 214–16, 224

Bantu 15, 177–80, 183, 190, 191

Bantu Education Act 190, 191, 197

Bantu Investment Corporation 178

Bantustans 177–81; *see also* homelands

Barrie, F. G. 235, 236

Bassick, Diane 174, 175

Basutoland 178

BBC 207

Beaumont Commission 70, 71

Beaumont, Sir William 70

Bechuanaland 178

Bermuda 46, 47

Besembos 124

Beukes, Mrs Aletta 43

Beukes, Dr D. P. N. 269

Beyers, General 62, 63

Biggar, Captain Alex 17, 19

Biko affair 221, 224–7

BOTSWANA

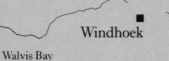

Windhoek

Walvis Bay

SOUTH WEST AFRICA/NAMIBIA

ORANGE RIVER

MA

Former British
Protectorate

Homelands

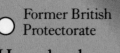 Ciskei

Transkei

 Kwazulu

Qwaqwa

 Swazi

Gazankulu

 Venda

Lebowa

BophuthaTswana

CAPE PROVINCE

Paarl

George

Cape Town • Stellenbosch

Simonstown

Miles

0 20 40 60 80 100   150